**BUREAUCRATS
AND
POLICY MAKING**

BUREAUCRATS
AND
POLICY MAKING

A Comparative Overview

Edited by
Ezra N. Suleiman

HM
HOLMES & MEIER
New York   London

First published in the United States of America 1984 by
Holmes & Meier Publishers, Inc.
30 Irving Place
New York, N.Y. 10003

Great Britain:
Holmes & Meier Publishers, Ltd.
Unit 5   Greenwich Industrial Estate
345 Woolwich Road   Charlton, London SE7

Book design by Stephanie Barton

Library of Congress Cataloging in Publication Data
Main entry under title:

Bureaucrats and policy making: A comparative overview

   Includes bibliographical references.
   1. Government executives—Addresses, essays,
lectures.   2. Civil service—Addresses, essays,
lectures.   3. Policy sciences—Addresses, essays,
lectures.   I. Suleiman, Ezra N., 1941–
JF1601.B87   1984   351.007'4   83-17171
ISBN 0-8419-0847-8

Manufactured in the United States of America

Contents

ACKNOWLEDGMENTS

I wish to thank the Centro de Investigaciones Sociológicas for sponsoring the conference at which the papers in this volume were originally presented. The conference was held in Madrid in December 1980 under splendid conditions. We are grateful for the interest shown throughout the course of this project by Dr. Rafael Lopez, who was Director of the Centro de Investigaciones Sociológicas at the time, and, together with Dr. Carlos Alba, was responsible for organizing the conference. All the contributors benefited from the comments and criticisms made by Miguel Beltran, Raphael Hadas-Lebel, Jean-Louis Quermonne, and Robert Putnam, who served as discussants.

E.S.

BUREAUCRATS
    AND
    POLICY MAKING

INTRODUCTION

Ezra N. Suleiman

The proper role that civil servants should play and the role they, in fact, do play in the policy process has been receiving considerable attention in recent years within different national contexts. The methodological approach to the study of the relationship between administration and politics has also varied, as one would expect given the complexity of issues that need to be examined.[1] Perhaps more important, however, is the fact that the focus of attention has shifted from the normative question of the role that civil servants *ought* to play to the behavioral one: What influence do civil servants exert on the political process?

The basis for seeking to go beyond the normative prescription, so clearly posited by Weber, of the appropriate relationship between civil servants and politicians is that it is at variance with the "ideal type" formulation.[2] The view that a number of scholars, including the authors of this volume, now take is that the "ideal type" Weberian formulation ought simply to serve as a backdrop to the analysis of the relationship between administration and politics. Hence, the central questions become: What is the degree of influence that civil servants exert on the political process? How is this influence exercised? And, finally, what are the effects of bureaucratic influence on politics?

These questions impose themselves on the observer because of the profound transformation that has occurred in the past century in both the political and administrative spheres. In the era preceding the establishment of a merit bureaucracy, the spoils system set political guidelines for the role that employees, hired for their political loyalty, would play. Political loyalty was a condition for recruitment, as it was for length of tenure. This was a system that, for all its negative aspects, responded to the limited role of governments. The expansion in the role of the state and the unionization of workers in both the private and public sectors accompanied, and in some cases preceded, the creation of a merit bureaucracy. The more orderly, uniform recruitment criteria placed civil servants, particularly those occupying the top posts in the bureaucracy, in an ambiguous situation. They had protection against political intrusion. Yet, they owed loyalty—and often their appointments—to the government of the day. Indeed, the ambiguity in the relationship between higher civil servants and the government in power persists in most societies today, as the essays in this volume suggest.

Politicians have had a strong hand in maintaining this ambiguity. They have generally wanted civil servants to be neutral yet responsive to the party in power. This contradictory expectation is found in societies as different as Chile, the United States, and France. Whatever politicians may consider to be the proper role of the bureaucracy, there is little question that they view it differently, depending on whether they happen to be in the opposition or in power. When in opposition, they seek neutrality; when in power they see the bureaucracy as a mere instrument. This is perhaps the only aspect that is unchanging across societies. It is a reality that we have come to accept. The only questions that then become meaningful for an investigator are the extent to which politicians in power succeed in rendering the bureaucracy an effective instrument of their power, and the effects of the bureaucracy's submission or resistance to or control over the politicans.[3]

Because civil servants have a hand in shaping public policies, it has become important to relate their administrative and political functions. The central theme that informs the essays in this volume is the political or policy role of higher civil servants. The essays have not sought to restate the obvious, namely, that civil servants do more than administer. Rather, they have sought to address the question of the kind of influence that civil servants exert in the political sphere. All the essays (with the exception of the one on Chile) cover advanced industrial societies where a civil service tradition has been in existence, even if, as in the case of the United States, such a tradition has been difficult to define. All the chapters have sought to cover the same basic points, though the emphasis placed on the different points varies.

Recruitment. The impact of the bureaucracy on the policy-making process is in some measure related to the system of recruitment of the higher strata of the civil service. The recruitment of higher civil servants is of course dependent on the political and social system that determines the recruitment of both civil servants and politicians. Most of the chapters have ascribed only a limited importance to the sociological data and have placed a greater emphasis on the possible consequences of particular socialization characteristics, on attitudinal data and, more particularly, on behavioral investigations. Crossnational comparisons of recruitment into the higher echelons of the bureaucracy are fruitful because they help to further one's understanding of how particular recruitment procedures can create conditions that favor (or hinder) bureaucratic influence.

Structures. The recruitment process must be viewed in relation to the structures into which the civil servants are recruited. The structures differ as do those who fill the top posts in these structures. There is no one group that can be credited with fulfilling the same functions in all societies. A high civil service post in France or Italy may be more or less equivalent to a political position in the United States, even though the responsibilities of the two positions may have much in common. This raises both a conceptual problem and one that is grounded in the hard reality of bureaucratic structures. We are faced with a situation where it is difficult to discern both a clearly identifiable group of higher civil servants in all societies and a set of functions that are performed in all the societies.

In order to tackle this complexity, some simplicity has been imposed by the literature on public administration and policy making. The simplicity has consisted in assuming a considerable degree of organizational unity, as well as a unity of interests within the bureaucratic structures. Indeed, the "bureaucratic politics" school, whatever it may overlook, has the merit of placing a much-needed emphasis on the importance of bureaucratic conflicts for public policy formulation. Crossnational comparisons can take account of structural differences of bureaucratic organization, which themselves make comparisons difficult, and of the variety of interests that a bureaucratic organization can represent.

The countries studied in this volume have developed civil services within a variety of organizational traditions—Napoleonic, Prussian, Anglo-Saxon—that have stamped their mark on the structures of their bureaucracies. This explains why it is often difficult to classify political appointees and civil servants within the same general category even when both may share a civil service status. Hence, the categories of ministerial cabinets in France, or of *gabinettos* in Italy, of under secretaries and assistant secretaries in the United States, or of *Politische Beamte* in Germany, imply a confusion of administrative and political roles that varies across nations.

Political Administration. Given these variations in structures, it becomes not only difficult to assess the political role of civil servants, but even more difficult to assess the causes for the variations in these political roles. If we know that civil servants influence the policy-making process, we still need to find out what kind of influence they exercise. The civil servants' level of involvement in the policy process varies across societies, and this may be due to organizational factors, to culture, to the party system. The essays in this volume attempt to assess, each within a specific national context, both the type and degree of involvement by civil servants in the policy process.

Accepting more or less as a given that civil servants play political roles and influence the policy-making process, the essays presented here attempt to grapple with the elusive question of the kind of functions they fulfill. This is a question that is in need of further attention because what becomes clear is that civil servants can influence policies in ways as different as providing information to (or withholding information from) their political chiefs to actually representing particular societal interests. Where bureaucratic agencies become representatives for specific private groups, this is generally attributed to a "weak" (or fragmented) federal structure.[4] Yet, this may equally be the case in centralized structures. In the latter cases, the bureaucracy can become identified with a private group and, as a result, simply becomes an interest group within the bureaucratic-political process.

Ideology vs. Reality. The above suggests that even when civil servants see themselves as representing the state or, at any rate, a constituency larger than one particular group, the reality is that the interaction between the bureaucracy and the society results in the submission of the former to a narrow segment of the latter. Because bureaucrats have different constituencies and because they have different levels of interaction with the political system and the political process, can it be said with any degree of accuracy that they represent the state? In view of the growing literature on state autonomy (or the limits to such autonomy), this question assumes a certain degree of importance and needs to be dealt with further.

Politicization of Bureaucracy. If the general view that civil servants influence the policy-making process, whether through moving into political posts proper or through accepting to represent a particular government or ideology, then the proposition that the bureaucracy has become politicized becomes plausible. If, on the other hand, the ties between the bureaucracy and the political system become strong, it may be equally plausible to speak of the bureaucratization of politics. In either case, a paradox appears: either the bureaucracy becomes an instrument of the government in power with its own ideological proclivities, in which case the notion of a neutral bureaucracy receives a severe blow; or, the bureaucracy plays the critical role in the allocation of resources, in which case the notion of the supremacy of politics (and the legitimacy of the electoral mandate) is undermined.

The relationship between politics and administration continues to raise nagging normative questions. The essays in this volume have not sought to resolve these questions. Instead, they have tried to identify and address the main issues affecting the relationship between administration and politics in a variety of national contexts.

NOTES

1. See Colin Campbell and George J. Szablowski, *The Superbureaucrats: Structure and Behavior in Central Agencies* (Toronto: Macmillan, 1979); Miguel Beltran, *La Elite Burocratica Espanola* (Madrid: Fundacion Juan March 7, Editorial Ariel, 1977); Mattei Dogan, ed., *The Mandarins of Western Europe: The Political Role of Top Civil Servants* (Los Angeles: Sage Publications, 1975); Joel D. Aberbach, Robert D. Putnam, and Bert A. Rockman, *Bureaucrats and Politicians in Western Democracies* (Cambridge: Harvard University Press, 1981); Richard Rose and Ezra N. Suleiman, eds., *Presidents and Prime Ministers* (Washington, D.C.: A.E.I., 1980).

2. See Max Weber, *Economy and Society* (Berkeley and Los Angeles: University of California Press, 1978), pp. 941–1005.

3. In regard to President Richard Nixon's attempt to control the bureaucracy, see Richard Nathan, *The Administrative Presidency* (New York: Wiley, 1983).

4. Grant McConnell, *Private Power and American Democracy* (New York: Vintage Books, 1966).

IN SEARCH OF A ROLE
America's Higher Civil Service

Hugh Heclo

 The first person to leave the earth and walk on another world was a civil servant. But Neil Armstrong was not paid for the summer day in 1969 when he walked on the moon. Like that of other Washington bureaucrats, his pay was subject to a congressionally enacted rule that limited the overtime payments to civil servants if such compensation would increase their salaries to a point approaching the pay scale of Congressmen and political executives. So although America had spent $25 billion to put him there, Armstrong could not legally receive overtime pay for the work he performed on a national holiday celebrating his moonwalk.[1]

 Astronauts are, of course, not typical members of the higher civil service, but the incident of Neil Armstrong's pay says something about the peculiar position in which highly qualified careerists can find themselves. The higher civil service in the United States is a study in ambiguities. Top bureaucrats' status, their role in policy making and politics, their relationship to the larger society—all these features are poorly defined in American central government and subject to immense counterpressures. It is even questionable whether or not there actually is a higher civil service in the United States, at least in the sense in which that term is used in other countries. To study the higher civil service in Washington, we need to think not only of hierarchies with formal, clear career lines, but also loose groupings of people where the lines of policy, politics, and administration merge in a complex jumble of bodies.

Washington seems to have everything. Look for the equivalent of French corps and you will find the closed, elitist model reflected to some degree in the membership of the Forest Service, Army Corps of Engineers, U.S. Geological Survey, Federal Highway Administration, or Justice Department Anti-trust Division. Within their own sphere, the State Department's Foreign Service and the president's budget agency have sought to duplicate a kind of British administrative class. Although not as self-consciously managed as their Japanese counterparts, administrative cohorts in Washington have been created by major events such as the New Deal of the 1930s, the Great Society/New Frontier initiatives of the 1960s, and the Nixon-Ford policies of the 1970s. Lawyers have carved out their own niche in the personnel structure of federal agencies[2] and frequently play the role of organizational negotiators along Norwegian lines. Likewise, strong bureau chiefs can claim the German title of "political bureaucrats" in advancing their programs with Congress, political interests, and department heads. And surely there is no lack of pettifoggery Italian-style in insulated pieces of Washington officialdom.

Each image can be found in America's higher civil service, but none is complete as a characterization of the whole picture. To suggest that one or another pattern predominates would be misleading. And yet to think that the senior bureaucracy is simply a random collection of people and styles would be obtuse. Like any montage, the U.S. higher civil service is best appreciated by its themes, not its individual pictures.

One such theme is the unmanaged quality of America's higher civil service. By that I do not mean that there is runaway growth or absence of legalistic constraints. Far from it. Growth in personnel has been meager, and restrictive personnel regulations abound. I mean that no one looks after the higher civil service as such, and certainly senior bureaucrats themselves do not (as in other countries) oversee its workings, traditions, and fate.

A second theme, related to the first, is the peculiar absence of a formal civil service presence in the central executive institutions of government, especially the president's office and the offices of major department heads. This situation appears to have been a gradual development of the last forty years or so: one part a "disappearing act" by senior officials who once made up such a presence, and one part a failure to discover effective new ways of using senior careerists as these central offices have grown over the years. But whatever the explanation, the result is clear. Compared to its counterparts in other countries, the U.S. higher civil service seems hollow at the center.

A final theme explored in this paper concerns a profound and probably growing duality in the higher civil service as an informal personnel system. Certainly, it is possible to identify a schizoid quality in the upper level bureaucracy of every country. This condition is the natural by-product of having to accommodate twin tasks in any higher civil service: overall supervision of the administrative machinery below and personal advisory relations with political ministers above. The effect in many countries is to create a kind of bifurcation in the civil service itself— service in the French *cabinets* and *grands corps* versus the more narrow career corps; German political bureaucrats who are state secretaries and the gradation of less political work below them; those at the top of the British administrative class and all the others; Japan's "politically sensitive" bureaucrats enmeshed in the web of conservative politics across the top of government versus the purer organization men below; and so on. The United States, on the other hand, has erected this dual need into a two-track system of top bureaucratic manpower, a formal civil service bureaucracy and an informal political technocracy.

The three themes are, of course, related. If the system as a whole tends to be unmanaged, how can there be any reliable civil service presence at the center or any coherent organization of the dual tasks at the top of the bureaucracy? If the civil service is largely excluded from the executive center, i.e., presidency, how can it be managed or even imagined to have a topside structure? With no real top but instead a duality of senior bureaucratic manpower, what is there to be represented at the center? And so the circle of ambivalence about the higher civil service continues unbroken in Washington. In the past several years, a new attempt has been made to reconstitute the senior executive personnel system of the bureaucracy, but as we shall see there are powerful historical and political forces working against any movement in the direction of a European or Japanese style of higher civil service. The real definition of America's higher civil service is being written, not in the language of formal personnel statutes, but in the quiet, informal understandings that shape people's careers in public service. In this as perhaps in no other country, the higher civil service is molded by forces external to itself. Its emerging structure, broadly understood, is shaped by changes in the larger political society, its character stamped by the unwritten no less than the written political constitution.

A Historical Anomaly

The ambiguous position of the higher civil service in the United States owes much to history. Taken as a whole, these background conditions add up to a situation that is uniquely American compared with the other bureaucracies discussed in this book.

In the first place, the national civil service was founded and developed only well after the basic constitutional framework of the nation had been established. The written constitution of 1787 was generally silent concerning the administrative nature of the new national government, leaving the eventual growth of the bureaucracy subject to successive feats of improvisation. Once the Founders had settled on the principle of a single executive head in the form of the president and his appointment of department heads with advice and consent of the legislature's Senate, their constitutional advice about the remainder of any administrative arrangements was, in effect, "leave it to Congress and [sotto voce] the President."[3]

Unlike its counterpart in other countries, the national bureaucracy in Washington had no roots in a preexisting monarchical or aristocratic government (as Britain, France, Norway, for example). Neither was it grounded in the struggle to attain nationhood (Germany, Italy) or to protect that nationhood against foreign threats (as in Japan). The first civil service law began to make itself felt in Washington almost a century after the constitutional design had been established and almost twenty years after the chief threat to that design—the War between the States—had been settled. During all this time the main threats had been internal, Federalists versus anti-Federalists, Abolition versus slave states. Rather than a rallying point for the defense of the nation, what small bureaucracy there was in those times became part of the spoils for which antagonists for different definitions of that nationhood contended. The result is that civil servants have appeared on the government scene in a way that seems somewhat detached from the accepted structure of American political institutions. That fact has helped foster ambivalent public sentiments about "Washington bureaucrats," although no one would want to claim constitutional history is the only factor at work.[4] Perhaps the most important effect of their detachment from constitutional history has been within the minds of bueaucrats themselves. There is less basis for American senior bureaucrats to feel sure of their place in government as civil servants as such (rather than as particular kinds of professionals, specialists, and so forth). Their profession as civil servants, their responsibility as representatives of the national state, has never been a part of the constitutional culture.

A national bureaucracy not only failed to develop in tandem with the constitution and nation-building process. It also lagged behind the development of more or less democratic forms of political participation. This is a second important distinction of the higher civil service in the United States compared with other countries. A popularly elected lower house of the national legislature was of course part of the original design for government in 1787, and Congress as a whole, not the president, retained the power to regulate the appointment of the bulk of the federal work force.[5] Within the next few decades, voting became an accepted right of virtually all adult white males, and mass political parties and organized interest groups were well under way. This gave the American national bureaucracy a more permeable, less elitist administrative structure than the European or Japanese cases and, for the same reason, heightens the similarity with the Chilean civil service. Before the higher civil service could establish its own coherent identity or defend its prerogatives, other political structures of modern democracy were in place and making demands.

Paradoxically, the fact that the U.S. civil service was born into a democratically mobilized world was a powerful impulse for seeking a clear separation between politics and administration. By the last quarter of the nineteenth century, the civil service concept was generally regarded as synonymous with the protection of administrative machinery against political influence. This approach severely inhibited any serious attention to defining the legitimate political functions of a higher civil service.

Yet the civil service reformers were more concerned about redeeming the "spoiled" quality of American politics than they were with insuring administrative efficiency.[6] Their impulse for a politically neutral civil service was redoubled in its impact by virtue of being combined with the simultaneous growth of industrial modernization. That the U.S. civil service developed after the growth of democratic participation but alongside this rapid economic change is a third distinctive quality compared with other countries (such as Chile). As the nineteenth century rolled into the twentieth century, coverage of the federal work force by civil service rules expanded. So, too, did doctrines of technical efficiency and scientific management. In the United States as in few other countries, the approach to public personnel policy became infused with the formalistic technology of written examinations, position classification, performance measurement, qualification ratings, and the like. The rapidly modernizing private sector provided a model, both for the efficient organization of routine functions and the aggressive use of professionalized specialists. It was a model that fit the expanding technical requirements of modern government, but it also fit the political needs of the situation. Bureaucrats were less vulnerable to the political crowds if they could justify their existence in terms of technical expertise. Congressmen could find the presence of high-paid bureaucrats politically acceptable on the same grounds.[7] Civil service reformers had paid little attention to the higher civil service because it would inevitably blur the line between politics and administration. The advocates of managerial modernization did likewise because it had little to do with either efficient routinization or technical specialization in the government work force. And certainly politicians in

Congress and the White House had little reason to jeopardize their credentials as democratic representatives by championing such an elitist concept. The higher civil service, therefore, has been an outstanding "nonsubject" in the development of American central govermment.

Here then is a combination of forces admirably suited to confuse the status of high level bureaucrats in Washington. *If* they had been identified with the creation and defense of the American nation-state, *if* they had been already in place to help socialize the emerging crowd of democratic politicians to understand their ways, *if* the Constitution sanctioned their existence with its mantle of authority, *if* they were expected to serve as aides to politicians as well as technical specialists or democratically programed bits of machinery—if some or all of these conditions were met, the political status of America's higher civil service would be much less problematic. Instead, the United States has, at most, tolerated the existence of Washington bureaucrats and evolved a complex system of high level administrative personnel that is both democratic and technocratic. Seen in relation to other countries, this is a remarkable combination of characteristics. No one could have invented it. America's higher civil service—broadly understood—is an unintended by-product molded between the internal demands of government and the external demands of the larger political society. Generations of personnel experts in the United States have envied the tidy bureaucratic system of Europe. Growing up around them, untidy and unobvious to be sure, has been a democratic technocracy that may have much to say about the prospects for self-government in many nations.

The Dual Structure

Seen as a whole, the Washington bureaucracy has a dual, or two-track system of administrative management: one growing out of the formal civil service rules of the personnel system and one based on an informal, but also technocratic quasi-bureaucracy of appointed manpower. Consider the gross structure of several departments as shown in table 1.

The general distribution is more important than the exact numbers and job titles. These American images of departmental management contrast with the situation found in other developed countries in these respects: there are (1) more appointive political positions that, (2) extend farther down into the administrative structure and, (3) commingle career and political appointments at some of the same levels in the agency hierarchy.[8]

During 1979, new rules for a "Senior Executive Service" brought somewhat more order to these arrangements. But this reform did not alter the basic *mixed* structure of career and political personnel in the bureauc-

TABLE 1.   Political (P) and Career (C) Positions in Selected Departments, by Rank as of 1975–76

| | DEPARTMENT | | | | | |
| | Agriculture | | Housing and Urban Development | | Justice | |
RANK	P	C	P	C	P	C
Executive Schedule						
I	1	—	1	—	1	—
II	—	—	—	—	2	—
III	1	—	1	—	3	—
IV	6	—	11	—	16	—
V	3	—	7	—	6	—
Supergrade Level						
18	10	11	5	2	17	6
17	15	37	21	15	42	15
16	36	162	17	67	88	64
Mid-level Grades						
15	20	1,151	28	571	14	1,096
14	7	2,422	14	1,075	39	1,959
13	6	5,451	10	1,756	56	5,047

Source: Unpublished data from the respective personnel offices of each department. For further details of position classification, see Hugh Heclo, *A Government of Strangers* (Washington: Brookings Institution, 1977), pp. 36–43.

racy. Approximately 8,000 managerial positions located predominantly in the supergrade level (but not 2,000 mainly scientific and professional jobs at the same level) compose the Senior Executive Service. Approximately 45 percent of these 8,000 positions are reserved for career civil servants by virtue of the political sensitivities associated with the work (e.g., Internal Revenue Service auditors, contract-awarding executives, and so on). The remaining 55 percent may be filled either by career or politically appointed executives, but the number of political executives may not total more than 10 percent (i.e., 800) of all Senior Executive Service appointments. The new senior executive system is obviously not the whole picture because presidential and other political appointees at the higher "Executive Schedule" level (see table 1, ranks I–V) can also be deeply engaged in administrative management of the departments and agencies. Governmentwide there are roughly 550 of these appointees, ranging from the 13 cabinet secretaries at level I to the over 400 appointees at levels IV and V who often do head major departmental divisions.

Who are these people? One may well ask. Certainly they are un-known to the general public and largely unmentioned in the news media. In some respects, political executives and career executives share charac-teristics that distinguish them from senior bureaucrats in Europe. In other respects, they differ from each other in significant ways. Table 2 lays out some of these key differences and similarities.

In general, the senior bureaucratic manpower of every country is unrepresentative in the sense of being drawn disproportionately from the university-educated, middle-class, and professional sectors of each na-tion's population. However, judging from a comparison of the parents' occupational status vis-à-vis the general population in each country, both political and career executives in America appear less unrepresentative than their counterparts in British, French, German, or Italian bureauc-racies. Their educational backgrounds suggest an American bureaucracy run mainly by people from the social, technical, and hard sciences com-pared with a European elite trained in the law and humanities. Most significant of all (and the information is scanty), both political and career executives in the United States betray little evidence of a family tradition in government service; as observers have noted for at least 150 years, Americans have been less apt than Europeans to create a "political class." All these data add to the picture of democratic technocracy that distin-guishes bureaucratic life in Washington from that in London, Paris, Bonn, or Rome.

And yet there are also important differences between the two tracks of senior bureaucratic manpower within the United States. One track, the de jure higher civil service, may be regarded as a grouping of persons at the upper end of government personnel systems characterized by civil service rules, in other words (in the U.S. tradition) by an open, competi-tive examination of nonpolitical qualifications. In this sense, we know a top civil servant when we see one by virtue of his or her place in a formal personnel structure.

Even under this formalistic description, the situation in the federal government is very complex. What really exists is a collection of civil services, for there are a number of personnel systems thriving at the periphery of the so-called general schedule civil service that can be said to use civil service-type rules in their operations. All of these "services" have resolutely opposed every attempt to integrate them into the larger system overseen by the Civil Service Commission (or, since 1979 reforms, the Office of Personnel Management). In March 1979, approximately 70 percent of full-time civil service employment (excluding postal workers) fell under the general schedule and the remainder in other self-contained pay systems. Thus, *the* higher civil service in Washington is something of a verbal artifact embracing the effectively autonomous leadership of units

TABLE 2. Selected Characteristics of Senior Bureaucrats in Different Countries, 1970–1971

	BRITAIN	FRANCE	GERMANY	ITALY	UNITED STATES	
					Career Executives	Political Executives
Father's occupational status						
high management and professional	51%	66%	46%	46%	39%	49%
lower management and professional	17	30	21	36	30	27
skilled nonmanual	16	3	19	16	11	11
lower nonmanual	5	0	2	0	7	7
skilled manual	5	1	11	3	7	4
semi- and unskilled manual	8	0	1	0	7	2
Bureaucrat's educational background						
below university level	14%	na	1%	0%	0%	3%
law	3		65	53	18	28
humanities	38		2	0	6	7
social sciences	12		17	36	29	38
technical, hard sciences	26		14	10	42	10
university major unknown	7		2	1	5	15
One or more relatives in politics or the civil service now or in past	48%	50%	80%	67%	37%	33%
Father employed in government	20%	na	32%	41%	9%	0%
Percentage who have spent at least one-quarter of adult life outside their respective national government	12%	37%	49%	2%	30%	78%
Percentage who have served in a national ministry other than present ministry	51%	na	32%	18%	27%	15%

Note: Compiled from information contained in Joel D. Aberbach and Robert D. Putnam, "Paths to the Top," paper presented to the Conference on Frontiers in Comparative Analysis of Bureaucratic and Political Elites, Waassenaar, Netherlands, November 1977.

such as the Foreign Service and Forest Service, FBI and CIA, National Park Service and Atomic Energy Commission, Veterans' Administration, Tennessee Valley Authority, and so on and on.

By and large, the senior bureaucrats of this de jure, conglomerate civil service spend the bulk of their adult lives working inside the national government, more similar in this respect to the British administrative class than senior bureaucrats on the Continent. But unlike the British elite—and more on the lines of top Italian and Japanese officials—the American career executives also tend to develop their careers within the confines of a single agency. This is generally both the base that supports their careers and the ladder on which they (again, though, unlike their Japanese counterparts on the bureau "escalators") either climb or stagnate. These American bureaucrats may be better educated and more white-collar than the mass of American citizens (also more white *colored* and male) but there is also something distinctly nonelitist in their more technical education and devotion to specialized programs. It is the bureau and its program that crosscuts any tendency there may be to aggregate the advantages of their diverse positions into a presumption of governmental or social privilege. Indeed, the program is more likely than not defined in terms of some type of service to one or another interest in the society at large, whether it be conservation for farmers or nuclear energy supplies to skeptical consumers.

But the vexing question remains, are these people the sum and substance of America's higher civil service? Certainly not in the sense that would be familiar to Europeans or Japanese. The career executives of the de jure higher civil service do not serve with any continuity as direct subordinates and assistants to the top appointed or elected political ministers. They do not oversee the general work of officialdom in their departments as a whole. Their work typically filters through a political subordinate of the minister—an executive aide, special assistant, assistant secretary, or the like—and for most career executives, a distinct sense of unease would set in were they to spend long hours working with "the political brass" as it is sometimes known. (As far as I can tell, every agency has a special name by which careerists refer to the usually separate complex of offices housing political executives, but the connotation is always one of a distant "them.")

It has not always been that way. As Leonard White noted there was also a dual system in the public service of the nineteenth century, but in that period more or less permanent staff was also present atop the departmental structures. The chief clerks were "the pivots on which daily business turned."[9] As ministers and their very few political assistants came and went, the chief clerks continued to superintend the departmental work force in the daily grind of government paperwork. When the minister (or cabinet secretary as they are known in the United States) was away, the chief clerk could be found filling in as acting secretary, not a rare occurrence in those unair-conditioned days in Washington. The chief clerk received the daily mail, distributed it to political officers and subordinate clerical staff, supervised the writing of all letters going out of the department, the distribution of publications, and the collection of subordinate clerks' monthly time sheets when that innovation was introduced. But this form of management could not hope to keep pace with the more complex, less routinized work of government, and by the end of the First World War this embryo form of higher civil service had largely disappeared amid a welter of problems and temporary officials.[10]

Yet there are people today who are regularly counted on to service cabinet secretaries and other top appointees and who oversee the working of departmental machinery. Indeed, it would be difficult to imagine how the work of government could go on if there were not such people. If we loosen our concept of the higher civil service so as to include indeliberately organized, loosely woven career lines, then the outlines of a second, de facto higher civil service begin to emerge.

The unilluminating term generally used for these persons is "In and Outers." This is not a helpful concept because it can apply to anyone with a temporary stint in government, especially the top political appointees whose tenures are short and sometimes (as one U.S. senator put it) possessing all the impact of a snowflake on the bosom of the Potomac. The *public careerists,* as I will call them, do occasionally rise to the ranks of secretary or agency head. In fact, as the role of political parties and their patronage power has declined, public careerists have become a more prominent source of senior political appointments. Approximately one-half of President Reagan's top appointees in the winter of 1980–1981 had held subordinate appointments in earlier administrations. But what truly distinguishes public careerists is not that they are part of any coherent, political career ladder, as is the case, for example, with the progression of British political executives (from parliamentary secretary, to junior minister, to senior minister).

What distinguishes the de facto, higher civil service of public careerists is their ability to combine top-level assistance to senior presidential appointees with some measure of familiarity about the issues and processes of government. What they know about policies—and public policy issues have become an increasingly complex area of technical specialization—makes the public careerists useful to the senior political executives. What the public careerists know about the ins and outs of government work and their own networks of personal contacts in Washington helps this de facto higher civil service use, if not administratively control in a classic bureaucratic sense, the machinery of government.

TABLE 3.   Political and Career Executives' Experience in the Federal
Government, 1970

YEARS OF GOVERNMENT EXPERIENCE	PERCENTAGE OF ALL		
	Presidential appointees	Noncareer supergrades	Career supergrades
under 2	69	40	3
2 to 5	19	7	11
6 to 10	6	14	9
over 10	6	39	77

Note: Adapted from Hugh Heclo, *A Government of Strangers* (Washington: Brookings Institution, 1977), p. 101.

It would be fruitless to try to draw clear lines around the careers of those participating in this informal system of bureaucratic executives. Some who participate in it are former career civil servants, especially those who are ambitious to expand their careers beyond the boundaries of their agencies. Some have worked in congressional staff positions. Some are academic experts with a penchant for government affairs. Any attempt to apply a single label, such as public careerists, does some injustice to the complexities involved. But the key point is that these are people who build their careers around problems of public policy and do so outside the confines of the formal civil service personnel system. They are not like career executives, who spend their lives within one or another government agency. Neither are they exactly like senior political appointees, who are often transient on the scene of public affairs and have little prospect for reentering government. Table 3 suggests something of the intermediary position held by public careerists: less experienced in government jobs than career executives but far better grounded than the normal run of presidential appointees. This latter feature is particularly striking inasmuch as the information shown is for a time when a new Republican administration had been in office less than two years and after a preceding eight years of control by the Democrats; yet over one-half of the noncareer executives had already had more than five years' prior experience in government at one time or another.

The potential recruitment pool for the de facto civil service is, indeed, immense. Since the mid-1950s the number of full-time permanent federal employees has remained unchanged at approximately 3 million persons, but the size of the so-called indirect federal work force has grown to an estimated 8 million persons; of these, an estimated 3 million are doing work that federal employees would have to do themselves to keep the government operating if the indirect employees were not there. I am certainly not suggesting that these millions of people themselves are public careerists as I have been using the term. But if one could look behind the numbers, deep into the tangle of relationships that is implied by this indirect or third-party government, what one would find are significant numbers who learn a great deal about particular policies and the administrative processes that go with them. Because of what they know and can do, at least by reputation if not in practice, they are likely to be called on when a new administration or new secretary begins "staffing up" and looking for "some good people who can help us," as the sayings go.

When not holding temporary positions in the executive branch or mushrooming congressional bureaucracy, public careerists can be found in academic departments, think tanks, interest group associations and public interest lobbies, law firms, consulting and policy research firms, and so on (rarely in state and local governments but sometimes in the lobby organizations for state and local governments!). The one thing that these places have in common is a stake in concrete problems of public policy and programing. The number of potential roosts for public careerists has grown phenomenally in recent years as the federal government has intervened in more policy areas and used various profit and nonprofit organizations—rather than the government work force—to do its work. The largely inadvertent result has been to expand a kind of on-the-job training by which persons outside the formal civil service system acquire policy expertise and a working familiarity with many aspects of government administration.

The evidence can be only impressionistic, but it seems that more and more bright young people who are interested in public service see their futures in terms of the loosely structured career lines of public careerists. To build a career in the formal civil service structure is likely to be regarded as plodding and unambitious. Better a stint teaching at graduate school of public policy and management or organizing the RFP process (requests for proposals to be funded by federal agencies) for some new policy evaluation firm. Better still to gain an academic position that combines only a little teaching with opportunities for extensive writing and consulting on particular problems of public policy, or to become a partner in a law firm or management consulting company dealing with particular policy issues. When back in government, public careerists will hold jobs that are formally designated as political appointments, but they are likely to know much more about the intricacies of given policies and their special brand of politics (with congressional staff, interest groups, the analytic community, and so on) than they are to know about political parties and elections. The best of these public careerists will know a great deal about the administrative machinery of government and so form a very useful link between senior presidential appointees and lower-level career bureaucrats in the agencies. The worst are in Washington to build a résumé and promote their particular policy preferences with little regard to administrative realities.

Policy and Politics in the Dual Structure

By now it should be clear that there can be no simple model describing the role of America's higher civil service in politics and policy making. Even the concept of a higher civil service is diffuse and subject to differing interpretations. "The" higher civil service is really an inadvertent by-product shaped by four immensely powerful political forces.

First, the higher civil service is part of an executive branch that the framers of the Constitution designed to have a single executive head, the president. Second, however, it is also part of an administrative structure that is beholden to a legislature—or more accurately various specialized parts (committees and subcommittees) of a legislature—that has enduring and independent power to shape administration. Congress can deny the civil servant and his organization funds, overturn decisions, specify actions, and generally make the bureaucrat's life miserable in a dozen ways. Third, administrative leadership is vested in a mix of permanent careerists and transient appointees who have only the most tenuous attachment to either presidents or congressmen as party politicians. Finally, the Washington bureaucracy has depended more and more on largely independent third parties in the private sector and subnational government level to accomplish its purposes.[11]

One way of summarizing all this is to say that the basic organizing principle—more unintentional than planned—of the higher civil service is horizontal. For members of both de jure and de facto systems, the lines of loyalty run outward through programs and policies rather than upward to bureaucratic or political superiors. That is, of course, a gross simplification of a very complex system, but it does encapsulate the essential difference of higher civil service work in the United States compared to other Western nations.

Thus, high-level career officials in the de jure civil service find it most useful to work closely with those in Congress and outside groups who have an enduring stake in the programs of their particular agencies.[12] Parochialism is its own reward, for in identifying one's career with a given bureau and its program lies long-run safety from political interference *and* personal advancement in the agency. Unlike the situation in France, which tends to eliminate risks for civil servants taking an overtly political role, the American system imposes extreme risks on any careerist performing the higher civil servant's role in working closely with top political ministers. Given the general American ambivalence about the Washington bureaucracy and narrowly technocratic assumptions about civil servants' work, given the transience and weak political position with Congress and the public of top presidential appointees, it is not surprising that career executives feel vulnerable if they are too closely identified with the department's "political brass." If France subsidizes civil servants to become politicians, America penalizes career bureaucrats for performing as higher civil servants.

The horizontal rather than vertical principle also applies to public careerists. Those closest to the cabinet secretary or agency head are not so much his political lieutenants as they are members of his personal entourage or liaison staff to outside groups. Public careerists mixed elsewhere in the administrative structure are political subordinates only in the most formalistic sense (job titles and pay scales) of that term. More realistically, they should be seen as peers drawn from collateral networks of analysts, lobbyists, and other activists in public affairs for whom politics is policy. This is true in foreign affairs no less than in domestic policy, where the horizontal alliances tend to be more obvious. Some flavor of the processes at work can be gained by looking more closely at one small example from the new Reagan administration. This portrait of a "defense intellectual" is drawn from the career of W. Scott Thompson, a thirty-nine-year-old professor and member of the Reagan transition team for defense issues.

> "The main challenge of conservative intellectuals is to beat down the New Class in the State Department and Defense Department." Thompson speaks in equally confident tones of sending the new message of toughness to the Russians. . . . Nine years ago he was on the foreign policy task force of George McGovern's presidential campaign. Thompson disagreed with McGovern's posture, but felt a need to occupy a formal place on his team. "It was an exercise in damage limitation," he says. . . . A few years later in 1975–76 he became a White House Fellow and served as assistant to Secretary of Defense Donald Rumsfeld, establishing Republican credentials. . . . When Jimmy Carter became President he shunned hard-line Jackson and Moynihan Democrats in making his foreign policy and defense appointments. Those shunned founded the Committee on the Present Danger. . . . Most members were old enough to have held high office in the Johnson and Kennedy Administrations, but there was a younger cadre, and Thompson was chief among them. "The Committee on the Present Danger has been the most influential elite-affecting institution in American history," says Thompson. "It has not tried to influence the masses." . . . The views of the Committee . . . were elaborated in an anthology . . . edited by Thompson and published in 1980 by the Institute for Contemporary Studies, a California based

think tank founded in 1975 . . . by, among others, Edwin Meese, now the President's counselor, and Caspar Weinberger, now Secretary of Defense. . . . In the 1980 presidential campaign, Thompson offered himself as an advisor to any and all candidates who shared his perspective. When Alexander Haig considered a run at the Republican nomination, Thompson secured a hearing for him . . . before the Massachusetts Republican State Committee. . . . Then he served as chief of John Connally's national security task force. But when Ronald Reagan emerged from the field, Thompson joined his camp. . . . He says he has been offered jobs he has turned down [in the new administration], and is mulling over others. "I'm on the standard lists," he says. "I'm on 20 lists. I like what I'm doing now, being a plugged-in intellectual."[13]

Other public careerists may be a little more adept at hiding their candles, but the same pattern repeats itself again and again in Washington: for large numbers of people at senior levels of the bureaucracy, engagement in public office and politics occurs through the vehicle of policy issues and networks of people associated with them. Far from increasing political control from the top of the department or the White House, adding more and more "political appointments" tends to diffuse control through the spread of horizontal loyalties.

Missing from this picture of mixed career bureaucracies and policy technocracies is "politics" in the traditional party-political meaning of that term. Neither career nor political executives have any tradition of serving in the national legislature, although some movement back and forth between legislative staff positions and the executive bureaucracy has become more common in recent decades. There is also little experience with senior bureaucrats serving in elective or appointive positions in state and local government (contra France and West Germany, for example). Career officials in the federal civil service are prohibited from engaging in all but the most routine grassroots, nonpartisan political activity.[14] Public careerists face no such prohibition but their policy interests generally lead them to shun the "nonsubstantive" and often tedious work associated with congressional careers or state and local government service. Likewise, career civil servants almost never rise to the top ranks of political appointments although, as we have seen, they can be found migrating into lower-level political executive positions, and there is some tendency for public careerists to form part of the potential pool for senior presidential appointments.

In this American system it is obviously very difficult to view the bureaucracy as an autonomous participant in policy making. At the senior levels of government, where matters of high policy are discussed and hopefully settled, the field of relevant "others" extends outwards, across institutions, through public careerists, and into the networks mobilized around particular policy issues. At lower levels, where policy lies disguised as problems of administration, career executives and the mixture of lower-level political executives have a field of discourse that also extends outward in a similar way, even if the subject matter is expressed in terms of hard program details rather than high policy. In this setting, the hardest problem is to make the conversation that is policy making extend upward and downward within the government. The sideways talk outside the state apparatus comes naturally. Only in America would "implementation" seem an exciting new frontier of policy analysis and academic fashion!

The Hollow Center

It is at this point—the nature of policy and administration as an up-and-down conversation within the machinery of government—that we come to the core problem in the search for a role in any higher civil service in Washington. The one institution with an inherent interest in taut vertical strength in the executive branch is the presidency. That is the inevitable consequence of a Constitution vesting the executive function in a single rather than a plural head chosen independently of the legislature. As the *Federalist Papers* put it,

> Energy in the Executive is a leading character of good government. . . .
> The ingredients which constitute energy in the Executive are, first,
> unity. . . . This unity may be destroyed in two ways: either by vesting the
> power in two or more magistrates of equal dignity and authority; or by
> vesting it ostensibly in one man, subject, in whole or in part, to the
> control and co-operation of others in the capacity of counsellors to him.[15]

The logic of the Constitution means that there can be no governmentwide, coherent higher civil service unless it is somehow attached to and led from the presidency. Anything less *must* represent less than the executive branch as a whole. Only the presidential office has a vested interest in integrating the diverse parts.

And yet there is a powerful political logic that has militated against the constitutional logic for the higher civil service. Everything said earlier about the difficulty of career executives working in close relations with senior political executives applies *in extremis* to the presidency. Secure in their horizontal loyalties, congressmen, departmental bureaucrats, and outside groups are deeply hostile to anything that smacks of permanent officialdom near the president. Likewise, presidents and their transient aides suspect any official who has been closely identified with the work of a preceding administration. And always in the background is the pervasive historical attitude that civil servants are at their best on narrowly technical matters and unfit for working in a political environment on questions of general policy—precisely the situation in the White House. It seems strange to say but it is true: the surest way for a higher civil servant to cut short his career in government is to work faithfully as a higher civil servant to the president.

This political logic means that the closer one approaches the person of the president, the farther into the background recede higher civil servants in both the de facto and de jure senses of that term. One searches in vain for anything even approaching a higher civil service presence in the Executive Office of the President as a whole. A closer look at the president's executive office will help clarify the paradox of a hollow center in the American higher civil service.

At the fringes of the Executive Office of the President (EOP) have traditionally been a number of special purpose units, usually put there at the insistence of one or another group who feels that the presidential seal of office will highlight the importance of its concerns. Consumer issues, drug abuse, and urban affairs are recent examples, as are the current environmental and science offices. Their staffs are generally a hodgepodge of personnel, some detailed from operating agencies, some from outside the government, but all having an evanescent quality as far as the larger working of the president's office is concerned.

Closer to the core of the EOP are four units, each with its own characteristics. The oldest is the Office of Management and Budget (OMB), and for some years after moving in 1939 from Treasury Department to the president's office, this unit approached being a general staff agency for the presidency with a fairly well defined structure of higher civil service careers. Much of that tradition has been lost in the past fifteen years, and several layers of political appointees now tend to insulate career staff from direct contact with senior presidential staff, much less the president himself. The political OMB appointees do reflect some of the characteristics of the de facto higher civil service discussed earlier but so far, the unpopularity of the budget decisions they must enforce has limited their chances for returning elsewhere in government. By and large, a generation of senior civil servants, whose careers culminated at the very top of the budget agency, has simply disappeared and not been replaced.

The National Security Council (NSC) and Council of Economic Advisers (CEA) constitute two more parts of the core EOP staff agencies. The personnel of each are drawn from powerful communities of policy professionals, the NSC in foreign affairs and the CEA in economics. Frequently young staff members will reappear later as more senior members of the NSC and CEA. Some, after a stint on the outside move on to departmental positions and vice versa. In other words, these staffs have something of the quality of public careerists discussed earlier, although it must be immediately added that their main interest is almost always on matters of policy rather than administrative machinery and process.

The Domestic Policy Staff (renamed Office of Policy Development in the Reagan administration) is a recent addition to central EOP operations, and its personnel have had the more diverse quality one would expect in a policy area where, unlike foreign affairs and economic policy, there is no well-developed community of specialists. Its staffs have generally been a mixture of personal acquaintances with an analytic bent and tie to the presidential candidate, young policy specialists from outside government, and detailed departmental staff to work on topical policy problems. Often their small numbers and inexperience in the ways of the bureaucracy have led to considerable dependence on the much larger, more institutionalized staff of OMB for in-depth staff work. At the same time, the loosely structured, highly maneuverable nature of domestic policy personnel, as well as their perceived closeness to the White House, facilitates dealings with high-ranking political appointees in a way that is no longer open to OMB careerists (who are likely to leave such matters to their own layer of appointees).

Taking these four units of central EOP machinery as a whole, one can say that each is (on the record of the past decade) likely to be headed by a senior personal assistant to the president, supported by a staff whose leading members are policy specialists drawn from outside and the fringes of the federal government. One might stretch terms and call these people informal higher civil servants (their careers are not heavily government based), but three things should be recalled before going very far with that label. First, their service is highly compartmentalized, limited to one of these four units at present or at any time in the future. An NSC staffman simply will not turn up later as a CEA, OMB, or domestic policy staffer, and the same applies for each of the other offices. Even if one accepts that there can be an informal type of higher civil service, that clearly does not apply to the EOP as a central entity, only to its parts.

A second reservation is that in all these offices, the general preoccupation is with policy problems and decisions, not with the administrative workings of government. Where there is administrative involvement it is likely to be concerned with checking to see that painfully arrived at presidential decisions are, in fact, being carried out. But this kind of "checking for obedience" hardly amounts to the oversight of administrative machinery normally associated with the functioning of a higher civil service. The one exception to these statements has been the Office of Management and Budget, which for a few brief periods in its history had an administrative management staff engaged in high level work. Since the early 1970s this staff work has lacked presidential backing, grown narrowly technical, and largely atrophied. The Office of Administration that appeared in 1977 is a newly created housekeeping unit for the EOP (mail service, library, and so forth) with a relatively large number of low-level civil service positions. To date all of the directors of this office have been aides to presidents Carter or Reagan, in their thirties, and with little or no prior experience in the federal government. It is revealing of the place of a "higher civil service" in the central machinery of government that with a change in political control of the White House in 1980, many staff changes in even this most routine of EOP units were thought necessary.

The third problem in speaking of an informal higher civil service within the perimeters of OMB/NSC/CEA/DC professional staffs is that these people simply do not interact directly with their chief client, the president. If he is their "minister," then they are not part of the strategic center of his activities. Only the head of each of these units is in *that* position, along with a number of other people in the White House. The White House Office, the second largest piece of the EOP, is, of course, itself a deviously complex bureaucracy. But none of the persons heading up the major units there is a civil servant in the de jure sense; that designation applies to only the lower-level clerical staff and by no means all of them. Neither can the nonclerical White House staff be fitted into the category of higher civil servants in the de facto meaning of the term. By and large there is no expectation that they will have or have had anything to do with the administrative machinery of government. With only very rare exceptions, they have never before worked in the immediate environs of a president and never will again (Bryce Harlow, James Baker, Fred Fielding and Lloyd Cutler being major exceptions in recent history). The White House is usually not a place for civil servants or public careerists.

It has not always been so. In the period roughly between the 1890s and the late 1930s, the staff immediately surrounding a president had acquired its own dual nature. The office of secretary to the president had a long and checkered career. Generally filled by personal friends, young political aides, and an occasional relative, the secretary's position gradually became more specialized and by the outbreak of World War II there were four personal aides performing different functions as FDR's secretaries. However, there was also a second side to White House staff assistance. As routine functions of the presidency expanded after 1890, a more permanent staff to deal with these tasks gradually took shape behind the scenes. By the end of the 1930s, the White House was virtually the only place left in the executive branch where the old chief clerk's role (see p.   ) still persisted. It did so in the person of Rudolph Forster. Forster's exact title varied over the forty-five years in which he served in the White House, but by the 1930s Forster was most commonly identified as executive clerk to the president and was responsible for supervising administrative functions of the White House much as chief clerks had done for departments. Under his jurisdiction fell the expanding offices for mail, correspondence, files, records, messengers, spending accounts, and personnel. Seeing the overwhelmingly routine nature of these tasks, presidential scholars have generally dismissed the role of the executive clerk and its eventual demise as unimportant.

In fact the executive clerk's position and what happened to it are central to understanding the absence of a higher civil service function in the central executive institution of government. Far from being routine, executive clerk operations were highly judgmental. Far from being relegated to lowly organizational levels, the executive clerk worked directly and intimately with presidents, their senior aides, leading political figures (even attending the president's senior political staff meetings every day during the Truman administration). Beyond the mechanical handling of paper lay extremely important functions of advice, warning, presidential protection, and institutional memory in an office chronically subject to disruptive changes. In short, there were the makings here of a higher civil servant's performance.

Rudolph Forster and Maurice Latta, who served as assistant clerk and succeeded Forster as executive clerk in 1944, both joined the White House in 1898 as civil service stenographers on detail from federal agencies. In subsequent years Forster and Latta shared two desks opposite each other directly outside the president's office (comparable to the still traditional position of cabinet office civil servants outside the British prime minister's office). All visitors to and from the president passed by their desks. All incoming correspondence and materials for the presidents passed over those desks. All presidentially signed documents and written instructions from the president (since the executive clerk had to pass them on to the messenger service for delivery) went past the eyes of the clerk. This continued not only in the drowsy days of presidential leadership in the 1920s but also during the tenure of Franklin Roosevelt.[16]

As the presidency acquired vastly greater responsibilities in the build-up to World War II, the position of executive clerk gradually faded in significance. It was a gradual process because Forster continued to be regarded by FDR as indispensable, and the smartest of the new "administrative assistants" to the president (created in 1939) used Forster's knowledge and advice about government processes to smooth their ways. But an executive clerk's office that merely perpetuated the traditional chief clerk functions had little chance of maintaining its position amid the growing responsibilities of the presidency. That much is obvious. Less obvious is the way that political forces stifled any chance that civil service presence at the center could keep pace with the presidency. Simply try to imagine the constraints at work if one were the executive clerk trying to keep up with the frenzy of presidential work and transitions. Any hold-over civil servants from a previous administration were inevitably subject to intense suspicion. Since one's loyalty is always in doubt, the best practical rule is to demean the services one might have offered, viz., do not push yourself; let the successive waves of presidential aides be assured that they, not you, know best. Wait for the phone to ring with questions as to how things should be done.

As the White House and Executive Office of the President became suffused with more and more temporary aides—visible to outsiders and confident of their proven loyalty to the president—the phone rang less frequently. In essence, there was no client for a higher civil service presence in the presidency: not presidents or their aides and certainly not congressmen or departmental bureaucrats. Hollowing out the center of any potential higher civil service was a process that fed on itself. No executive clerk could reasonably feel justified in trying to attract high-quality civil service staff to the White House. Working hard, doing well, and serving an incumbent faithfully would very likely lead to nothing with the next administration. Far from helping one's career in the government service, it was a road that offered political vulnerability or routine paper shuffling in deference to the ever growing number of political appointees in the White House.

Events have confirmed the political logic. Perhaps the easiest way to see the overall trend is simply to observe the physical position of the executive clerk in the never-ending struggle for White House office space. The time-honored position had two administrative careerists seated together in the office directly outside the president's door; one of these was executive clerk, the other his senior assistant. When Forster died, the Forster/Latta duo was replaced by Latta and another careerist, William Hopkins, who had already been in the White House fourteen years; Hopkins succeeded Latta during the Truman administration and remained executive clerk until retiring under Nixon. While the personnel continuity is impressive, so, too, is the loss of office stature. Early in the Eisenhower administration, the president's new staff secretary was added to the clerk's office, forcing the clerk's assistant to an office downstairs and breaking the traditional career duo. Later in the Eisenhower years, a new staff secretary's office was carved out, a wall built, and a walkway created between the president's office and that of his senior assistant. No longer was the executive clerk at the point of access to the president. In the Johnson administration the space needs of even more presidential aides took over what had once been a washroom (turned into a private room for rest after Eisenhower's heart attack) and combined this area with the remnant of the executive clerk's office. The clerk then moved upstairs in the White House to what had been a telephone room. In the

Nixon administration, assistants to presidential aides acquired the upstairs space and the executive clerk ended up in the basement. In 1977 it was the political head of the new Office of Administration (cousin Hugh Carter) who took over the chief clerk's White House space. In 1982 the last vestige of a career head for White House administration disappeared when the political head of the Office of Administration acquired his own politically appointed deputy to deal with the few remaining long-term employees who head administrative divisions. These scattered remnants of institutional memory for the presidency dwell in the basement of the old Executive Office Building across from the White House.

Trivial as these developments seem, they illustrate a larger point concerning the problematic nature of any civil service functions in proximity to the president. What the executive clerk's office could not become was a locus of continuing responsibility for the operation of *the* central executive machinery of government, that is, the presidency as an institution. Failing to perform that function, "the" higher civil service can only be regarded as a term of art in American central government.

A Prologue to Democratic Technology

America's higher civil service is an unmanaged affair, weak in the central executive apparatus and extensive in horizontal links to the larger political society, The two faces of the higher civil service, de facto and de jure, are really both reflections of the profound duality in modern government—at once inward-oriented by the immense technical complexity of modern policy *and* outward-directed by the broader social cooperation on which its policies depend.

The profile of the senior bureaucracy is, therefore, etched by the interaction of powerful external agents on the hard surface of government expertise. The great strength of this system is its capacity to make government accessible to those who are actively interested in affecting its work. The great dangers are that the government will be unable to act as a collective enterprise with institutional continuity and with some sense of purpose that is more than a reflection of the preferences held by those who happen to be mobilized to affect its work. No nation seems likely to reverse the growing need for technical expertise at all government levels. What America's "non system" of public careerists may have to offer are some hints about tilting the inevitable technocracy in more broadly democratic directions. What Washington has yet to discover is a means of meshing its formal and informal higher civil service with presidential leadership and with the need for a longer and broader attention span in government.

In 1978, President Carter signed into law the first comprehensive Civil

Service Reform Act since the passage of the original statute in 1883.[17] It would clearly be premature to try and judge the full impact of this major act, but there are four features that reaffirm the thesis of this paper. The real definition of America's higher civil service is being written not so much in formal personnel laws as in the ambiguous, informal understandings that shape people's careers in public service.[18]

First, the new law has disbanded the old Civil Service Commission. In its place is an Office of Personnel Management, headed by a director appointed by the president and confirmed by the Senate to a four-year term, and a separate bipartisan board to police the mass of routine civil service jobs. But the new personnel office was not placed in the Executive Office of the President, largely because of the congressional criticism that was feared from increasing the number of staff in the presidency.

Second, the new law places considerable emphasis on competition for financial rewards at both the middle and the upper levels of the formal civil service system. Each department and agency develops its own performance appraisal system and pays out cash rewards to the top "performers" from a limited pool of funds. Here again are the familiar echoes of technical efficiency and scientific management in government personnel policy, as if the work of higher civil servants were an unambiguous product to be measured and ranked. This provision for linking financial rewards to performance measures has occasioned charges of favoritism and a major congressional reaction against the law, insofar as bonuses for top bureaucrats might produce a higher annual income than that received by congressmen. If a moonwalk could not qualify, high-performance civil servants with more terrestrial achievements were probably foolish to bank on the new bonus system. In fact many did and now feel betrayed by the haphazard implementation of performance pay.

Third, a new Senior Executive Service was created, as noted earlier, to provide more mobile and systematic management of career and political executives below the level of top presidential appointees. What is noteworthy so far is that management of the new system has devolved mainly to the bureau level within the separate departments and agencies. No central means exists to control or even facilitate the assignment of senior executives on anything like a departmentwide—much less a governmentwide—basis.

Finally, there is simply no meaningful system for using the higher civil servants of the Senior Executive Service in the Executive Office of the President. The Office of Management and Budget, with 40 percent of all Executive Office staff, has its own procedures for its own purposes. Several other units do likewise, and the White House Office, with 30 percent of total Executive Office manpower, has no systematic means for using Senior Executive manpower. As far as the operation of the presidency is concerned, the new, reformed civilian career system is largely a non-event.

The conclusion seems inescapable. Neither the historic constraints, nor the 1978 reforms, nor current practice, point toward a significantly different future for the formal, de jure concept of a higher civil service in American government. Yet there is a system, and it carries with it the strengths and dangers of a democratic technocracy. To find a higher civil service function developing we must loosen our categories, take a deep breath, and keep an eye on the public careerists.

NOTES

1. The rule in question is Section 5547 of Title V of The United States Code. I am grateful to James W. Fesler of Yale University for bringing this example to my attention. The astronauts fell under a personnel system administered by the National Aeronautics and Space Administration, which, in standard government usage, is counted as part of the civil service merit system but not subject to rules of the general competitive examination system administered by the Civil Service Commission or, after 1979, the Office of Personnel Management.

2. At the insistence of Congress, government lawyers have been kept in a separate "schedule" of the civil service system in which examinations for entry are prohibited and political removal is easier.

3. A useful overview is contained in James Q. Wilson, "The Rise of the Bureaucratic State," *The Public Interest,* Fall 1974. For a more comprehensive review of the issues discussed in this section of my paper, see House of Representatives Committee on Post Office and Civil Service, *History of Civil Service Merit Systems of the United States and Selected Foreign Countries,* 94 Cong., 2d sess. (GPO, 1976).

4. There is little comparative information regarding public attitudes toward the higher civil service in different countries. The most relevant studies contain some hints that, during the 1960s at least, Americans were more trusting of national administrators than they appear to be today, more confident than citizens of Western Europe that they could organize to influence administrative decisions, and less cynical about the integrity of public bureaucracies than were citizens in less developed countries. See M. J. Jennings et al., "Trusted Leaders," *Public Opinion Quarterly* 30 (Fall 1966); 368–384; Senate Committee on Government Operations, *Confidence and Concern: Citizens View American Government,* 93 Cong. 1st sess. (GPO, 1973), part 2. Gabriel A. Almond and Sidney Verba, *The Civic Culture* (Princeton: Princeton University Press, 1963), pp. 70–73; Samuel J. Eldersveld et al., *The Citizen and the Administrator in a Developing Democracy* (Glenview, Ill.: Scott, Foresman, 1968).

5. Article II, section 2 of the U.S. Constitution.

6. Cf. William Dudley Foulke, *Fighting the Spoilsmen,* (New York: G. P. Putnam's Sons, 1919).

7. Creation of higher grade positions in the civil service, as for example with the addition of supergrades in the Classification Act of 1949, has always been debated and politically accepted in Congress largely on the grounds of attracting specialists and experts into the government service and *not* as a means of promoting a system of more high-level, general assignments for the existing bureaucracy. See, for example, *Congressional Record,* daily edition, Sept. 14, 1950, and Sept. 21, 1950, pp. 15036–15037, 15558.

8. Further details comparing U.S. executive structure with that in France and Britain are contained in James W. Fesler, *Public Administration: Theory and Practice* (Englewood Cliffs, N.J.: Prentice-Hall, 1980), pp. 132–135.

9. Leonard D. White, *The Jacksonians* (New York: Macmillan, 1954), p. 352.

10. The only other time that a departmentwide civil service begins to come into view is during the 1950s and early 1960s. Following recommendations publicized by the Hoover commission on government organization, the major executive departments established posts that were usually termed assistant secretary for administration. The original expectation was that these positions, although filled through presidential appointment, would be held by careerists from the general civil service and that they would serve as each secretary's chief deputy for internal departmental management. Most of these offices therefore encompassed budgeting, personnel, and procurement functions. The intentions for these assistant secretaries were clearly not realized during the 1960s and 1970s for reasons discussed in Heclo, *A Government of Strangers* (Washington, D.C.: Brookings Institution, 1977), chapter 2.

11. This point is discussed more fully in Frederick C. Mosher, "The Changing Responsibilities and Tactics of the Federal Government," *Public Administration Review,* Winter 1980–1981; and Samuel H. Beer, "The Modernization of American Federalism," *Publius,* Fall 1973.

12. See, for example, Joel Aberbach and Bert Rockman, "The Overlapping Worlds of American Federal Executives and Congressmen," *British Journal of Political Science,* vol. 7, no. 1, January 1977.

13. Sidney Blumenthal, "Portrait of a Defense Intellectual," *Boston Sunday Globe,* Feb. 8, 1981, p. C–2.

14. Permissible political activities are spelled out in 5 U.S. Code of Federal Regulations, sections 733.111 to 733.122. The prohibition has been challenged several times, most recently in 1973, but has been upheld by the Supreme Court as being constitutional. *United States Civil Service Commission v. National Association of Letter Carriers, AFL-CIO,* 413 U.S. 548 (1973).

15. *The Federalist,* Number 70.

16. A lively, popular account of the presidential secretaries is in Michael Medved, *The Shadow Presidents* (New York: Times Books, 1979). Enticing hints of Forster's work, despite his passion for anonymity, and of FDR's regard for him are in FDR's "Memorandum to Bill Hassett," Sept. 4, 1942; and "M. H. McIntyre

to Rudolph Forster," May 1, 1937, all in Rudolph Forster papers, Box 1, Library of Congress, Washington, D.C.

17. The Act and its passage are described in Felix A. Nigro, "The Politics of Civil Service Reform" (reproduced), paper presented to the 1979 Annual Meeting of the American Political Science Association, Washington, D.C.

18. In 1984 Congress reviewed the first five years of the Senior Executive Service. As I interpret this evidence, it demonstrates a failure to create anything like a creditable higher civil service and does so largely due to failures of implementation by temporary political appointees. See *Hearings before the Civil Service Subcommittee,* Post Office and Civil Service Committee, U.S. House of Representatives, Washington, D.C., November 7, 1983; February 16, March 20, April 12, and April 13, 1984.

THE HIGHER CIVIL SERVICE IN ITALY*

Sabino Cassese

On the relations between politics and administration at the summit of Italian bureaucratic structures, very different observations can be read. For example, in recent times, two foreign scholars of notable competence, such as Robert D. Putnam and Sidney Tarrow, have arrived, by different ways, at completely discordant conclusions. According to Putnam, "the fragmentation of the Italian political class has allowed and encouraged the bureaucracy to 'rise above politics,' responsible to no higher authority and fundamentally unresponsive. And to complete the vicious circle, the inability of successive Italian governments to make the bureaucratic machine respond has condemned them to ineffectiveness." Tarrow, on the contrary, highlighted the central role carried out by parties and politics in relations between central and peripheral administrations.[1]

There is no doubt that these two points of view grasp some obvious

*The author wishes to thank the following for the precious help they gave him in the research phase or with comments on the text: Comm. Claudio Caponetto, Dr. Gaetano D'Auria, Dr. Domenico Macri, Prof. Onorato Sepe, Avv. Nino Terranova, and Dr. Francesco Saverio Vestri. The author also thanks Prof. Robert Putnam for his attentive reading and his comments.

contradictions of the Italian situation: in a country in which party politics is everything, how is the evident detachment between bureaucratic summits and governments possible? How to explain, in the main collaborators of politicians, a diffused, defensive attitude and—often—resentment with regard to parties and politics? Is it not schizophrenic, the attitude of those who despise politics but make use of it, mistrust ministers but serve them?[2]

This article will analyze the problem of the role of higher civil servants and their relations with ministers on the basis of the thesis set forth here in summary form. If the relations between politics and administration are determined in a different way from one country to another, so that there is not one model, or even prevalent models, the peculiarities of the "Italian case" can be set forth in the following logical sequence:

1. Higher civil servants are not integrated in politico-economic leadership: unlike in France (and, partly, also in Great Britain), there is a separation between the first and the second.

2. Relations between higher civil servants and political leaders are based on a relationship of exchange in which the former have obtained a guarantee of their post and their career in exchange for a loss of prestige and power; in fact, the Italian higher civil servant, as compared with his foreign colleagues, is more certain of his post, but less influential; the higher civil servants, therefore, have accepted a lesser role, in order to have a free hand as regards their own fate.

3. The political leadership, however, tempers the relative rigidity of the relationship that is established in this way with four correctives:

- by increasing indirectly the remuneration of some higher civil servants by giving them external assignments
- by setting against the heads of departments the *gabinetto* (private secretariat of a minister), for which frequent recourse is had to state councillors
- by having recourse to the "promotion" of heads of department to the State Council or the Audit Office, in order to remove them
- by setting up administrative organisms outside the ministries.

These correctives modify the situation as it exists at the outset and give rise to "parallel administrations," which enable the political leaders to govern.

4. Higher civil servants, though they are—partly—themselves the cause of this situation, realize that their behavior and the reactions that follow as a result put them on a dead-end track; hence their attitude of mistrust and (sometimes) of protest with regard to political leaders, an attitude unfavorable to innovation, and preference for the "application of the laws";

5. In order to be able to overcome this "impasse" (but also under the thrust of other pressures), the government multiplies its activity of legislative proposal. Of the two instruments to guide the administration—the

law of Parliament and the command of the government—the former tends to be emphasized. More laws, however, mean, not only a more controlled higher civil service, but also more power of Parliament over the administration, at the expense of the government itself. The result, therefore, is a loss of influence, not only of the higher civil servants, but also of the ministers themselves. The administration remains without guidance.

To illustrate the sequence set forth, we will examine, in order, the following aspects:

1. The historical-constitutional background of relations betwen government and administration (and Parliament-society-administration) is ambiguous: historically several models are superimposed upon one another, while the Constitution does not make a choice.

2. The higher civil servants, if they are functionally part of the ruling class, are not so structurally.

3. The higher civil servants have few powers and many guarantees.

4. The ministers overcome and go over the heads of higher civil servants in various ways, but without causing irremediable breaks.

5. The "monopoly of jurists" and the abundance of laws end up in a limit also for the government; the administration has two masters (Parliament and government), but no guide.

6. The prospects seemed to be opening with the introduction of the regions; today, however, the regional experiment, from this point of view, should be judged with caution.

Let us begin with *the constitutional background*. The 1948 Constitution accepts the parliamentary model according to which the administration is the set of offices serving the government, which is put in charge of them. After having laid down in article 94 that "the government must have the confidence of the two Chambers," the Constitution establishes, in fact, in the following article, that ministers are responsible for the acts of their ministries. On the other hand, in articles 97 and 98, the Constitution seems to make a different choice in favor of a conception of the administration as a public apparatus in the service of the collectivity. In these articles, in the first place, the fundamental concern is that of administrative impartiality and, therefore, they contain norms that aim at avoiding the political aspect induced by the presence of the government at the top of administration. (For example, the organization of the offices must be determined with a law and not with an act of government; it should be kept in mind that in Italy, unlike France, there are "reserves of law," but not "reserves of regulatory power.") In the second place, it is laid down that "civil servants are in the exclusive service of the nation." In this way, having recourse to a term extraneous to Italian juridical culture (unlike the French one) and to constitutional vocabulary itself, the idea of the civil servant as "Crown's servant" is abandoned.[3]

Before going on the examine the higher civil service more closely two other observations should be added regarding the change in politico-administrative relations in the historical evolution and the general conditions of the administration of the higher civil service at the present time.

The first period after the union of Italy (1861–1900) was characterized by a great "mobility if not exchangeability of political roles and administrative roles."[4] The osmosis (if not the union) of political roles and administrative roles in that period was followed by a certain attenuation in the first two decades of the twentieth century: the phenomenon continued, but it was of lesser proportions. Fascism, on the other hand, led to a break: access to political roles was given to men belonging to the party and the Fascist movement, or else to technicians, industrialists, and so forth; in any case, not to civil servants. In the period after the Second World War, owing to the preeminent role assumed by the parties, the situation did not change. The number of higher civil servants present in the political arena in Italy is certainly one of the lowest among Western countries.

As for the second aspect, let it suffice to recall the condition in which the administration found itself, between the widespread initial conditions of underdevelopment (especially in the South), on the one hand, and an accelerated growth of administrative services, on the other hand. In the last thirty years, public expenditure has increased twice as much as in other industrialized countries. Since 1930, expenses for education have more than doubled and those for social services have increased tenfold in percentage of the total. "Italy—it can be said—a late comer first to industrialization and then to welfare, has tried to catch up with the other countries as quickly as possible."[5]

Deprived of bridges with politics and subjected to strong tensions imposed by the rapidity of growth, the higher civil service found itself in a position "objectively weak and subjectively lacking in aggressiveness." It has been pointed out that, generally speaking, it operates in irrational structures, and with few means; and it consists of persons poorly motivated who entered the civil service in the absence of other possibilities of work. Therefore, "it can be considered that the Italian administration is unable and unwilling to carry out a dominant role in the political field."[6]

Who are the heads of departments? It should be mentioned, for this as for other subjects that will follow, that the absence of researches and data is such as to make it necessary to have recourse, on the one hand, to the help of a series of indications; on the other hand, to direct nonsystematic observation.

Before proceeding, it is necessary to clarify that reference is made (and will be made from now on) to the heads of the main sectors of the ministerial central administration of the state, the departments *(direzione generali)* and offices equated with them. Excluded, unless otherwise indicated, are the heads *(direttori generali)* of the six autonomous concerns and administrations, which are part of the central administration but are engaged in productive activities. Excluded, also, are heads of nonstate administrations.

It is well to clarify, furthermore, that the heads of departments that we are examining amount today to about 150 in number.[7] In the postwar period, from 1948 to today, there have been altogether about 1,000 persons. It must be kept in mind, however, that, in the postwar period, the number of heads of departments was not always 150 every year, but lower (in 1960 there were about 100): just think that at least 4 ministries have been added—in 1947, in 1956, in 1958, and in 1975. To make a comparison, it is recalled that, in 1963, there were 120 directors in France; while British higher civil servants (including permanent secretaries, deputy secretaries, and under secretaries) amounted to 860–900 in 1976 and 770 in 1979. From 1946 to 1969, in France, 440 directors have been calculated.[8]

In Italy, heads of department are *not only integrated functionally but not structurally in the ruling class, but they are not even a body* (unlike France, where the contrary happens for both aspects). The following indications make it possible to measure the separation of higher civil servants and political leaders: commune and region of birth; age; absence of a system of induction in the administration; tasks and role of the higher civil servants in the decision-making process.

Table 1 gives a comparative picture, in 1962, of the commune of birth of heads of departments, of the Italian ruling class, and of the resident population.

Table 2 indicates in more detail the commune of birth of heads of departments according to classes of demographic size.

Table 3 gives a comparative picture of the region of birth of heads of departments, deputies elected in the third legislature, and the resident population.

These data[9]—the only ones available, and going back to 1962—show that

TABLE 1. Demographic size of the commune of birth of heads of departments, of the ruling class, and of the population

DEMOGRAPHIC CLASS OF THE COMMUNE OF BIRTH	HEADS OF DEPARTMENTS	RULING CLASS	POPULATION
under 100,000 inhabitants	67.7%	34.3%	79.6%
over 100,000 inhabitants	32.3%	64.1%	20.4%

TABLE 2.   Demographic size of the commune of birth of heads of department.

DEMOGRAPHIC CLASS OF COMMUNE OF BIRTH	HEADS OF DEPARTMENTS
under 50,000 inhabitants	60.4%
from 50,000 to 500,000 inhabitants	16.7%
over 500,000 inhabitants	22.9%

- the heads of departments are in inverse proportion to that of the ruling class, according to commune of birth,
- about two-thirds of the heads of departments were born in communes with under fifty thousand inhabitants,
- the South gives a number of heads of departments almost double that of the "political class," i.e., the members of the Parliament (and as compared with the population).

It should be added that the phenomenon of southern origin is repeated, to the same extent, for civil servants of the administrative class *(carriera direttiva),* who, in 1961, were distributed as follows: North: 10.58 percent; Center: 24.45; South: 62.67. Considering that the heads of departments are part of the wider category of civil servants of the administrative class and since the distribution of the latter according to region of birth, in 1961, corresponded, with only slight variations, to that of the heads of departments in 1962, the conclusion can be drawn that the phenomenon noted twenty years ago remains stable in time. And that is confirmed by other recent researches and estimates.[10]

From the quantitative data concerning heads of departments, compared with those for the population, ruling class, and political class, there emerges the poor territorial "representativeness" of the higher civil service in a rather long period, as well as the gap between it, the ruling class, and the political class. Let us now consider more closely the predominance of southerners in the higher civil service and what that entails.

As is known, in the higher civil service in Italy, the Piedmontese

TABLE 3.   Region of birth of heads of departments, of M.P.'s, and of the resident population

REGION	HEADS OF DEPARTMENTS	M.P.'s	POPULATION
North	11.5%	40.4%	36.8%
Center	26.0%	19.0%	25.6%
South	62.5%	38.1%	37.6%
Abroad	—	2.5%	—

influence predominated throughout the nineteenth century. Even though there were complaints about the predominance of southerners at the beginning of the twentieth century, it was not yet a fact in those years and, in any case, it did not concern the top class. It was only later that the southern element became predominant there. There is a growing distinction between a "productive" country (the North, where graduates go into industry) and an "unproductive" bureaucracy (the South, where young graduates are obliged, owing to the absence of other prospects of work, to choose the civil service). The predominant southern influence in the higher civil service is not just an exclusively territorial phenomenon. In the first place, the South, an agricultural area underdeveloped economically, has always been influenced, in particular, by idealism, which in Italy has always been tinged with an authoritarian hue. (The Bertrando brothers and Silvio Spaventa, Benedetto Croce, and Giovanni Gentile are southerners.) In the second place, the difficulties of the work market and lack of mobility cause young graduates from the South to seek, above all, security of employment and the guarantee of a career. Finally, for the same reasons, an ambiguous attitude is cultivated in regard to politics, which people are ready to exploit (when it serves the purpose, with its patronage powers, of giving a job), but also ready to reject (when it may cause interferences in careers, so that the tranquillity and security offered by hundreds of laws inspired by automatism are preferred).

This is the profile of a firm category coming from a part of the country that is far from industry, closed to innovation. Yet it is not immobile, and anything but insensitive to social needs (but to those of employment, not to those of production, as we will see).

Let us go on to examine the *age* of heads of departments, comparing it with that of the ruling class. In this case, too, we will note a considerable difference.

As regards age we have at our disposal data for several years. Let us limit ourselves to the data for 1961 and for 1979. Table 4 indicates the percentage number of heads of departments according to age brackets in 1961 and in 1979.[11]
It is easy to note that

- Hardly anything has changed in the twenty-year period,
- 90 percent of heads of departments are over fifty years of age,
- About 55 percent of heads of departments are in their last decade of activity (they retire at the age of sixty-five).

In this case, too, a comparison with the data for other social sectors shows the great difference between the latter and the higher civil service. From a survey carried out in 1961 in the ruling class and already utilized,

TABLE 4.   Heads of departments by age brackets in 1961 and in 1979

AGE BRACKETS	HEADS OF DEPARTMENTS (1961)	HEADS OF DEPARTMENTS (1979)
35–50	9%	10%
51–55	36%	33%
56–60	23%	29%
61–65	32%	28%

it emerges that about 27 percent of the ruling class are under fifty years of age, while only 73 percent are over fifty (as against the 90 percent of heads of departments). A Doxa-Censis survey on private managers, carried out in 1967, shows that 34 percent were under forty, 55 percent between forty and sixty, 11 percent over sixty.[12]

It has been seen up to now that the higher civil service, as regards territorial origin, mentality, and age, is not structurally integrated in the ruling class. And the question has already been raised how this *separate structure* should be called to carry out a *function of service* of the ruling class, in which it is not integrated.

It has been said before that the Italian higher civil service is not only not structurally integrated in the ruling class but is not even, in the strict sense, a body. To clarify this aspect, it will be well to recall that the higher civil service comes from civil servants[13] of the eighth functional category—*direttore di divisione aggiunto* (see below). Before the recent reform of law n. 312 of 11 July 1980, these civil servants belonged to the administrative class *(carriera direttiva)*. The 1972 reform (of which I will speak further) introduced the managerial category (and career), divided into three fundamental levels: *primo dirigente, dirigente superiore,* and *dirigente generale.* (The last level interests us here.)

To give a precise idea of the career, let us consider an example, taking as reference the system preceding the very recent reform of July 1980. A future head of department will have entered the administrative class *(carriera direttiva)* after graduating from the university, in the same ministry in which he is today. To enter, he will have passed a public competition for qualifications and examinations (written and oral). It will not have been his only competition: he will have attempted others, not being content until he has passed the one he considers most interesting. Interest will have been determined principally by the place of work and the remuneration, not by the type of work, in view of the poor motivation of persons who enter the civil service (they do so mainly because there is nothing else and because of the stability of civil service jobs). In the administrative class, after three years in the position of *consigliere* (counselor), he will have passed *a ruolo aperto* (whether or not there is a position vacant) to that of *direttore di sezione* (bureau director) and, after selection, to that of *direttore di divisione aggiunto* (adjunct division director). Then, after an examination for comparative merit, he will have become *primo dirigente* (at the age of forty to fifty), with the task of head of a division. He will have passed then, according to seniority (after three years of service without a blameworthy act) or with a competition for service qualifications (before the three years) to the post of *dirigente superiore.* Finally, he is nominated by the Council of Ministers *dirigente generale* (which, apart from some exceptions, involves being at the head of a department).[14]

It should be pointed out that (apart from the exception mentioned) this slow (and necessary) progression takes place *a ruoli chiusi* (that is, when the post in the superior category is available). That the main element of the career is seniority, which is considered the only neutral one, which cannot be influenced from outside. That annual judgments on activity have slowly been abolished and competition is regarded unfavorably. That the career takes place entirely in one ministry, the one in which the competition was passed. That, finally, the appointment and selection of the personnel—but what counts more, the career and assignment to posts—are the work of the higher civil service itself, without any interference, or with the minimum interference, on the part of ministers.

The career type now described is about to change—but only a little— with the law of July 1980, which divides the administrative class into two levels only, the seventh and eighth, without it being necessary, however, to pass through the seventh to reach the eighth, at which candidates can arrive also with a direct external competition.

From the description just given, it is clear, in any case, that, in Italy, there is no system of induction into the administrative élite comparable to the French National School of Administration (ENA, the role of which is too well known to have to be recalled) or the English Oxbridge system (from which 66 percent of general higher civil servants come).[15] Recruitment is influenced by what the market offers when the competition is announced, and selection is determined by automatic norms and terms. The persons who succeed, in the end, in arriving at the top, stay there a very short time (as we will see) because they arrive there late. But this is a way of ensuring several aspirants the possibility of being in charge and, therefore, of satisfying once more the deep aspiration, in the Italian higher civil service, to a noncompetitive society of equals.

Other aspects could be recalled (such as the difficulty of organizing a trade-union association of higher civil servants, with a homogeneous following in the various ministries), but, for the moment, let us limit ourselves to the aspect regarding recruitment and selection.

The picture of the separation between the higher civil service and politics would not be complete if, in addition to indications of structural character, mention were not made of the functions carried out by the higher civil service, which has, in general, less important tasks than the higher civil servants of other countries.

In the first place, in fact, either it does not take part in the policy-making process or it plays a secondary role. For example, the drawing up of bills to submit to the approval of Parliament is—normally—the work of the minister's office. And it is the latter, moreover, that maintains contacts with other ministries.

In the second place, the expertise provided by the higher civil service is regarded with mistrust by the ministers (also because it is often used to win new bureaucratic space: expansion of the office, its promotion to higher levels, more employees, and so forth). It is now a rule that the minister should have his own advisers. This happens in two ways: with commissions of experts (generally university professors) operating for more or less long periods (from a few months to some years); or by "borrowing" qualified persons (and far better paid than civil servants) from public agencies and public corporations *(enti pubblici)* or from the Banca d'Italia. There has been news, recently, of a minister who, to make his staff of advisers more stable (mainly coming from the university and from industry), has set up a limited company (it is not known with what financial resources). One of the reasons that accentuate this isolated position of the higher civil service in Italy lies in the frequent changing of ministers. The latter prefer to have their personal advisers who follow them from ministry to ministry, rather than heads of departments whom they do not know very well in most cases.

There is no doubt that this absence from the policy-making process (often rightly explained by the absence of capacity, exclusively juridical training, and so forth) leads to a further weakening of the higher civil service, which sometimes reaches paradoxical extremes: some years ago, a director general of the Ministry of the Treasury confessed that for years he had not been able to see the minister on whom he depended. There is no doubt, in any case, that, generally speaking, the names of the higher civil servants are the ones that figure least frequently on the agendas of ministers, who prefer to avail themselves of their office as a filter.

What, then, does the higher civil service do? The task of *execution* remains for it. Which is not easy, in an overregulated country like Italy. For this reason the higher civil servants become interpreters of the law. But even in this task the separation of politics and administration makes itself felt. The higher civil service, called to carry out routine tasks, takes "revenge" by operating slowly, as a real and proper braking power. Evident indications of this are the "debit funds," that is, the sums allotted by Parliament, "pledged" by ministers, and not actually spent: they constitute, every year, around 30 percent of the total amount of expenses foreseen by the budget. It is interesting to point out immediately that, in their turn, political leaders try to overcome this obstacle by getting round it: instead of entrusting to state offices the tasks of making public investments or other tasks, they have recourse to public agencies or to state-controlled corporations. Let it suffice to recall that the informative systems of income (Ministry of Finance) and of expenditure (Ministry of the Treasury) are entrusted to private companies controlled by a public agency, Istituto per La Ricostruzione Industriale (I.R.I.). There is, consequently, an increase of transfers, that is, the sums that pass from the state to other public apparatuses. And so the role of the higher ministerial civil service is reduced even more.

The only function that the higher civil service does not renounce (and the one that mainly occupies it) is management of the personnel (career, transfers, and so forth). The importance assumed by this function can be explained with many reasons. The main ones are the following. The chronic lack of jobs in the South results in a high proportion of southerners within the civil service: this, in turn, results in posts in the North remaining free and gives transfers from one locality to another an enormous importance. Furthermore, the civil service is regulated by an overprotective "statute" and is divided into a thousand *ruoli* (categories), each with its own regulations. Consequently, the most gifted civil servants spend their time in a laborious chase among the various regulations.

To conclude this part, it is well to recapitulate the main observations and try to formulate some hypotheses of a more general character.

Italian higher civil service is not a body or homogeneous group, but has homogeneous characteristics at its base. If it lacks, as unifying element, a common system of induction and formation, it is kept united, however, by social origin.

Alongside the "elite" model (of the French, or also British type) and the "representative" one (unlike France and Great Britain, in the United States only a quarter of the under secretaries come from Yale, Harvard, and Princeton),[16] there must be put another one, not yet well defined, but characterized by a particular social-territorial extraction of higher civil servants and their origin from underdeveloped areas. This happens in countries that are only partly developed and, therefore, characterized by strong social-territorial inequalities. Under these conditions, if the civil service becomes the place of access of social classes coming from the underdeveloped area, it tends to reproduce within it the egalitarian aspira-

tions of these classes and their tendency to exclude any factor (innovations, intervention of "politicians," and so forth) that would modify the
promotion mechanism ensured by the civil service. Management becomes
bureaucratic, but not owing to external variables, such as the prevalence
of law, the public purpose, the control of Parliament, but owing to an
internal variable, characteristic of the bureaucratic personnel, since the
latter find in the bureaucratic organization and management satisfaction
of the aspirations to the protection of their own status and of the recruitment mechanism that made it possible. Any disturbance represents an
interference, not only in the work of the civil service, but also—and
especially—in the social system in which it has its place.[17]

The higher civil service, in this model, is more homogeneous socially
than in other countries, but less bound by espirit de corps. Urged by the
difficulties of the work market, it puts the job in the first place, of which it
tends to have a patrimonial conception. Its attitude is of the "noninterventionist" type (for the higher civil service, in fact, none of the five factors
are required that, according to John A. Armstrong,[18] are always correlated
to the development of an "interventionist" role: metropolitan influence,
territorial experience, administrative integration, scientific-technological
education, systematic economics training). Therefore, the higher civil
service is little interested in *productive needs*. But that does not mean it is
immobile, because it is, on the contrary, very sensitive to the *needs of
employment*. All that pertains to the personnel, from the creation of new
posts to the career, is constant concern of this type of administrative
"elite." It feels far less the head of a concern producing services than a
part of a social class, called in by the state to offer posts to its own kind
and to manage their successive fates.

We have seen so far the differences between the administrative elite
and the political leaders. If we were to stop at this point, the question how
two such different segments of Italian society succeed in collaborating
could reasonably be raised. Let us now go on to examine what holds these
two parts together, what is the functional bond or the division of work that
unites them.

The thesis set forth at the beginning is the following. The political
class uses its own politico-constitutional preeminence (and, in particular,
the power of appointing higher civil servants, which it has reserved for
itself) as a means of exchange in order to obtain consent of the higher civil
servants: the higher civil servants know that they must conform to the
choices (and the nonchoices) of the ministers, if they want to be sure of
the abstention of the ministers from the "career" (in the broad sense). The
higher civil service exchanges, therefore, power for security. The ministers, in their turn, ensure the implementation of their programs, through

the minister's office, public agencies, and so forth, leaving it to the higher civil servants to manage their own career.

Actually, only some ministries approach this model. To understand it fully, just think of what happens in other countries. Greater possibilities of work or a greater homogeneousness of the higher civil service with the political class (work market and political class are the two determinant factors) make it possible for higher civil servants to run the "risk" of disagreeing with the minister, thus having greater power, but less security. Making this comparison, we realize how differently the same constitutional model functions, the one according to which politics guides administration in the ministries. In Italy, this power is neutralized, made innocuous by consent and submission, in exchange for security. Where risk is accepted, the power of appointment and dismissal (on which the preeminence of politics on administration relies) is a real power, not "frozen" by a preliminary agreement between the parties.

Before proceeding with examination of the functional position of the higher civil service, it is well to give greater clarifications on the regulations that have followed one another and the changes that have taken place in the period 1948–1980.

The changes (especially the legislative ones) in the postwar period are considerable. To make them understandable, I will set them forth as if they had taken place on different planes (actually, they cut across one another, both as dates and as regards effects).

In the *first* place, we have seen that the higher civil service is part of the administrative class *(carriera direttiva)*. That class was regulated, up to 1956, by royal decree n. 2395 of November 1923. It was a text adopted with the full powers of the first Mussolini government, which aimed at "putting order" in the civil service. There followed the law made under delegated power number 1181 of 20 December 1954, which made possible the promulgation, by the government, of the Decree of the President of the Republic no. 3 of 10 January 1957, containing the unified text of the measures concerning the statute of civil servants. This text was of the guarantee type, for civil servants. While the essential part of this statute remains, there have been in successive periods many "revisions" of careers, the most important of which are the ones carried out with Decree no. 1077 and no. 1079 of the President of the Republic on 28 December 1970 and with law no. 310 of 11 July 1980.

In the *second* place, with law no. 775 of 28 October 1970 (amending law no. 249 of 18 March 1968) there was planned, and with the Decree no. 748 of the President of the Republic of 30 June 1972 there was set up, among civil servants of the administrative class (carriera direttiva), a higher category, called the managerial level *(dirigenza)* and subdivided into five levels, of which only three, however, are found in all the ministries *(primo dirigente, dirigente superiore, dirigente generale)*. At this point, in Italy, the top class of civil servants (about eight thousand persons) has its own differential statute. (Even though, being part of the administrative class of civil servants, most of the regulations that concern it are to be found in the previously mentioned "unified text" of 1957.)

A *third* change concerns persons. In fact, with the aforesaid decree of 1972, which set up the dirigenza, and with decree law no. 261 of 8 July 1974 (converted into law no. 355 of 14 August 1974), the "voluntary exodus" from the civil service was facilitated. With very considerable economic incentives of various types, civil servants were induced to retire in advance. (The pension attributed was higher than the last salary received.) These regulations have had great effects in administration. Unfortunately, no one knows the exact number of persons who left the civil service as a result of these regulations. The quantification would be particularly interesting for the higher civil service, because it underwent, in its turn, a process of physical renewal of marked extension in the 1970s. Robert D. Putnam wrote in 1970, in fact, that 95 percent of Italian higher civil servants had entered the civil service before the war and that, in five or eight years, they would be entirely changed.

In the *fourth* place, there should be added the influence of a certain institutional "thaw" (perhaps due to the presence, in the second half of the 1960s, of the Socialists in the government), which led to a great opening to the outside—for example, the parliamentary regulations (of the Chamber, art. 143; of the Senate, art. 47), which provide for the hearing of higher civil servants, albeit "decreed" by the competent ministers. That represented the actual recognition of the crisis of ministerial responsibility, of the widespread weakness of government power as compared with certain public apparatus.[19]

It does not appear, however, that these changes have brought about a change of the model of relations between politics and the civil service. Not the change of persons, because, beyond the physical structure, there is a continuity due to the common territorial origin, and to the acceptance, by the new recruits, in the long wait due to gerontocracy, of the traditional models. Nor the change of powers and advantages, because the measures of the 1970s (exodus and dirigenza) can be interpreted in two very different ways. On the one hand, as the reaction of the political class to the "sabotage" by the civil service of the programs of the 1960s, which called, in particular, for an acceleration of the administrative process of decision and of public expenditure. On the other hand, as measures of compensation, deliberated by the political class, for the higher civil service, which had been "expropriated" of a considerable number of competences with the institution of the regions (1970).

It is necessary to consider at greater length the decree made under delegated power of 1972 on the dirigenza.

It has already been said that this decree came out slowly, after the law made under delegated power no. 775 of 28 October 1970. The decree, furthermore, had a tormented passage, due to the difficulties put forward by the Audit Office which—for constitutional reasons, but actually driven by "envy" of the increases of remuneration granted to higher civil servants—did not register the decree, so that the government had to have recourse to registration with reserve.

The decree regulates the functional position of higher civil servants and aspires to redefine the relations between government power and administrative power. The examination will be divided into ten points:

1. The decree differentiates in the administrative class (carriera direttiva) a so-called superior category called "managerial" *(dirigenziale)*. However, it limits itself, substantially, to "photographing" the situation existing in 1970–1972. The number of dirigenti that emerged was high (about 8,000), because it was necessary to recognize as such (with a complicated procedure) those who at the time were *direttori di divisione, ispettori* (inspectors) *generali,* and *direttori generali.* Not all the holders of these offices became dirigenti. But the above-mentioned norms on the exodus took steps to satisfy them. It can be said, therefore, that the attempt to identify a few persons with really managerial tasks was frustrated by the pressure of the higher civil service, which transformed the initial plan in its own favor, increasing the number of dirigenti and creating a real and proper managerial career.[20]

2. The decree makes provision for dirigenti generali for the central roles (only in a few cases also for peripheral ones, and only for Health and Defense are technical dirigenti generali envisaged). A subsequent measure (law no. 382 of 29 July 1975) laid down that the dirigenti should be incorporated in one category, independent of the ministry. The dirigenti of the most important administrations—General Accounting Department of the State (of the Ministry of the Treasury), Ministries of Home Affairs, Foreign Affairs, and Defense—had succeeded in avoiding the incorporation in one category, independently of the ministry, with an express exception in the law itself. Well, this measure was looked upon with disfavor by the dirigenti, who were afraid they would lose the career expectations created in the administrations and that there would be a competition in which the ultimate decision would be left to the political class. The measure, though it has not been repealed, has never come into force.

3. The decree makes provision for an original system of *access* to the level of primo dirigente: heads of sections (direttori di sezione) must, in order of seniority, sit for a competition for service qualifications, carried out annually for the number of posts available, increased by 50 percent; a unified commission at the presidency of the council admits applicants to a unified course for all ministries, lasting for fourteen months, run by the superior School of Public Administration; at the end of the course, a commission of teachers of the school selects two-thirds of the candidates, the ones who will become primi dirigenti.

There are three new elements in this procedure. First: the competition and course are the same for all the ministries. Second: selection is highly competitive. Third: the selection of the basic cadres of administration is not carried out by each ministry, but by a different organism, the School of Public Administration.

Precisely for these reasons, the decree was not applied and, with a delay, law no. 583 of 30 September 1978 lays down that, provisionally, access to the class of primi dirigenti will be had by means of assignment of judgments on comparative merit carried out in the ministries to which candidates belong.

Subsequently, the procedures were started in 1978, with a decree of the president of the Council of Ministers of 27 October, but blocked by the bill no. 792 Chamber of Deputies (not yet approved by Parliament), which makes provision for courses of only thirty days, organized and carried out by each ministry under the supervision of the School of Public Administration, which indicates one-third of the teachers and two of the five members of the examining commission. It is laid down that, "on the request of the administrations concerned," the course, thus abbreviated, can be carried out by the School of Public Administration.

Once more we see an act with force of law that remains nonapplied owing to the resistance of the higher civil service, not ready to accept new "rules of the game" (selection made on competitive bases and with rigid criteria, "expropriation" of the power of co-optation that higher civil servants have with regard to lower ranks). In this case, too, the acquiescence of the political class with regard to the higher civil service is met with.

4. The decree envisages the possibility of conferring, for a two-year period, the office of head of department to persons *outside* the civil service or to civil servants of other ministries. The measure was intended to create a certain mobility between a civil service career and other careers, which today are separated, but the regulation has not been put into practice.

5. For access to the final stage of civil service personnel, which concerns us here, the decree makes provision for a procedure that is divided into two phases: appointment as dirigente generale on the proposal of the

competent minister, with a deliberation of the Council of Ministers (and decree of the president of the Republic); appointment to the office with a decree of the competent minister, after hearing the president of the Council of Ministers. This is, without any doubt, the greatest power of the political class with regard to its direct collaborators. It has been said that access to the level of primo dirigente (which should be according to the criterion of merit, impartially evaluated) is a power attributed to the higher civil servants of each ministry. It has been seen that access to the class of dirigenti superiori depends on seniority (or alternatively here, too, by co-optation). For the last stage, the choice is left to the minister. Already, with the preceding regulations, the head of department (direttore generale) has been nominated by the government. In this case, however, there is a double decision: appointment to the class and attribution to the office, the first attributed to the whole government, the second to the individual ministers, in agreement with the president of the Council of Ministers. The intention (as we will see better later) was, according to some, that of introducing a "relationship of trust" between minister and head of department (so that when the minister was changed, the heads of departments could be changed too). Confining our attention, for the present, to the appointment, it should be said that the choice of the government, in general a free one, is, in actual fact, limited in the most powerful ministries, such as Defense and Treasury, where the minister usually proposes the most senior dirigente superiore. Where this happens, the political class renounces operating its principal instrument of direction. As has been seen, this, too, is a *use of the power of appointment, even though a negative one,* because it does not entail the abandoning of this power, which functions as a "threat" to impose collaboration.

The explanation given of this in the administrations is that a careful selection of the personnel has already been carried out first, in access to the preceding levels, by the higher civil servants themselves. In the less important ministries, the higher civil service is less strong and government choices freer.

6. For the same reasons indicated in regard to appointments to outsiders, the decree lays down that civil servants of other classes or other administrations or persons not in the civil service can be appointed head of department.

This power seems to have been exercised in very few cases, of which only some concerned persons not in the civil service.[21]

7. As already mentioned, the decree made provision for considerable remunerative increases for heads of departments, of about 90 percent. But, in addition to this, it laid it down that the remuneration was comprehensive of everything, in the sense that it was forbidden to give heads of departments "allowances, proceeds or compensation due, in any ca-

pacity, in connection with the office or for services rendered in any way in representation of the administration to which they belonged, unless they have a character of generality for all civil servants" (art. 50). After a short period, this regulation, thanks to a series of complaisant interpretations by the Council of State and by the Audit Office, has been applied in a contrary sense, favorable to the attribution of allowances, which, as we will see later, heads of departments particularly enjoy.

8. The 1972 decree has certainly revised the tasks of heads of departments. Article 155 of the 1956 "statute" made provision for the following powers for the head of department: to see to matters delegated to him by the minister; to assist the minister in carrying out administrative action; to prepare the elements for the report to Parliament on the budget; to direct and coordinate the activity of subordinate offices, ensuring their legality, impartiality, and correspondence with the public interest; to promote the best organization and improvement of services. Article 2 of the 1972 decree lays down: "Heads of Department attend to the following tasks: the direction, with the connected power of decision, of wide divisions of the central administrations, . . . ; study and research; consultation, planning and programming; the issue, in connection with the general directives imparted by the ministry, of instructions and dispositions for the application of laws and regulations; propulsion, coordination, vigilance and control, for the purpose of ensuring the legality, impartiality, economic convenience, speed and correspondence with public interest of the activity of dependent offices; the participation in collegial organs, commissions or committees operating within the administration; the representation of the administration and care of its interests with the agencies and companies subject to the vigilance of the State, in the cases laid down by the law."

In particular, art. 7 lists in 14 points the attributions of heads of departments, which are today of three types: auxiliary functions of the minister, own functions, delegated functions. (The latter is regulated by art. 14; it seems, however, that so far no power has been delegated by ministers to heads of departments.) Moreover, art. 19 lays down that higher civil servants are responsible for observance of general ministerial policies, for respect of the laws and attainment of the results of administrative action. It is interesting to note that the specific functions of heads of departments are established by referring to the monetary value of business. For example, a head of department can decide with regard to contracts for work, supplies, and services up the amount of 300 million lire.

It has been pointed out, in general, that these measures have widened the powers of heads of departments. That is certainly not true in some ministries, where the head of department, by virtue of preexisting regulations, already has wider powers. In general, furthermore, the following doubts can be pointed out: a comparison of actual powers cannot disregard an examination of what, albeit formally as proposals for the minister, heads of departments were able to decide before the 1972 decree. Was the attribution of powers of their own a widening of the powers of heads of departments, or was it not desired by the political class itself in order not to be overcome by the too many decisions to be taken? Is not the indication of specific attributions, made with recourse to the monetary value of business (even though this value has subsequently been revalued), a hypocritical way of conferring powers that, it was known from the beginning, would be eroded by inflation? Can decisions that range between a value of 60 and 300 million lire be considered important? Finally, there is news of frequent cases in which the heads of departments do not avail themselves of the power of decision envisaged by the regulation, preferring to "pass the buck" and to please the minister, to bring the documents concerned for him to sign.

It should be pointed out finally that the extension of functions for which provision was made by the degree on the dirigenti, has been used mainly for tasks connected with personnel management. This confirms the thesis that the function of the higher civil service is, substantially, limited to government management.

9. The 1972 decree (art. 3) makes provision for the following important functional ties between the minister and the heads of departments:

- The minister establishes the general directives, the preliminary programs, and the scale of priority of the action to be carried out;
- the minister makes, with his decree, a list of the measures adopted by the heads of departments that must be communicated to him and fixes the ways of the communication;
- the minister can, on his initiative, within forty days of their promulgation, annul (for flaws of legitimacy) and revoke or reform (for reasons of merit) the measures promulgated by the heads of departments and communicated to him.

The annual "reports" of the Audit Office on the general statement of the state from 1974 and the "report on the state of public administration" of 1977 have pointed out that

- very few "directives" have been issued, and they are more generic indications of goals than plans of activity;
- in some rare cases, the list of documents to be communicated to the minister has also been prepared;
- there has been no annulment, revocation, and reform.

This further nonapplication may only be an indication of the fact that there is no need of ministerial interventions of control because it is always the minister who makes the decisions or because the decisions left to the heads of departments are of little importance.

10. Finally, the 1972 decree envisages governmental powers of dismissal of heads of departments. We have already considered the responsibilities of higher civil servants. In the same article 19, the decree lays down that

- "in particular cases," heads of departments can be "placed at disposal" by the Council of Ministers; after three years in this position, they are pensioned off "by right"—that is, they must leave the job. But heads of department "at disposal"—those who do not have a regular, assigned task—cannot exceed 10 percent of those on the staff;
- "in the case of great seriousness or repeated responsibility," the Council of Ministers can directly decree the "pensioning off."

These two regulations confer powers that the government previously had only with regard to particular categories of personnel (the first, with regard to diplomatic personnel and prefects; the second, with regard to questors and to inspectors general heads of police).

Up to now, this power of dismissal has been used only once (in 1979, at the Ministry of Transport, for the question of air traffic controllers). The failure to use it is all the more extraordinary if it is compared with the frequent application that is made of the power of dismissal in a country such as Great Britain,[22] where it certainly cannot be said that relations between the minister and higher civil servants are inspired by the criteria of the relationship of trust.

The long and analytical examination of the decree made under delegated power[23] concerning the higher civil service has made it possible to note that a regulation that seems, at first sight, to establish a different relationship between the political class and the higher civil service (the latter less irresponsible and more open to the outside, the former less engaged in day-to-day management), has been substantially transformed in concrete application.

What is striking, in particular, is the large number of quiescent governmental powers; but alongside these, also the "retreat" of higher civil servants. In other words, a singular modus vivendi seems to have been established between government and higher civil service, based on the fact that each of the two withdraws, adopting a policy of self-restraint. All that is against the law, but without repeating it formally, so that the "pact" founded on mutual renunciation is guaranteed by those quiescent powers that, in case of nonconformity with the tacit agreement, each side could bring back to life.

It seems equally clear, from the examination made, that the "pact" between the political class and the higher civil service is based on a different order of relations, which gives special importance to the values that, by tradition, each party prefers: the former, power; the latter, security.

We have seen how the higher civil service is becoming more secure. We must now return to the other point, that of its lack of influence, to clarify this aspect better. The absence of osmosis between politics and administration, the lack of internal circulation, very low external mobility, and (comparatively) low remuneration are the indications that must be commented on.

While, as pointed out at the beginning, in the first forty years of unitary history and in the first twenty years of this century (age of Giolitti), there was frequent *access of higher civil servants to politics* (let it suffice to see how many of them sat in Parliament and became ministers), in the Fascist age and in the second postwar period *there was no longer osmosis between administration and politics.* The only example of a minister coming from the ranks of higher civil service—apart from Carlo Sforza—is Gaetano Stammati, and it does not seem that any heads of departments became members of Parliament.[24] In spite of the experience of the so-called experts or technicians in the government made in more recent years, there has been no "fonctionnarisation de la politique" (bureaucratization of politics).[25] In fact, apart from the case of Stammati, it was always a question of university professors and not of higher civil servants. As a more general indication of the little political weight of the higher senior service, let it suffice to say that, in the last forty years, the total number of civil servants in Parliament has fluctuated between 3 percent and 5 percent of the members of Parliament. (For the sake of comparison, it can be added that the number of lawyers accounted for between 20 percent and 29 percent.) Apart from very rare exceptions, there are not even heads of departments who are members of regional and local deliberative organs.[26]

It should be recalled that this fracture finds no explanation in the laws, which, in fact, are among the most liberal. In fact, for *enrollment in parties,* art. 98 of the Constitution makes provision that limitations can be established with laws to the right of enrollment in political parties only for magistrates, professional soldiers in active service, police officers, and agents and diplomatic and consular representatives abroad. For the first and the last of these, no laws have been promulgated, so that there are no limits for them. For the rest, civil servants must respect the principle of impartiality (art. 97 of the Constitution) and art. 88 of the 1956 "statute" regarding official secrets.

For election to Parliament and in regional, provincial, and communal organs, the discipline of the civil service does not contain norms. It is, on the other hand, the laws concerning those organisms that lay down:

1. If elected to the Chamber of Deputies or to the Senate, civil servants are put on leave of absence (art. 4, law no. 1261 of 31 October 1965 and art. 2, 1. 27 February 1958 no. 64); the Constitution (art. 98) lays down that civil servants "if they are members of Parliament, cannot obtain promotions except by seniority";

2. if elected to deliberative organisms of regions or provinces or large communes, civil servants can, on request, be put on leave of absence (law no. 1078 of 12 December 1966);

3. for minor local bodies, suspension of work is not even contemplated, but authorizations can be obtained for absence from the office.

From time to time journalistic literature and political gossip ascribe one or other higher civil servant to this or that Christian Democrat faction. It is probable that this may be true, for the higher civil servants are not "dead souls." But, on the one hand, the phenomenon is overestimated. On the other hand, this political militancy takes place without particular, visible external signs (as would be necessary if the administrator wished to go over to politics).

To lack of political commitment (particularly important in a country in which the parties are seen as one of the major channels of promotion) are added the almost nonexistent *internal mobility* (the names can be recalled only of Gaetano Stammati, who passed frrom Finances to State Holdings and to the Treasury, and of Giuliano Passalacqua, who passed from the Treasury to Finances)[27] and *closing toward the outside.* (In France *pantouflage* involves 30 percent of higher civil servants in bodies such as that of the Mines and of Finances. In Great Britain about a quarter of the permanent secretaries go to the private sector,[28] while in Italy transfers to the private sector, which take place generally after pensioning, are of appreciable entity only at the Post Office, Defense, and Finances; there are a few rare cases at Industry, Agriculture, Public Works, and Foreign Commerce.)

The last sign of the lack of influence of the higher civil service is its remuneration. It has obtained frequent revisions and is certainly not low. But here it is of interest not in absolute terms, but as compared with the low levels. Now, if we examine the remunerative range between the receptionist, usher, or concierge, at the bottom of the bureaucratic pyramid and the head of department, at the top, and its variation in time, it is seen that the head of department, who in 1861 was paid 8 times more than an usher, in 1971 was paid 5.68 and in 1979 only 3.60 times as much as an usher.[29] The flattening of remunerative levels is a general phenomenon in Italy but, in this case, it is particularly marked. Furthermore, the ministerial higher civil service compares its own (relatively) low salaries with the high ones of public corporations (especially economic ones) and finds in this a motive of frustration and further mistrust with regard to politics.

The higher civil service in Italy seems, therefore, especially if compared with that of other countries, a category with little influence and weight. Another sign of this, though ambiguous and though a weaker sign than the preceding ones, is *the low number of conflicts* (those that have external echoes) *between ministers and higher civil service.* Moreover, those conflicts mainly concern questions of "respect for the career," for which the impartiality of the political class is invoked (that is, abstention is requested). Just think of the question raised—also with letters to newspapers—in 1977–1978 by higher civil servants of the Treasury, when the possibility was ventilated of a person outside the civil service being nominated head of the Treasury. Or of the protests in 1979–1980 for the nomination, at Public Works, of primi dirigenti as dirigenti generali (thus passing over the intermediate grade).[30]

On the other hand, in the case of the higher senior service in Italy, can it be said that the ministers pass but the service remains? In the postwar period, the average duration in office of heads of departments, for the reasons that have already been set forth, is low: about three to four years, as against the six years for the British permanent secretary.[31] Then, too, we have seen the age at which heads of departments are appointed, and it is evident that their maximum duration, reached and surpassed by only some twenty persons in the period 1948–1967, is ten years.[32] There are, it is true, ministries with more rapid careers, such as Finances (because of the abundance of categories of civil servants, which are 69), Cultural Goods (because of its recent institution), the Post Office (because central departments have been brought to the level of heads of departments), Home Office (because of the high number of prefects), the General Accounting Department of the State (because of the temporary posts that it actually has at its disposal).

The minister and his direct collaborators (the *gabinetto,* which we will consider shortly) are, in spite of governmental instability, relatively stable, with an average stay in office of two years.

In conclusion, it can be said, therefore, that the higher civil service asks, in the name of impartiality, the political class to abstain, to let it alone as regards its own fate; it pays for that with a loss of power, which it renounces, in order to have what interests it most. As has already been mentioned, however, it keeps an important power, the one regarding personnel: recruitment and co-optation are in the hands of higher civil servants, who tend to favor social and patronage demands that give most importance to employment, which becomes an interest of the bureaucratic class. The latter, increasing the number of its subordinates, thinks it has more power. Actually, it does nothing but represent the interests and the aspirations of that southern middle class, hungry for jobs, from which it comes.

Consequently, it cannot be said that, in its own way, the higher civil service is without powers and without a policy. It has only a policy that is different from the productive one, a policy that is usually defined, in Italy, as *assistenziale*. This is, moreover, the meeting point between higher civil service and politics, which, as has been seen, are separate in so many ways. Both are interested in satisfying "clients" and "relatives."

How does the political class react to the inevitable rigidity of the relationship analyzed?

Before analyzing the principal ways already indicated let us ask ourselves how this situation has been able to occur. In Italy, one party, the Christian Democrat party, has been in the government for about forty years. In almost twenty ministries (for a duration of nearly six years) all governmental posts went to this party. In other governments (so-called coalition governments) it has always had most ministers and always the most important ministries. Nearly everything that has happened in Italy in this period is attributed to Christian Democracy. How has the higher civil service been able to "escape"? Has there not been, for it, that "vassalization" that has taken place in so many other fields (banks, public agencies, and so forth)?

Apart from some correctives that political leaders have used and that modify the initial situation, several explanations can be given for the lack of attention of this party with regard to the higher civil service.

In the first place, the frequent changes from one ministry to another have not made it possible to concentrate on a work that is necessarily long.

In the second place, the lack of interest of ministers in the apparatus they were to govern must be kept in mind. The real center of their interest is divided between the constituency and the party, owing to the importance that the latter has maintained in the Italian political system. A cultural element must not be underestimated either: poor administrative preparation, a widespread conviction of the unimportance of administration from the political point of view and of the importance, on the contrary, of consensus, the inability to understand the connection between administrative implementation and social consensus, and so forth.

In the third place, it should be stressed that, owing to the importance assumed by Parliament in the regulatory process (the abundance of laws, the habit of regulating everything by law and of considering laws rather than administrative action as the product of the minister's action), the minister is engaged in parliamentary work more than his foreign colleagues (even if the results are, on the whole, less good).

In the fourth place, we must consider that after the fall of fascism political leaders inherited a strong bureaucracy, but one whose technical level had already been lowered, since the tradition of "servants of the state" of the first fifty to sixty years of unitarian history had been lost. For this reason the purge was very limited. But it was necessary to have recourse to external personnel, from the public agencies, the Banca d'Italia, and so forth. Once this second channel was created, interest was lost in the first one.

Hence the remedies, which consisted in particular in recourse to public agencies and to the minister's office. The situation, already in 1971, was described as follows.[33] A politician who wishes to make innovations or merely to obtain the prompt application of a law, will find himself up against "executors" who are, generally, contrary to his policy; the latter will have at their disposal the means to sabotage or nullify the minister's policy, protected from all consequent negative sanctions. A minister who wishes to react to this state of affairs can take two paths: get round the obstacle or personally (or by means of persons whom he trusts) take the place of the civil servants who refuse to act. "In practice, if the 'getting round' solution prevails, we will have, and we have, alongside the traditional public administration, a series of semiautonomous and highly politicized public agencies which should act in a simplified way and in good time. . . . If, on the contrary, the 'replacement' solution prevails, we will have the spread of the practice which could be defined as 'reaching down,' as a result of which the minister reaches down the hierarchical scale and arrogates to himself practices or groups of practices which he will have 'carried out' according to his own criteria or, under his own supervision, by the confidential assistant of his office."

In this way we have already passed to discussion of the correctives that the political class has made with regard to the initial situation. Let us now consider them more closely.

As is known, in Italy the number of public bodies is high. Among them are a thousand or so of particular importance. Now, ministers often appoint their heads of departments to the board of directors of the bodies. There are also cases in which that is even laid down by law. But, for the subject examined here, the hypothesis in which the minister, being able to choose, has appointed a head of department is more important.

This political patronage acts with regard to those who avail themselves of it and those who aspire to avail themselves of it. The allowances to which members of boards of directors are entitled are not negligible; in the more important economic bodies they are high; the heads of departments of the ministries and departments that count, especially the economic ones, are usually members of several boards of directors, and they can, in this way, arrive at doubling or tripling their income. The minister, therefore, has a considerable power, which has two characteristic aspects.

In the first place, this form of political patronage is not addressed to outsiders, but to persons who are already, by law, the most direct collaborators of the ministers. In the second place, appointment to the boards of directors does not confer either a load of work or much greater powers (in the bodies, the people who count are the presidents and the general managers of the bodies themselves); it is substantially, therefore, an economic incentive. In the two aspects, we find again elements already known. The necessity for the minister to "win" the collaboration of his own institutional collaborators is another sign of the separation between the higher civil service and the political class. But the latter is not ready, as we know, to grant the former more than what is necessary to ensure their passive adherence, of mere implementation. He gives, therefore, "money without power."[34]

A second corrective of the relations described is the one that the ministers introduce by means of the gabinetto.

The gabinetto is still regulated today by the royal decree law no. 1100 of 10 July 1924. It is usually composed of three offices: head of the minister's office, head of the legislative office, special secretariat of the minister. Other offices are frequently added (deputy head of the minister's office, press attaché, the minister's advisers). The number of the personnel—of all levels—varies from some tens to a hundred or so persons.

The regulation cited defines the gabinetti as offices that "collaborate in the minister's personal work . . ., but cannot hinder the normal action of the administrative offices, or take their place." In fact, however, the head of the minister's office, speaking in the minister's name, may have a power of guidance over heads of departments, with whom he is almost institutionally in competition.

It is interesting to recall that the regulation of 1924 laid down that the whole personnel of the gabinetto should be taken from officials of the respective ministry. Only a year afterward, another regulation (royal decree law no. 1791 of 15 October 1925) made an exception for state councilors. Other exceptions were made subsequently. Only for the Ministries of Defense and of Foreign Affairs does a regulation lay down that the head of the minister's office should come from the respective administrations. The same thing holds good for the Home Office and Education in practice (with some exceptions), while the office of the Ministry of Justice is traditionally attributed to a magistrate.

Table 5 indicates in percentage terms the origin of the heads of the

TABLE 5.   Origin of heads of ministers' offices and of heads of legislative offices in the postwar period

ADMINISTRATIONS OF ORIGIN	HEADS OF MINISTERS' OFFICES AND OF LEGISLATIVE OFFICES
Ministry	30%
Other ministries or bodies	5%
State councilors	30%
Audit office	3%
State office of lawyers	6%
Ordinary magistracy	9%
Universities	2%
Not identified	15%

minister's office and the heads of the legislative offices in the postwar period (out of a total of about 350).

It will be noted that about a third of the heads of ministers' offices come from the same administration, and the state councilors are in the same proportion. Even if, during the postwar period, the number of state councilors has increased slightly, it should be pointed out that the phenomenon is not so conspicuous as the continual criticism of heads of departments of the intrusiveness of state councilors seems to make it appear. (In fact, of the hundred or so state councilors, up to 1970, about six were heads of ministers' offices; in successive governments, their number went up to about ten).[35]

What is striking, rather, is another phenomenon: the creation (in actual fact, of course) among state councilors of a small number of *gabinettisti,* present in several ministries, successively, following the ministers in their moves, or continuously present in a ministry because they are confirmed by the ministers who follow one another. At this point, for ten to fifteen years and sometimes longer, the position of head of the minister's office becomes "a real and proper career."[36]

To understand the dimensions and weight of the phenomenon it should be added that, alongside the official presences of state councilors, there are the unofficial ones, who are not formally envisaged by the decrees on the composition of the ministerial gabinetti. It is a question in this case of state councilors called to ministers with tasks of trust that are not specified. That emphasizes the political, and not only technico-juridical, importance of their collaboration.[37]

This is even more evident in the case of heads of the legislative office, whose average duration in office is three to four years. The figure of the deputy head of the minister's office is being slowly introduced; this office is nearly always filled by an official of the ministry in question, with the function of ensuring continuity of work in the minister's office. The deputy head of the minister's office, in fact, remains in office for a long time, regardless of changes of ministers.

It is not possible to illustrate here the nature of the body of state councilors. Moreover, in this role of *pépinière des grands commis* (nursery of higher civil servants), the Italian Council of State is no different from the better known French one. It should merely be recalled that, for access by means of competition to the Council of State, it is necessary to have been in the civil service for some time. And that the Council of State (or at least its first three sections) carries out an administrative function (consultative, not jurisdictional). (As we will see in a moment, there is another way to have access to the Council of State—or to the Audit Office: appointment by the government.)

If the use of state councilors as heads of ministers' offices often serves to create competition between the heads of departments and the heads of the ministers' offices, which is useful for the ministers, the appointment of heads of departments as state councilors and councilors of the Audit Office[38] may have several purposes—in most cases, that of taking a person away from a department. It should be recalled, however, that the decision often takes place with the full consent of the person concerned (for the better remuneration; the duration in office to the age of seventy; the prestige, especially in the Council of State). In some cases, the purpose of the appointment, for a minister, is to ensure for a collaborator of his in a ministry the mobility that heads of departments do not have; with the nomination as state councilor or councilor of the Audit Office, the head of department leaves his department, but can follow, as head of the minister's office, the minister in the various ministries. It can be said that many of the most eminent political personalities have done so in order to be sure of a trusted collaborator who will follow them in their various offices.

To have a precise idea, see the distribution of members of governmental nomination in the two bodies, by origin, illustrated in table 6.

Table 7 indicates the ministries of origin of most councilors of governmental nomination.

The preceding tables (which refer to the period 1945–1980 for the Council of State and to the period 1947–1977 for the Audit Office) are not sufficiently clear if it is not specified that

- they refer to 177 state councilors in all and to 150 councilors of the Audit Office;
- the expression "ministerial officials" refers to higher civil servants,

TABLE 6. Councilors of state and of the Audit Office of governmental nomination in the postwar period, by origin (percentage data)

ORIGIN	COUNCIL OF STATE	AUDIT OFFICE
Ministerial officials	50	70
Ordinary magistracy	4	2
State office of lawyers	4	5
Professionals	4	15
Others (members of Parliament, employees of public bodies, military, university professors)	14	6
Nonclassifiable	24	2

but not always heads of departments. The latter represent just *under* half of the ministerial officials for the Council of State, and just *over* half for the Audit Office.

If these facts are kept in mind, it is possible to evaluate at about 10 percent the percentage of the total number of heads of departments nominated in those two organs. Taking into account, moreover, what was said about governmental nomination, which often does not have the purpose of removal, it can be said that the power of dismissal of higher civil servants exercised by the postwar governments has been contained in relatively limited terms. The overall marginal use of this power confirms the thesis, sustained here, of a tacit modus vivendi reached between the political class and the higher civil service in the postward period.

A mere mention will be made of the fourth corrective, that constituted by the *public bodies.* An adequate treatment of this subject would require, in fact, an essay to itself. Historically, public bodies have often been instituted in order to avoid the rigidity of the provisions in force for

TABLE 7. Ministries of origin of ministerial officials nominated in the postwar period to the Council of State and the Audit Office (percentage data)

MINISTRY	COUNCIL OF STATE	AUDIT OFFICE
Home Office	42	17
Treasury	5	16
Finances	9	13
Education	10	10
Public Works	7	9
Other ministries	27	35

the state. Among them, in particular, it was desired to avoid the "guaranteeism" of work relations, which prevents dismissal and makes the mobility of the civil servant difficult. The system of public bodies has created an area partly free of conditionings, in which the policy, but especially the ministerial political patronage, is possible, unlike the ministries. Governmental appointments concern, of course, the president and the board of directors of the bodies. The directors of public bodies, though not civil servants, are employees, and often they enter by means of a public competition.

The importance of the task carried out by the "parallel administrations," as those of the public agencies are defined, has long been stressed by all observers. In 1964, Meynaud pointed out "la tendance des gouvernements successifs à doubler l'administration ordinaire d'une bureaucratie extraordinaire en laquelle ils ont davantage confiance pour réaliser leurs desseins" (the policy of governments to set up, alongside the ordinary administration, special agencies on which they rely for implementing their policies). A decade later, it was pointed out that "in Italy the special administration undoubtedly plays a more important role than does the ordinary bureaucracy in bringing about whatever outputs the system produces." The first is "structurally privileged," "prone toward activism and intervention," while the second is "old and formalistic, lacks modern technical skills, is entangled in its own procedures, doubts its own efficacy."[39]

In a word, use of public agencies in this sense (as well as recourse to the gabinetti) serves to change considerably the initial conditions of political leaders, who, however, operating by getting round the higher civil service, in a way respect its position, though depriving it of the most important tasks. The system functions along two ways, which are different. While the position of the higher civil service is stable, that of the collaborators of ministers and of the public functions, attributed mainly as a concession to public agencies, is changeable. While the former carries out routine activities, the latter are called to carry out new and innovative tasks.

The higher civil service, weak and outflanked, accustomed to be on the defensive, takes refuge in *legalism*. If in 1954 some 36 percent of higher civil servants had degrees in jurisprudence, in 1961 the percentage had gone up to 40 percent (while graduates in economics account for about 10 percent). But these data say little. In general, more attention should be drawn to the faith in control, mistrust, or suspicion with regard to innovation, the search for precedents, the motivation of activity carried out only with reference to the law, and so forth. Even persons not educated in law assimilate in the civil service its concepts, mentality, and procedures.

The sign of the attitude of defensiveness and protest, even if unexpressed, can be seen in the reaction of higher civil servants to the new laws, which are interpreted in the light of the old ones.

The government, in its turn, reacts to this situation by multiplying the laws, in the hope of straightening out the situation. The Italian Parliament normally produces four times as many laws as its British counterpart. The laws in force, not consolidated or put in order, constitute a mass that is certainly not less than 100,000.

Of the two aspects of its activity—the one addressed to administration and the one addressed to Parliament, the first of administration, the second of legislation and policy—government gives its preference decidedly to the second, both when it operates collegially (Council of Ministers) and when it operates individually (single ministers). This particular attention to Parliament and laws, which is due to many causes, not least in the frequent succession of government crises brought about by Parliament (and by the parties belonging to it), makes, on the contrary, the ministers inattentive within administration. The more and more frequent laws create new constraints in which the very ministers who wanted those laws remain caught up in a circular process in which everyone complains of the absence of guidance in administration, the constraints created by the laws that should serve for that guidance and which block even the ministers are multiplied, while administrative activity becomes more and more a "slalom" among the bans, rules, and constraints of the laws.[40]

Let us cast a glance backward, at the system just described. In the last century, there was full homogeneousness between political leaders and administrative leaders. This was broken at the beginning of the century, when the widening of electoral suffrage increased the pressure of civil society for more public services, protection of workers, and so forth. At this point, on the one hand, the administrative leadership underwent the influence of the South, becoming different from the political leadership. On the other hand, administrative leaders felt a need of protection with regard to political leaders. Fascism would sanction the definitive break.

The premises were thus laid for the model that has been described—a model that presents fewer advantages than drawbacks.

Among the advantages, mention should be made of the fact that the separation between the political class and the higher civil service ensures a neutrality of the civil service that is not easily reached. In a country in which the strongest bond and the widest net are political, it is rather strange that those who are closest to the ministers are so little influenced by them (in general, of course, because the government has recourse to correctives that partly modify the picture).

Another interesting aspect is the strong social and territorial cohesion expressed by the administrative leaders, who have been a channel of promotion of a social flow that benefits young graduates from the South, coming from the lower middle class.

This work, grandiose in its way, with which a category not interested in *development* has at least given *help* to a social class that is particularly weak and vulnerable, such as the southern middle class, has been drying up, however, in the last few years. The higher civil service has gradually been supplying itself and has become endogamous: just think of the Romanization of the civil service and of the fact—pointed out in sector surveys—that one-third of civil servants are children of civil servants.

Thus the negative aspects come to the fore. The system described is, in fact, precarious and insufficient. Precarious because—like the government itself, moreover[41]—it is written on water: it keeps going through the play of mutual silence, without a solid basis, a law that is respected. Inefficient because, in a continual sequence, it multiplies the compensations and, therefore, the constraints. It is supported by an ingenious circular system of weights and counterweights, in which the last weight finds a compensation in the first counterweight.

Made mainly to run what already existed, this system underwent a heavy shock during the 1970s with the transfer of state functions to the regions, carried out in 1972 and in 1977. Regionalization has broken the system, throwing it out of balance, because whole administrative apparatuses, managed by heads of departments, are now divided into fifteen parts (the number of regions with an ordinary statute) and managed by politicians (regional councilors). Regionalization has involved mainly the Home Office, Public Works, Agriculture, Tourism, Education, as well as Transport, Labor, Health, and Industry, and it has entailed the abolition of fifteen departments.

The diminution of powers for the higher civil service was considerable, to such an extent that it has been possible to put forward the hypothesis that the decree made under delegated power of 1972 on higher civil servants served as "compensation for the damage."

It is too soon to express a judgment on the experiment as regards the aspects that are interesting here. For the present, two or three phenomena can be observed in progress.[42]

In the *first* place, the space lost by the center in terms of spheres of competence has been regained in terms of finance. The fiscal reform started in 1971 and the subsequent affirmation of the idea that the state must be the only organism of the public system (which comprises also national public bodies, regions, local bodies, and so forth) with a deficit balance, have led to a very important centralization of finances, so that, albeit with many constraints, the final decisions pass to the central government, which divides the funds.

This tends to bring about a *second* phenomenon. Whereas the leading department with regard to the periphery was, previously, the one that controlled it (Home Office, through the prefects), today it is the one that finances it (Ministry of the Treasury). There is, therefore, a change of importance in the central administrations.

To these first two changes, which regard mainly the structures, there is added a third one, which has direct effects on the relations between the political class and the higher civil service. It is a question of the institution, in the health, agriculture, and housing sectors, of anomalous, mixed, state-region organisms. The minister and the regional councilors of the sector belong to them. The minister, as a member of these organisms, exercises powers that belong to him institutionally, but as minister. It follows that he may or may not avail himself of the ministry. It is no longer true that the minister's powers are equal to the ministry's powers. The ministerial apparatus and the heads of departments concerned are involved only by proxy and on the initiative of the minister in questions that regard these organisms. They are, therefore, cut out of the institutional circuit. The initial, nineteenth-century situation of the head of department as a mere auxiliary of the minister is, in a way, recreated. These minister-collaborator relations were characterized in the past by the absence of a bureaucratic apparatus of vast dimensions under the civil servant. The development of these apparatuses and of an abundant legislation that concerns them had strengthened the higher civil servant as compared with the minister. Today, a century later, the same situation is recreated in a corner of the civil service system.

NOTES

1. Robert D. Putnam, *The Political Attitudes of Senior Civil Servants in Britain, Germany and Italy,* in Mattei Dogan (ed.), *The Mandarins of Western Europe: The Political Role of Top Civil Servants,* Sage Publications, New York, 1975, p. 111. This essay has been translated into Italian with the title *Atteggiamenti politici dell'alta burocrazia nell'Europa occidentale,* in "Rivista italiana di scienza politica," 1973, A. III, n. 1, p. 145 f.; the passage that concerns Italy is also in Sabino Cassese (ed.), *L'amministrazione pubblica in Italia,* II ed., Bologna, Il Mulino, 1976, p. 255 f. Sidney Tarrow, *Between Center and Periphery: Grassroots Politicians in Italy and France,* Yale University Press, 1977 (translated into Italian by Il Mulino).

2. On the attitudes of higher civil servants, Luciano Cappelletti, *Burocrazia e società,* Milan, 1968, and ISAP, *La burocrazia periferica e locale in Italia,* in several volumes, Giuffrè, Milan, 1969.

It should be said right now that the only existing statistical collections are two. The first one *(una tantum)* is: Presidency of the Council of Ministers, *Albo dei dipendenti civili dello Stato, Carriere direttive,* Istituto poligrafico dello Stato, Rome, 1963; the second one (annual) is: Ministry of the Treasury, *Dipendenti delle amministrazioni statali al 1 gennaio 1979,* Istituto Poligrafico e Zecca dello Stato, Rome, 1979.

The most important general public documents are: Audit Office, *Decisione e relazione sul rendiconto generale dello Stato* (published every year in the parliamentary proceedings, documents series) and Presidency of the Council of Ministers, *Relazione sullo stato della pubblica amministrazione* (from 1972; the latest one, not yet published, is of 1977).

3. See Sabino Cassese and Rita Perez, *Manuale di Diritto Pubblico,* Laterza, Bari, 1981, and Luigi Arcidiacono, *Profili di riforma dell'amministrazione statale,* Giuffrè, Milan, 1980, p. 23.

4. Riccardo Faucci, *Finanza, amministrazione e pensiero economico: Il caso della contabilità di Stato da Cavour al Fascismo,* Torino, Fondazione Einaudi, 1975, p. 97 f.

5. SABINO CASSESE, *Esiste un governo in Italia?* Roma, Officina, 1980, p. 11.

6. Franco Ferraresi, *Modalità di intervento politico della burocrazia in Italia,* in "Studi di sociologia," VI, 3 (September 1968), p. 247 f. See also by the same author, *Burocrazia e politica in Italia,* Bologna, Il Mulino, 1980.

7. It is necessary to specify that the number is evaluated by taking into account only persons placed at the head of organisms of the central administration, directly under the minister. This is specified because, after 1972, in addition to the latter, the rank of *dirigenti generali* is given also to first-class ambassadors and plenipotentiary ministers, prefects, and regional superintendents of public works, though they are not at the head of departments.

8. The data regarding France were taken from Ezra N. Suleiman, *Politics, Power and Bureaucracy in France: The Administrative Elite,* Princeton University Press, 1974, pp. 63 and 64. On Great Britain, Yvonne Fortin, *Hauts fonctionnaires et superstructures des administrations centrales en Grande-Bretagne,* in "Revue du droit public et de la science politique," 1979, juillet–août, n. 79, p. 1088.

9. Taken from Alessandro Taradel, *La burocrazia italiana: provenienza e collocazione dei direttori generali,* in "Tempi moderni," 1963, A.VI, aprile–giugno, n. 13.

10. Expansion of the subject, Sabino Cassese, *Questione addministrativa e questione meridionale—dimensioni e reclutamento della burocrazia dall'unità ad oggi,* Giuffrè, Milan, 1977.

According to calculations on a small sample, in recent periods higher civil servants coming from the South have increased to about 70 percent; while the North has gone down to about 5 percent. (Only 33 percent of the total number of civil servants, however, worked in the South [*Servitori dello Stato Intervista sullo pubblica amministrazione a Sabino Cassese,* ed. Redento Mori, Zanichelli, Bologna, H 1982.])

See Ministero del Tesoro, *Dipendenti delle amministrazioni statali,* Istituto Poligrafico dello Stato, Roma, 1980, *passim.*

11. Since, as has been said, the Ministries of Foreign Affairs, the Home Office, and Public Works have at the head of peripheral offices, which are not departments, persons of the same level as heads of departments, and since the official statistics do not make it possible to consider the latter separately, the three ministries indicated have been excluded from the data that follow. If they are taken into account, carrying out an inclusive calculation, the situation appears worse, because in 1961 persons over fifty-five amounted to 57 percent; in 1979, to 68 percent.

12. The results are partly published in "Formazione e lavoro," 1976, I, n. 77.

As a note to this section on age, it may be interesting to add that for the first time in history the Council of Ministers on 18 January 1980 appointed two women dirigenti generali: Teresa De Cornè and Liliana Forcignanò Brossi, respectively at Foreign Trade and at the Treasury.

13. In addition to civil servants, the following categories of personnel depend on the state: magistrates, teachers, professional soldiers, personnel with particular systems.

14. A summary has been made, simplifying it, of a type of career at the end of the 1970s. The first part of it was changed by law n. 312 of 11 July 1980. However, the career was slightly different even previously: for example, instead of one, there were, in the 1950s and 1960s, three levels of *consigliere;* before 1972, instead of the three managerial levels, there were the levels of director of division, inspector general, and director general.

15. Y. Fortin, p. 1101.

16. See also the second volume of Ezra Suleiman, *Les élites en France: grands corps et grandes écoles,* French trans. Seuil, Paris, 1979, as well as V. Subramanian, *Representative bureaucracy: a reassessment,* in "American Pol. Sc. Rev.," 1967, vol. LXI, p. 1010, and Kenneth John Meier, *Representative bureaucracy: an empirical analysis,* in "American Pol. Sc. Rev.," 1975, vol. LXIX, n. 2 June, and Richard A. Chamman, *L'élitisme dans le recrutement des hauts fonctionnaires en Grande-Bretagne,*in "Revue Française d'administration publique," 1979, octobre–décembre, n. 12, p. 687 f.

17. S. Cassese, *Questione amministrativa,* p. 95.

18. John A. Armstrong, *The European Administrative Élite,* Princeton University Press, 1973, p. 305.

19. Andrea Manzella, *Il Parlamento,* Bologna, Il Mulino, 1977, p. 149.

20. That can be noted also by comparing art. 12 of law n. 775 of 28 October 1970, which contained the authority for the government to discipline the higher civil servants and the directive criteria.

21. Before the regulation on higher civil servants that has been quoted, only six cases can be recalled. After 1972, only nine.

22. Y. Fortin, p. 1092.

23. See however, in general, SABINO CASSESE, *Organizzazione statale e disci-*

plina dell'impiego pubblico and *Elite amministrativa e potere politico: la dirigenza,* both in *L'amministrazione dello Stato,* Giuffrè, Milan 1976, p. 33 and p. 47 f., as well as the bibliography quoted there.

24. It may be interesting to note that an inspector general, Giovanni Pitzalis, was a member of Parliament, for Christian Democracy. He was secretary of DIRSTAT (autonomous trade union of higher civil servants) and the law regarding the passing *a rudo aperto* (that is, without having to wait for a vacancy) to the rank of inspector general.

25. Gérard Timsit and Céline Wiener, *Administration et politique en Grande-Bretagne, en Italie, et en République Fédérale d'Allemagne,* in "Revue française de science politique," Vol. 30, n. 3, 1980 juin, p. 520 f.

26. The phenomenon also concerns state councilors, with regard to whom it has rightly been pointed out that the tendency to abstain from direct political activity (from the first to the sixth legislatures state councillors were elected to Parliament twenty times, but it was a question only of seven persons) is accompanied by an increase of politico-administrative offices: G. Paolo Storchi, *Materiali per una analisi del ruolo politico del Consiglio di Stato. Gli "incarichi esterni" dei magistrati amministrativi,* in "Rivista trimestrale di diritto pubblico," 1977, n. 2, p. 596.

27. The passing from ministry to ministry, but through the *gabinetto* (minister's office) is a different case—also exceptional. For example, Sensini, a prefect, passes to the Foreign Office gabinetto with minister Arnaldo Forlani; another prefect becomes deputy head of the minister's office at the Ministry of Industry, under Antonio Bisaglia.

28. E. Suleiman, *Les élites en France,* p. 232 f. and Y. Fortin, p. 1094.

29. ISTAT, *Sommario di statistiche storiche,* Istat, Rome, 1968, p. 129; Ermanno Corrieri and Giovanni Dossetti, *Inflazione e sistema retributivo,* in "Il Mulino," 1979, July–August, n. 264, p. 567, and Paolos Sylos Labini, *Chi guadagna e chi perde con l'inflazione,* ivi, p. 581 ff.

30. See the publication of the trade-union association of higher civil servants—DIRSTAT, "Riforma amministrativa," 1980, January, n. 1, p. 1.

31. Y. Fortin, p. 1095.

32. Michele Bottalico and Paolo Albertario in Agriculture; Giuseppe Dall'Oglio and Luigi Attilio Iaschi at Foreign Trade; Alfonso Pirozzi at Defense; Benedetto Bernardinetti at Finances; Nicola Fini at Justice; Antonio Padellaro at Industry; Rosario Purpura, Giovanni Carapezza, and Angelo Altarelli at Labor; Romolo De Caterini at the Post Office; Francesco Bubbico, Mario Pantaleo, Guglielmo De Angelis D'Ossat and Guido Arcamone at Education; Ludovico Nuvoloni, Vincenzo Firmi, Carlo Marzano, and Giuseppe Caccia at the Treasury.

33. Vittorio Mortara, *Tendenze conservatrici e rapporti con la politica degli alti burocrati* (1971) in Sabino Cassese (ed.) *L' amministrazione pubblica in Italia,* II ed., Bologna, Il Mulino, 1976, p. 263.

34. Alongside these forms of utilization others must be added: higher civil servants *assigned,* as collaborators, to the minister's office; *detached* from a peripheral office to the ministry; *detached* from a ministry to other administrations; called to *special* tasks.

These kinds of utilization, which are not frequent, are criticized by the autonomous trade union of higher civil servants (DIRSTAT): see Domenico Accorinti, *Distacchi e incarichi vanno stravolgendo la figura del dirigente voluta dalla legge,* in "Riforma addministrativa," 1980, May, n. 5, p. 4.

35. G. P. Storchi, p. 601.

36. Ibid., p. 613–614.

37. Observations by Onorato Sebe, contained in an unpublished article on the political leaders.

38. In which, however, the Council of Ministers is not completely free, since it must have the prior agreement of the body for which it wishes to provide for the nomination.

39. The first quotation is by Jean Meynaud, *Rapport sur la classe dirigeante italienne,* Lausanne, Etudes de science politique, 1964, p. 49; the others by *Stefano Passigli, The Ordinary and Special Bureaucracy in Italy,* in Mattei Dogan (ed.), *The Mandarins of Western Europe. The Political Role of Top Civil Servants,* Sage Publications, New York, 1975, p. 233.

The essay of Giuliano Amato, *La burocrazia nei processi decisionali,* in "Rivista trimestrale di diritto pubblico," 1975, A. XXIV, n. 2, p. 488 f., should also be read. Amato maintains, in general terms, that the "mistrust" of the second postwar period was subsequently followed by a "collusive faithfulness" between the higher civil service and the government leaders. The study summarized by him, on the ministry of agriculture, shows, however, that the apparatus of the ministry has remained confined to routine, while there is "a phenomenon of getting round the bureaucratic machinery, by means of a kind of parallel administration."

40. The phenomenon becomes more marked when the higher civil service itself prefers the law. One of the reasons for this preference is the interest in avoiding the opinion of the Council of State on the regulations, so that it is found more convenient to accept the longer passage through Parliament than the more attentive examination of the Council of State.

For an examination of the consequences of the absence of a political guidance of the administration (prevalence of the Ministry of the Treasury, which supersedes the Home Office, and reduces the administration to unity thanks to the marginal but pervasive power of control of expenditure), Sabino Cassese, *Introduzione* in Sabino Cassese (ed.), *L'amministrazione pubblica,* p. 32–33.

41. Sabino Cassese, *Esiste un governo in Italia?,* Officina, Rome, 1980, as well as Mauro Calise E Renato Mannheimer, *I governi "misurati." Il trentennio democristiano,* in "Criticia marxista," 1979, n. 6, p. 47 (for a careful measuring of the duration of governments and governors).

42. Donatello Serrani, *L'organizzazione per ministeri—L'amministrazione centrale dello Stato nel periodo repubblicano,* Officina, Rome, 1979, p. 149 f.

ORGANIZING FOR EFFICIENCY
The Higher Civil Service in Japan*

T. J. Pempel

As most of the advanced industrial countries are chastised for their alleged ungovernability, Japan emerges as contradictorily governable. As students of public policy lament the allegedly unmanageable complexity of modern social problems, Japan stands out as a defiant exception. As most of North America and Western Europe struggles with geometrically burgeoning public expenditures and bloated national bureaucracies, Japan luxuriates at the bottom of the OECD scale in both the size and the cost of its government.

By what twentieth-century alchemy are such miracles achieved? Different observers have posited a wide array of social, economic, organizational, cultural, and psychological phenomena to unravel the apparent mystery of Japan's seeming successes and its ostensible exceptionalism. Others have also suggested that contemporary Japan, if successful on many dimensions, is doing so only at great cost to individuality, social welfare, cultural heterogeneity, freedom, or some other set of values held

*The author thanks Peter Katzenstein for his suggestions on the manuscript.

to be more precious. A bargain with the devil, it is suggested, has been struck: ephemeral triumph at the cost of the soul.

Intriguing as it may be to peel back the layers of causality in search of some "ultimate" prime cause, or to debate the merits of competing philosophical values, there is no denying that, at a very proximate level, many of Japan's public policies have been highly efficient, both in the instrumental sense of achieving targeted goals and in objective comparison with other industrialized countries. Japanese policies have reflected a generally politically successful fusion of public and private activities that I have elsewhere referred to as "creative conservatism" (Pempel, 1982).

Much of this political success can be attributed to the country's national bureaucracy. Though industry deserves its share of the credit, Japan's economic successes during the 1950s, 1960s, and 1970s were also due to the highly successful policies of industrial transformation generated and enforced by the Ministry of International Trade and Industry (MITI) and the unstinting budgetary and monetary oversight of the Ministry of Finance (MOF). The Ministry of Transportation is rightly proud of Japan's world-famous supertankers, while its high-speed super express trains (commonly known in the West as "bullet trains") stand as the capstones of one of the world's best-developed systems of transportation. Japanese crime rates have been declining for two decades and have long been but a fraction of those in the United States and most of Western Europe, an outgrowth of highly effective police and Justice Ministry policies. At the end of the 1960s, Japan's air, water, and soil pollution were unquestionably the worst in the industrial world. By the beginning of the 1980s, rigid enforcement of new laws and ordinances by both local governments and the national Environment Agency had dramatically reversed these conditions. Cross-national testing in grammar and high schools almost always shows Japan's students to be at or near the top internationally, a fact which the Ministry of Education loses no opportunity to cite as an example of the highly successful national school system it runs. The picture is the same at the level of the "street level bureaucrat." Japan's mail is delivered rapidly; trains and buses run on time. Teachers frequently go out of their way to make sure that students are not hanging out in coffee shops or pinball parlors; they generously provide extra instruction, visit their pupils in hospitals, or attend student sporting events on their own time; they contact parents when their charges appear to be having academic or personal problems. During the massive university protests of the late 1960s, a pitched two-day battle took place at Tokyo University between over 10,000 police and students barricading themselves in the main hall. When the police finally broke through all of the barricades, they pulled back temporarily, allowing the students about five minutes of nationally televised flag-waving and protest songs before making calm and injury-free arrests. In doing so they distinguished themselves markedly from their U.S., French, or West German counterparts. During the same period, conductors occasionally held up trains to allow student protestors to finish their marches without missing the last trains back to campus. Despite the occasionally surly, misinformed, or lethargic official, for the most part, teachers, policemen, city and town officials, bus drivers, welfare agents, and other bureaucrats conduct their duties with a grace, efficiency, and sense of duty that Japanese citizens take for granted and that disarm the foreign observer.

Why is it that when "bureaucracy" has become a virtual synonym for red tape, inefficiency, self-service, and blockage, the situation in Japan appears reversed? The answer to this question may well emerge from an examination of the reasons for many of the negative qualities currently associated with bureaucracy. Although many specific factors might be adduced to explain bureaucratic inefficiency, most can be reduced to either the quality of the personnel that staff bureaucratic agencies or to internal bureaucratic structures that constrain, rather than enhance, efficiency. Both of these in turn derive from the character of relations between bureaucratic agencies and other important political actors.

Many agencies throughout the world are staffed by persons whose attributes are far inferior to those of the nation's most talented individuals. The reasons for this may be many. Among the most easily cited are patronage control over many positions, boring jobs attracting compatible individuals, or the operation of the "Peter Principle," whereby individuals who prove competent in one position are continually promoted until they reach a level at which they can no longer function effectively. A host of others might be added. Whatever the many possible causes, there can be little doubt but that many agencies function poorly because they are staffed by poor-quality personnel. This phenomenon may be referred to as the problem of the Drones. It has been widely cited as endemic to many big city governments in the United States (Shefter, 1977; Banfield and Wilson, 1963). Italy, too, is seen as plagued by this problem (e.g., Cassese, 1981; Graziano, 1978). So, too, are many Communist and third-world governments (Moore, 1965; Riggs, 1963).

Where personnel are competent and efficient, a converse problem frequently plagues bureaucratic agencies: namely, the inability to instill a sense of loyalty to the agency and its mission. Instead of serving the agency and its goals, talented individuals frequently reverse the desired order, using the agency to advance either their personal ambitions or programmatic and ideological aims at odds with or far outside the purview of the agency's stated mission. In contrast to the problem of the Drones, this problem is that of the Queen Bees. Agencies staffed preponderantly by either Drones or Queen Bees are almost certain to have problems with efficiency. Washington's "in and outers," Britain's "high flyers," and members of the French *Grands Corps* can be easily criticized as prime examples of this problem.

Beyond problems of personnel, many bureaucratic agencies falter as a result of organizational and structural failures. Numerous agencies with competing missions may engage in activities that duplicate or, worse still, completely contradict, those of other agencies. Agency A does not know what Agency B is doing or, if it does know, it works in total disregard of the second agency's activities. Coordination at higher levels is weak or ineffective. The result is the proliferation of autonomous subgovernments. McConnell (1966), Lowi (1969) and others have characterized the United States in such a fashion. Lægreid and Olsen's phrase "Key Actors—On Different Teams" suggests the same phenomenon for Norway. Moulin (1975) and Lorwin (1971) have identified the problem as endemic to the Belgian civil service.

In contrasting cases, there is the equally stifling problem of excessive guidance or control from above. Rules made blindly somewhere "above" in a hierarchical chain of command can easily lose touch with the specific problems being faced by individual agencies and individuals "down below." This tension between "government" and "subgovernment" is one that Michel Crozier has ably argued has been a perennial problem in French bureaucratic organization (1963).

These rather serious problems of personnel and internal organizational structures contribute greatly to the inability of many bureaucracies, individually and collectively, to operate effectively. Yet personnel and organizational structures do not emerge in a political vacuum. Rather they are the consequences of the manner in which the bureaucracy relates to the political system as a whole. This relationship, both directly, and indirectly through its influence on personnel and structure, can also contribute to inefficiency. Again dichotomizing, the major problems appear to be related to those long labeled in China as the conflict between "red" and "expert." When a system is "red," political expedience takes precedence over functional expertise; the politically loyal individual or agency is valued more highly than those that are administratively efficient. Instrumental inefficiency consequently becomes an inevitable component of overall bureaucratic activity. Such political dominance of the civil administration has been a direct and ongoing contributor to inefficiency in many Communist systems (Granick, 1954; Moore, 1963). Cassese (1981) and others have effectively demonstrated its importance in lowering efficiency within the Italian civil service. The many layers of political loyalists at the top of most Washington agencies also impede efficiency within the United States (Heclo, 1977). A related problem occurs when there are frequent changes in policy direction. These occur most often with changes in the ruling party, or in the balance in the governing coalition. Politically loyal bureaucrats must then shift their policy gears, abandoning lines followed under the previous government, whether these are incomplete or well established. Britain, in particular, has been plagued by this problem (Beer, 1965; though cf. Ashford, 1981). But it appears also to have vexed the West German civil service following the transition to socialist rule in 1969, and it certainly occurred in Sweden following the ouster of the Social Democrats in 1978.

Less directly, a high level of political responsiveness by the civil service in any country typically contributes to a comparably high degree of political patronage and the corresponding problem of technically unqualified individuals holding many important posts. Where competing political groups have colonized different segments of the civil service, it also adds to the problem of proliferating subgovernments. Thus, both directly and indirectly a high degree of political penetration of the civil service can work to impede administrative efficiency.

In contrast, under an "expert" system, political sensitivity is down-played in the search for the technocratically perfect solution to discrete problems. Here, because the realities of social power and political in-fluence are ignored, bureaucratic solutions often prove to be practically unworkable or impossible to implement. Coordination of diverse efforts becomes difficult; what is technically correct in one area is technically catastrophic in its secondary and tertiary effects. "Expertise" frequently becomes the bureaucratic excuse for incrementalism and lethargy when new vision and rapid change are called for. Prerevolutionary France and Russia were characterized by this problem. The Labour Party has fre-quently complained that its efforts at rapid social transformation have been impeded by such a mentality within the British civil service and the political system of which it is a part. So, too, have other governments attempting rapid and radical transformations of past activities. Thus, an excess of expertise may be little more conducive to efficiency than an excess of political sensitivity.

These three dimensions whose extremes reflect different forms of bureaucratic inefficiency present a highly schematized and perhaps overly taxonomic approach to the myriad ways in which agencies may demon-strate incompetence. At the same time, they capture three central ten-sions whose resolution is essential if bureaucratic organizations, and the political systems of which they are a part, are to function effectively. Efficiency demands a "correct" balancing of these three lines of tensions: a country's bureaucracy must avoid the extremes of "red" and "expert" in its relations to the political system as a whole; meanwhile, internally, bureaucracies must be organized to avoid the problems of Drones and

Queen Bees, and the problems inherent in excessive government or sub-government.

The argument that I will make with regard to Japan is that the comparatively successful functioning of the Japanese bureaucracy and of its political system can be attributed largely to the fact that on all three dimensions the country appears to have avoided the extremes that lead to inefficiency. Its individual bureaucrats are highly talented but rarely leave the bureaucracy before retirement age, and rarely are capable of advancing their own careers at the expense of bureaucratic goals. Although most agencies are highly autonomous, strong personal and structural mechanisms provide overall guidance and coordination to these individual agencies, ensuring that their autonomy does not run strongly counter to broader national objectives. In the final analysis, however, such intrabureaucratic successes are possible only because the bureaucracy as a whole has been integrated into the political system in ways that avoid the extremes of "red" versus "expert." Instead, throughout its modern history, Japan has sustained a creative tension between the competing demands of technical expertise and political loyalty. It is when such balances have not been maintained that inefficiency has been most noticeable. Nevertheless, as I will explore at the conclusion, efficiency as a goal is not always reached. Even more importantly, its achievement often entails undeniable costs that must be calculated in one's assessment of Japan's undeniable successes.

BETWEEN "RED" AND "EXPERT"—THE AMBIGUOUS RELATIONSHIP TO POLITICS

No modern bureaucracy is ever divorced from politics. As Rose notes elsewhere in this volume, senior-level bureaucrats, at least, engage in a variety of political activites. As Putnam (1976) and Muramatsu (1978, 1981) have suggested, few top officials remain "classical administrators," involved exclusively with the technical problems of carrying out directions issued from some isolated political sphere. Rather, top-level civil servants in all industrialized countries are invariably "political administrators" whose activities and guiding principles must reflect a sensitivity to the broader power and political relationships of their environment.

With such a realization, it makes little sense to ask whether higher civil servants in Japan, or elsewhere, perform political functions. They obviously do. The more interesting questions concern the degree and arenas of such political functions, and the ways in which they form part of the broader matrix of relationships within the political system as a whole.

What is most striking about the case of Japan is that, for most of its modern history, the political weight of the civil service has been extremely high and broadly comprehensive. Bureaucratic influence has typically been greater than that of other political actors, including Parliament, parties, and interest groups. At the same time, exerting such influence has rarely put the bureaucracy in a position of having to become either "red" or "expert." Rather, it has been so centrally a part of Japan's governing coalition that any suggestion of a dichotomy between its expertise and political loyalty would completely miss the reality. This integration without polarization has been central to Japan's efficiency.

Bureaucratic strands wind through Japan's history from at least the Nara Period (710–784), but the establishment of a modern bureaucracy dates from the opening of Japan by the West in the middle of the nineteenth century. At that time, European and U.S. commercial and military interests forced their way into a Japan that had been isolated from the international economic system for 250 years.

In the short period from the signing of the first commercial treaties in 1854 to the Meiji Restoration in 1868, it became clear to important segments of the Japanese leadership that the country's sole hope for preventing the West from subdividing Japan, as it was doing in China, lay in national unity, rather than in the feudal divisions that prevailed. This unity meant military modernization rather than a reliance on a narrowly based and antiquated warrior caste; and large-scale industrialization, rather than a continued reliance on agriculture and small commerce.

A well-trained, elite, national bureaucracy under the direction of a small oligarchy was to be the key tool in effecting these massive changes. Even by the final years of the Tokugawa regime (1600–1868), many of the more forward-looking fiefs had begun to institute the shift toward modern bureaucracies. Demonstrated competence in such areas as military science, finance, foreign language, engineering, and technology soon became keys to an individual's success.

With the restoration, there was a demonstrable and nationwide shift toward greater centralization of administrative powers and toward the development of a modern, rationalized, national service. The ending of feudalism in 1871, the establishment of a land tax in money in 1873, the creation of a standing conscript army in 1873, and the ending of all samurai privileges in 1877 worked collectively in the direction of consolidating the power of the national executive. With the creation of a cabinet in 1885 and the promulgation of Imperial Ordinance 37 in July 1887, and the introduction of the Meiji Constitution in 1889, the main outlines of a political system with a strong national bureaucracy modeled on that of Prussia were established (e.g., Rosenberg, 1958).

A national higher educational system was begun with the primary purpose of training a cadre of talented individuals capable of bringing about all phases of the nation's modernization. Staffing the national bureaucracy was a central concern. Tokyo Imperial University, the first university in Japan, and particularly its Faculty of Law, became the key institution for the preparation of government officials.

The logical corollary to the Meiji leadership's concern for a collective, hierarchical, well-trained civil service, single-mindedly devoted to the advancement of a presumably clear-cut national interest was its hostility toward the specificity, self-interest and diffuseness of "politics." A powerful Parliament, local autonomy, and government by election and party were all perceived as major threats to the strong state needed to ensure national unity, industrial development, and international influence. Thus, the leadership group took great pains in shaping the Meiji Constitution and the political system that resulted to ensure that the national bureaucracy would be kept both powerful and autonomous from the particularistic threats of partisan politics. Bureaucratic agencies were created well before parliamentary institutions. Only one house of Parliament was chosen by election, and the franchise was strictly limited to a minute proportion of the well-to-do citizenry; universal male suffrage was not introduced until 1922. The early political parties were subjected to stringent controls and frequent harassment by the Justice Ministry, the Home Ministry, and the police; when Socialist parties and labor unions attempted to organize in the early part of the twentieth century, these controls were even more strictly enforced. The elected House of Representatives had a rigidly circumscribed arena of responsibility. Local government was almost exclusively appointive through the national Home Ministry.

Thus, from its early modern history, the Japanese state had the national bureaucracy at its core, while electoral and parliamentary politics remained at the periphery. Unlike Britain, the United States, and even France at this time, Japan's civil service was not subject to major checks from the electoral and parliamentary sphere.

Not only was governmental power vested in the bureaucracy at the expense of the Parliament, but civil servants themselves were sharply proscribed from becoming enmeshed in partisan affairs. Yamagata Aritomo, one of Japan's foremost state builders and the man generally regarded as the father of the Japanese bureaucracy, took a number of steps to keep government as "transcendental" of partisan politics as possible. As "servants of the Emperor," Japan's bureaucrats were sharply proscribed from any involvement in electoral and party politics. For the military bureaucracy, the "National Rescript to Soldiers and Sailors" served as an imperially sanctioned ban on all partisan political activity by members of the military. Then in 1899, Yamagata, in conjunction with the

Privy Council, pushed through a Civil Service Appointment Ordinance that set stringent restrictions on the scope of free, politically based appointments that could be made within the bureaucracy.

Reality was always somewhat removed from this ideal of separating "bureaucracy" from "politics." The parties were prevented from gaining patronage controls over administrative positions, and low-ranking bureaucrats were kept out of electoral and party politics. But the primary consequence of the Meiji system was to reduce the influence over government exerted by parties, the Parliament, and elections. When they did gain some measure of influence during the 1910s and 1920s, it was only insofar as they were willing to accept and operate within the basic ideological framework that had been shaped in the preceding forty to fifty years. Meanwhile, although the civil service was kept rather insulated from penetration by political parties at least until that time, it by no means kept out of governmental politics. Personal and organizational relations among government leaders and top civilian and military bureaucrats were inevitably intimate. In part these were based on family, marriage, educational, and other background commonalities. In part, they were the outgrowth of relatively close interaction in a single capital city, Tokyo, which was the headquarters for virtually all of the nation's important activities. Most fundamentally they rested on the commonality of views all held on the major policy direction most advantageous to the country.

Senior-level bureaucrats, despite their alleged isolation from politics, were intimately involved in most aspects of policy formation. Thus, both civilian and military bureaucracies exerted extensive power over the formulation of most facets of national policy. Although Article 37 of the Constitution provided that every law required the consent of the Diet, few laws actually originated there. Most were drafted within the various agencies of the national bureaucracy and then presented to Parliament for ratification. In addition, Imperial Ordinances, technically issued by the Emperor, provided an extralegislative channel for direct bureaucratic control over wide areas of public policy making. This was a control that carried the important legitimation provided by the Imperial seal. The military bureaucracy had further powers inherent in the so-called Right of Supreme Command (Tosuiken). This provided that the Emperor had supreme command over the armed forces and that they reported directly to him. Thus, civilian authorities, be they bureaucrats or politicians, were circumscribed from exerting effective political control over many aspects of foreign policy, arms procurement, military promotion, and the like. This right also gave military officials an important device by which to influence the composition of cabinets.

Senior-level bureaucrats were not isolated from other aspects of politics either. Upon retirement, many former civil servants could look forward to appointment to the House of Peers, from which they gained, not only additional prestige, but, if they desired, not a small measure of influence over the nation's policies. Still others entered the political world directly, although rarely through electoral politics. Some such as Ito, Goto, Okuma, Hara, Kato, and others left the bureaucracy to accept leadership posts in political parties. Far more were appointed directly to cabinet positions, or to prefectural governorships. Thirty-six percent of the prewar cabinet ministers, for example, were former bureaucrats, and only eight of the forty-four cabinets formed between 1890 and the end of World War II were formed by the heads of political parties (Pempel, 1978: 319).

Party patronage and the spoils sytem were minimal even after parties, elections, and Parliament began to gain in influence. The first party cabinet of Okuma and Itagaki in 1898 had seen an early flirtation with patronage as a means of ensuring political control over the bureaucracy, and the political and bureaucratic consequences were almost uniformly negative (Scalapino, 1962: 140–141). However, the ordinance of 1899 effectively curtailed the prospects for such activities. As the parties and the Diet increased their influence, bureaucratic-party links improved, and top positions in various ministries were at times reallocated following changes in government. But for the most part this meant replacement of one career civil servant by another deemed somewhat more favorably inclined to the government. And since so few prewar governments were party governments, such changes rarely involved purely partisan replacements. Few civil servants were formally affiliated with political parties even during the 1920s, the heyday of party influence during the prewar period. Rarely did a career politician skilled only in the matters of practical politics find himself holding a second, third, or lower tier position within the central administration. Thus, to the extent that prewar Japan had links between politics and bureaucracy, most of it involved bureaucratic penetration of the political world rather than political penetration of the bureaucratic.

The effect of this all was to contribute greatly to both political and bureaucratic efficiency during the bulk of the period following the Meiji Restoration. The remarkable transformation of the country socially and economically has been widely chronicled. For most of the period following the formation of the modern bureaucracy, it was well integrated into the political system, and functioned effectively. The times when such efficiency was most noticeably lacking were those when the pendulum seems to have swung too far in the direction of a purely political or an excessively apolitical and technical bureaucracy. During the first few sessions of Parliament, for example, efforts to stifle the embryonic political opposition typically backfired and resulted in governmental paralysis (Scalapino, 1962). Similarly efforts to suppress leftist groups, no matter how moderate, that occurred two and three decades later had comparably negative results. Conversely, most efforts by the parties to gain patronage controls over the bureaucracy aided party growth but impeded governmental efficiency (Masumi, 1965–1968). And the rise of a highly politicized military linked to right-wing extremist groups during the late 1920s and early 1930s also had profoundly negative consequences. Still, for most of the period, the bureaucracy was closely interwoven into the fabric of politics, accepting the basic outlines of policy formulated by the government of the day, yet not surrendering its technical expertise in order to carry out such policies.

The American Occupation reinforced this pattern of bureaucratic involvement in political matters. In contrast to Japan, the United States had a long tradition of political parties exerting a predominant role in government and public policy. Moreover, in theory and in practice, legislative influence was strong. Nevertheless, during the middle and late nineteenth century, there had been a strong reaction to the influence exerted by parties over both local and national governments and their bureaucracies. The progressive movement sought to purify the government's civil servants from the negative influences of political parties, and most explicitly from the influences of patronage. National, state, and local civil service commissions sprang up to provide position classification, hiring, and promotion through competitive examination, the creation of retirement and pension plans, efficiency evaluations, and the like. Administration was to be kept as separate from partisan politics as possible, particularly in the areas of promotion and dismissal (Kaufman, 1956; Shefter, 1978; Pempel, 1984). This tradition in politics was bolstered by the trend in private industry toward adoption of the principles of scientific management advocated by Frederick Taylor and Leonard White. Expertise was to be prime.

The thrust toward scientific management and instrumental efficiency was vigorously pursued by the U.S. Personnel Advisory Mission, a group sent to Japan in November 1946 to make recommendations on bureaucratic reform. Its members were all experts in scientific management and personnel administration, and its proposals uniformly centered around establishing detailed standards for recruitment, training, position classification, compensation, employee evaluation, health, safety, welfare, recreation, employee relations, retirement, employment statistics, and so forth. These changes were brought about through a National Public Service Law (NPSL) designed to regulate such matters within the national civil service. A newly created National Personnel Authority was to deal with the implementation of such matters, much along the lines of the U.S. Civil Service Commission. Meanwhile, matters of administrative rationality and managerial efficiency were given over to the Administrative Management Agency, a newly created body under the Prime Minister's Office.

But while one aspect of U.S. policy pushed in the direction of keeping administration highly technical and completely separate from politics, another was pushing in precisely the opposite direction. Initially supportive of "democratization" and "demilitarization" in Japan, the United States, for reasons of domestic and international politics, soon became the vigorous supporter of Japan's "political stability" and "economic recovery." To implement this shift in goals, the Occupation carried out numerous policies aimed at curbing the political left and ensuring continued dominance by conservative forces. As a corollary, it was essential to ensure that the bureaucracy would be compatible with these conservative political goals and with the conservative coalition that the Americans were helping to gain predominance. Thus, the National Public Service Law contained a provision that made ineligible for civil service examination or appointment any person who "advocated or belonged to an association or political party which advocated the overthrow by force of the Constitution of Japan. . . ." The same section of the law prohibited strikes by any member of the government service and subjected strikers to loss of all rights guaranteed under the law's protective provisions. These and other measures had a stifling impact on the development of the embryonic public service unions, and on the left more generally.

The overall shift toward conservatism on the part of the Americans served to create and reinforce the formal and informal linkages between Japan's top-level bureaucrats and its conservative leadership, both in and out of political parties. General loyalty to conservative principles became a prerequisite for higher civil servants; the bureaucracy as a whole ironically retained its prewar conservative tincture of "red," but without having to surrender its characteristic as "expert."

Parties and Parliament became far more central to Japanese politics following World War II. At the same time, bureaucratic penetration provided the top ranks of the conservative parties with an infusion of apolitical "expertise." The political purges in the years immediately following the war temporarily removed many top party leaders from the conservative political parties. Former officials like Shidehara, Yoshida, and Ashida moved into the vacuum. With the elections of 1949 and 1953, significant numbers of former officials (25 percent of the Liberal Party in 1953) began to win seats in the House of Representatives.

It was under such leaders that much of postwar conservative politics took shape. And with the consolidation of the country's conservative parties in 1955, a bureaucrat mindful of success, either in bureaucratic office or in a subsequent career, had to be a close ally of, or at least a person who could be compatible with, conservative party officials, and top business leaders.

In 1955 the two major conservative parties in Japan, the Liberals and the Democrats, merged. The resultant Liberal Democratic Party (LDP) has since then maintained a continuous parliamentary majority, and has controlled all cabinet seats. The margin of LDP control declined rather consistently from the mid-1960s to the end of the 1970s, when it was forced to enroll several conservative independents to insure its continued majority. The first two elections in the 1980s saw continued LDP majorities in both houses of Parliament. Even more important in understanding the hegemonic position enjoyed by the LDP during this period is the fact that no other single party ever held as many as one half the number of seats held by the LDP. A fragmented opposition was as much a contribution to LDP control as were its own electoral successes.

Despite this apparently unassailable strength, the LDP did not undermine the autonomy or instrumental efficiency of the national bureaucracy in traditional political ways. There have been no serious moves to inject patronage appointees, while a number of steps examined below concerning recruitment, agency competition, and administrative reform through personnel cutbacks have all been highly conducive to apolitical or conservative-political efficiency.

Unlike many other countries, Japan's civil servants do not enter the political world very overtly while in office. Unlike in France, Japanese civil servants do not serve as formal advisors to the cabinet, to ministerial cabinets, nor to elected local officials. Nor is there a *Grands Corps* concept allowing Japanese civil servants to move freely between administrative and political posts, or to run for office while retaining bureaucratic status. Unlike those of West Germany, Japan's bureaucrats cannot sit simultaneously in Parliament. In contrast to the United States they do not serve on "presidential teams" made up of politicians, administrators, and admixtures of both. The lines separating politics and administration are, in principle, clear and hierarchical. Each ministry or agency is staffed by members of the civil service, the sole appointed political officials being the minister and the parliamentary vice-minister.

Nor do most Japanese bureaucrats have an overtly political conception of their roles. For example, one survey showed that nearly 90 percent of the top officials surveyed felt it was bad for elected officials to intervene in public administration, and a slightly higher percent held that administrative vice-ministers and senior bureau chiefs should not change when the cabinet changes (Watanabe, 1974: 439–440; see also Muramatsu, 1981: 102–124). At the same time, as one moves up the bureaucratic ranks, political sensitivity becomes an important part of one's thinking. Efficient operation demands such sensitivity for, in fact, the Japanese bureaucracy plays a highly political role in the country.

This political role is most pronounced in the formulation of public policy. There, bureaucratic agencies and individual bureaucrats have numerous devices to exert a major influence over the conceptualization, discussion, and implementation of most governmental choices. Senior bureaucrats and those on the rise spend a great deal of their time, particularly during the evenings, in meetings of "study groups," typically composed of a mixture of journalists, academics, bureaucrats, politicians, and businessmen. These groups are normally devoted to a specific problem in which all share a common interest, and usually some influence and expertise. The problems might be as broadly defined as "Japan in the Pacific" or "Coping with the Leisure Boom" or as narrow as U.S.–Japanese textile trade, countering student protests, or constructing a bridge from Shikoku to Honshu.

There are other opportunities for bureaucrats to interact with those in other spheres. Personal connections are vital: class reunions are a particularly important device for members of different elite circles to interact. At a slightly more formal level, most government agencies have numerous advisory councils (*shingikai* or *kenkyūkai*) designed to provide advice to ministers on a variety of broadly or narrowly defined problems within the agency's sphere of activity. Although politicians have become rarer as appointees to such groups, they or their surrogates are still appointed. Present or former bureaucrats are the most numerous groups included, along with individuals representing a variety of relevant groups, institutions, or interests. Ministerial staff oversee the actual investigations and typically write up the final reports (Pempel, 1974).

Out of these multiple groups come the bulk of the ideas and the specific proposals that eventually go on to become public policy. The bureaucracy plays a key role in drawing up most national legislation, for example. Approximately 90 percent of all legislation passed since 1955 was drafted within a government agency, and top-level bureaucrats typically serve as behind-the-scenes managers of these bills once they are up for parliamentary consideration. It is most often the civil servant, rather than the minister, who undergoes the meticulous questioning and browbeating that passes for parliamentary interpellation in Japan. And once a bill is passed, it frequently includes a proviso that allows the specifics of implementation to be regulated by bureaucratically generated ordinances. Furthermore, ministerial and cabinet ordinances far outweigh laws in Japan, and have become numerically more important (Pempel, 1974: 657).

Although they do not regard themselves as "political," Japanese higher civil servants perceive themselves as the ones most responsible for public policy formation. One comparative survey showed 80 percent of

Japan's top bureaucrats agreeing that it was they, rather than the elected politicians, who were solving the country's general policy problems. This figure compared to only 21 percent of the British and 16 percent of the West German bureaucrats surveyed (Kubota and Tomita, 1977: 192–9311; also Muramatsu, 1981: 169–206).

The reasons for this bureaucratic influence are many, but one of the most important factors is the way in which Japanese cabinets are formed and the relationship between ministers and civil servants that results. The primary consideration that goes into the formation of a Japanese cabinet is the factional situation within the ruling LDP. For the most part these factions exist to advance the political fortunes of their leaders and, ultimately, their followers (Watanabe, 1958). Ideological and policy differences are very rarely salient among the factions. Occasionally, it is clear that a particular issue, such as energy, normalization of relations with China, curtailing student protests, or foreign trade liberalization, is likely to dominate the political agenda in the short-term future. When this occurs, the minister most directly involved will usually be picked for his talent to cope. Since the formation of the LDP in 1955 there have also been two or three instances in which non-LDP parliamentarians have been appointed to cabinet posts. But in most cases, cabinet posts and the post of parliamentary vice-minister, are distributed as the fruits of party factionalism.

Furthermore, the average life of a cabinet in the period since 1955 has been less than a year. Occasionally a minister will be reappointed. But far more typically, the two political overseers of an agency will remain "in control" for a bit less than a year, when they will then be rotated out. Under these circumstances it is rare for an individual minister to attempt major policy initiatives. Again there are exceptions, often involving a "strong man" with prime-ministerial hopes. Kono Ichiro was a major influence on the Ministry of Agriculture, and, later, on the Ministry of Construction. Ikeda Hayato was instrumental in convincing the Ministry of Finance to utilize a variety of its available fiscal tools more forcefully. Nakasone Yasuhiro pushed forward various armament expansion proposals when he headed the Self-Defense Agency. Nagai Michio (incidentally one of the nonparliamentarian ministers) managed to stimulate the Ministry of Education to generate, and the Parliament to pass, several major reforms in higher education. For the most part, however, these cases stand out as exceptions to the more general pattern in which a minister becomes the advocate of proposals pushed up to him by the top civil servants of the agency he heads. In these respects, the more permanent and technically expert bureaucratic staff of an agency is usually in a far better position to influence the details of policy than the politically appointed cabinet minister.

Bureaucratic influence, either by individuals or by agencies, does not take place in a conceptual vacuum. The continued rule by the Liberal Democratic Party, and the continuity of its socioeconomic base, has set broad boundaries around most areas of public policy. Hence, government support for rapid and large scale industrialization during the 1950s and 1960s meant that, try as it might, the Ministry of Health and Welfare could generate little support for environmental control or for child allowances. A similar commitment to low defense expenditures worked to check proposals by the Self-Defense Agency for expanded armament purchases. Political bargains struck between President Nixon and Prime Minister Sato took precedence over the inclinations of senior bureaucrats concerning Okinawan reversion and purchases of the Lockheed Tristar.

Furthermore, the influence of the minister, and more importantly, the influence of the LDP, over the careers of the highest ranking civil servants and the character of policy is by no means negligible. Technically all promotions in the civil service are governed by civil service regulations and the norms of neutrality. All promotions to bureau chief and above, however, must clear the cabinet and, in fact, are subject to additional scrutiny by LDP headquarters. But, in fact, the choice of top bureaucratic positions is usually made by former top officials in that agency, and only ratified by the cabinet. Still, most ministers will insist on having individuals below them with whom they can work, and will use the denial of cabinet approval if necessary to ensure this. As a result, the actual promotion of individuals to top positions in the bureaucracy is by no means devoid of political sensitivity, and actual movement to top ranks involves gaining leverage, not only within the ministry itself, but also with top-level members of the LDP. Loyalty to the general aims of the LDP and the dominant coalition is only one of the many prerequisites to gaining a high position.

In a comparable vein, alliances with outside interest groups develop as an essential part of most top officials' careers. The Ministry of Trade and Industry, for example was organized for most of the postwar period into product-related bureaus—textiles, steels, machinery, and so forth (Johnson, 1982). The Ministry of Transport is organized into bureaus for shipping, aviation, railways, and roads. Although these bureaus in both agencies are charged with "controlling" such sectors, in fact, close alliances were more forthcoming than hierarchical control (Honda, 1974). The Food Agency in the Ministry of Agriculture and Forestry works closely with the farmers' cooperatives *(Nōkyō)* (Donnelly, 1977). The same types of alliances are formed between the Medical Affairs Bureau of the Ministry of Health and Welfare and the Japan Medical Association (Steslicke, 1973) or the Social Insurance Agency and groups of the elderly (Campbell, 1979). The list is one that is easily multiplied and that probably does little to distinguish Japan from most other countries (Kosaka: 1981).

Any bureaucrat or any agency that seeks to gain increased political

influence must take such factors as givens. But once these broad boundaries are accepted, the room for political influence by top bureaucrats is
considerable.

Just as successful performance in office demands the ability to work
well with elected officials and with outside interests, so, too, does a
successful postbureaucratic career.

Early retirement serves to rejuvenate the bureaucracy continuously
as channels of promotion open up frequently for talented individuals in
lower ranks. At the same time, it creates the problem of finding subsequent employment for those of proven competence in the prime of their
working lives. With government pensions low and financial responsibilities high, most retired bureaucrats find second careers, very often in
private industry or in public corporations overseen by the agencies with
which they previously worked. In most cases such second careers are the
result of links developed in direct consequence of the individual bureaucrats' official work. Technically, the National Personnel Authority is sup-
posed to rule on the legitimacy of such "descents from heaven" by former
officials into jobs in private sector firms having "a close connection" to
the agency the official has left (Johnson, 1974: 974). In fact, official enforcement of the law is extremely lax, and the official interested in a
successful postbureaucratic career in business almost inevitably has this
concern in mind during his final years in office as he interacts with the
private sector, and with political officials.

The same holds true for the official considering a political career.
Compared to the total number of bureaucrats retiring every year, the
proportion who go on to careers in politics is relatively small. Yet those
who do are an influential group in national and local party politics. Almost
without exception, politically oriented former bureaucrats join the ruling
Liberal Democratic Party. Slightly more than one quarter of the LDP's
freshman candidates in the 1976 election for the House of Representatives
were former career officials. Approximately 20 percent of Japan's postwar cabinet ministers have been former bureaucrats. Eighteen prefectural
governors serving in the mid-1970s were former high-ranking national
government officials; an additional seven had been career officials in local
governments. Even more significantly, in the twenty-five years following
the formation of the Liberal Democratic Party in 1955, the office of prime
minister was held for only five years by men who could be described as
professional politicians. During the remaining twenty years, former bureaucrats occupied the office (my calculations from *Asahi Nenkan,* annual).

In all of these ways, therefore, the bureaucracy in Japan enjoys an
ambiguous but unmistakable relationship with party politics, and with
outside pressure groups. At most of the lower levels of the bureaucracy,

there is relative isolation. But as one moves to higher echelons, close personal and programmatic interactions are essential. The top levels of the bureaucracy are integrally woven into the web of conservative politics that has dominated the country during the postwar years with bureaucratic influence being high. The long dominance of the LDP has meant that agencies and individual civil servants in Japan must become imbued with political loyalty if they wish to survive and succeed. Freed from the ambiguities that result from alterations in the governing party, this political loyalty can remain consistent over time, and bureaucrats can approach technical problems from a generalized conservatism well meshed with the political orientations of the dominant political coalition. Moreover, as long as the current web of conservative politics remains intact, bureaucratic efficiency in carrying out the broad policy directions of the coalition is ensured by the fact that, at the top levels, the civil service is in fact itself part of the coalition.

Bureaucratic efficiency in Japan is unquestionably helped by the mixture of political loyalty and expertise that has been characteristic since its origins. Yet features internal to bureaucratic recruiting and bureaucratic organization independently bolster the overall effectiveness of the civil service. It is well to explore these two dimensions individually to understand how they complement the fusion of "red" and "expert," and contribute to bureaucratic efficiency.

No Drones; No Queen Bees—High Quality Personnel; Collective Mission

Throughout most of its modern history, Japan's civil service has attracted some of the nation's most talented individuals. At the same time, it has managed to channel their individual talents into collectively agreed upon directions, most typically agency or national goals. Attracting talent has not required the surrender of control over ends. Broad strategic aspirations have not stifled individual creativity in the selection of strategies to achieve them.

From 1869 on, a rigorous examination system has governed entry into the civil service. Nearly all national government posts are covered through such examinations, the most stringent of which monitor entry into the senior civil service. The exam for the higher civil service has involved a combination of written and oral questions, geared to the generalist. A broad education with a focus on administrative law has always been the standard preparation. Passing the exam guaranteed entry into the top ranks of the civil service and almost ensured continual and rapid advancement to top positions. Virtually all of the written evidence suggests that the examinations were free from any taint of serious corruption in the prewar period (Spaulding, 1967: 293–305). At the same time, law faculty members of Tokyo Imperial University and, to a lesser extent, Kyoto Imperial University had predominant responsibility for drawing up the questions and administering portions of the oral examination. Thus many of the questions of a professor's final examination in, say, constitutional law could reemerge several weeks later on the higher civil service examination. This created a clear element of favoritism for students from such schools. Not surprisingly, virtually the entire corps of prewar higher civil servants were graduates from one of these universities.

One study of Japan's *Who's Who* in 1937 shows that 74 percent of the senior civil servants had graduated from Tokyo Imperial University; a full 47 percent from the university's law faculty. An additional 9 percent came from the next best source, Kyoto Imperial; only 18 percent of these top officials lacked a degree from one of these two institutions (Inoki, 1964: 295–297). In addition 85 percent of the prefectural governors serving between 1900 and 1945 were graduates of Tokyo Imperial University (Silberman, 1974: 194). Yet without question, these institutions attracted and graduated a highly skilled cadre with little direct class bias.

Open testing in both the universities and the civil service spurred the creation of a reasonably meritocratic bureaucracy. Unlike most of the European civil services at the time, Japan's had a disproportionately low percentage boasting noble birth. The same survey mentioned above, for example, showed that 72 percent of these top civil servants had a commoner's background (cf. Armstrong, 1973). The openness of Japan's bureaucratic elite to all with the right educational backgrounds and the requisite knowledge to pass the higher civil service exams, undoubtedly contributed to the widespread public support for the system, and the high prestige enjoyed by the individual civil servant during this period.

Bureaucratic power and prestige were strongly reinforced during the U.S. Occupation. First of all, the Americans took great pains to eliminate the power resources of most competing prewar elite groups. The military underwent a virtually total purge, as did the top echelons of the political and economic leadership. Landlords lost their power base through land reform. Yet the bureaucracy was left virtually unscathed. It was used by the Americans instead to carry out a variety of transformations in fields as diverse as education, broadcasting, health, and industry. The top levels of the bureaucracy thus had the comprehensive national mission of protecting the best of the past, dealing effectively with the Americans, ending the Occupation, and transforming the country by removing the most baneful elements of the prewar regime. Its powers were thus reinforced, not diminished.

During the earliest phases of the Occupation, several proposals were made for reducing the political power of the national civil servants. There was particular criticism of the important role exerted by Tokyo University graduates (for example, Maki, 1947; Esman, 1946). One measure designed to diversify backgrounds involved declaring all existing personnel "temporary" until they passed an adequate civil service exam designed under the aegis of the newly created National Personnel Authority, a body fashioned after the U.S. Civil Service Commission. When the exam was, in fact, given, toward the final years of the Occupation, it proved to be a hollow shell devoid of its original purposes. Officials were given unlimited time to complete their examinations; tea breaks were frequent; pressure was limited and, most significantly, resulting personnel changes were almost nil. Nearly 80 percent of the incumbent officials were retained, and at the uppermost levels of the civil service the retention rate was 88 percent (Shirven and Soeicher, 1951: 57).

In the period since then, broad general education at a top quality university, plus passage of a rigid examination, continue to be the prerequisites to joining and moving through the senior civil service. Competition on the Principal Senior A-Class Entrance Exam is intense and has become increasingly so with time. Most who pass can anticipate eventually achieving a post in one of the civil service's top three grades, which represent approximately 1,500 positions, of which about one-half are truly important. Between 1970 and 1979 alone, the number of applicants tripled from 20,000 to 60,000 despite the fact that only 1,311 individuals would gain posts. Whereas in 1964, there were fewer than 10 applicants per position, by 1979 the competition ratio had more than quadrupled to nearly 43 applicants per position (Jinjiin, annual).

In principle, any Japanese citizen is eligible to compete. But only a small number successfully negotiate the many hurdles before passage. Educational background still plays the largest part in this success, and the oral exam serves as an additional check on quality plus political acceptability. In 1976, for example, 53,935 applicants took the senior civil service exam, of whom only 1,336 passed. Of those who were successful, 461 (35 percent) were graduates of Tokyo University and 193 (14 percent) were from Kyoto University. The next highest numbers were achieved by Tohoku (51), Nagoya (42), and Kyushu (41) Universities. Only 12 other universities out of Japan's more than 400 placed 10 or more graduates on the passing list. Despite slight variations from year to year, the general pattern was the same into the 1980s. Although contemporary dominance by Tokyo and Kyoto Universities is far less than it was during the prewar period, it still remains exceptionally high.

Such educational homogeneity becomes even more pronounced in the senior ranks of the national civil service. In the early 1970s over 60 percent of those holding the rank of section chief or above were graduates of Tokyo University. The bulk of the top civil servants also have back-grounds in legal studies. In 1972–1973, 77 percent of the bureau chiefs and 91 percent of the administrative vice-ministers were graduates of law facilities.

If the civil service does not necessarily acquire Japan's *most* intelligent young men, it selects at least a group that has proven its ability to pass a series of exacting "tests by educational fire"—the entrance exams that are a part of all Japan's high-quality schools from kindergarten through university, and then culminating in the civil service exam itself. Accidents of birth provide some measure of assistance in becoming a top civil servant, but only in the broadest sense that they help to determine careers in most societies.

Top-level Japanese officials themselves perceive the process of bu-reaucratic recruitment as open and nonascriptive. In reply to a question concerning whether people from a certain segment of society are inher-ently suitable to become leaders of the state, the negative replies of Japa-nese bureaucrats far outdistanced those of their counterparts in England, West Germany, and Italy. One hundred percent gave negative or more or less negative replies in contrast to response rates ranging from 50 percent in Italy to 80 percent in England (Kubota and Tomita, 1977: 195).

Importantly, Japanese civil servants also evince a high degree of self-sacrifice in speaking about their high prestige jobs. Asked to choose from ten possible reasons for choosing their careers, virtually none of Japan's top-level civil servants answered that they took the position for the pow-ers it held or as a possible springboard to a career in politics. The most cited reasons were "suitability to one's own character" (21 percent), "breadth of vision" (18 percent), "to serve the state" (16 percent) and "to serve the public" (12 percent). Only after these did "security of the posi-tion" come into play (10 percent) (Watanabe, 1974: 429). In a related vein, when asked what features of their job were most enjoyable, nearly 50 percent cited service to the public, a figure three times larger than any other reason (ibid.). Far and away the most negative feature of the job as they saw it was "poor remuneration" (52 percent) while "political pres-sures" proved a weak second (10 percent) (ibid.: 432).

Careers are predominantly limited to a single agency, and advance-ment within that agency involves a mixture of seniority and demonstrated talent. Reassignments occur once every two years or so, and members of an entering cohort tend to move up as a cluster through a variety of positions in the agency. The most successful individuals can expect to achieve the position of section chief after approximately fifteen years of service, assistant bureau chief after twenty-two to twenty-five years and bureau chief after twenty-five to twenty-eight years. The top position, that of administrative vice-minister, is available only to a single individual out of two or three cohorts. It usually takes twenty-eight to thirty years for an individual to reach this level. Typically, he then holds this position for two or three years, after which he and any remaining members of the group that entered the ministry with him will retire. Their age at this time is most often fifty-one to fifty-five.

While the process of advancement is frequently compared to that of riding an escalator, an individual's talent and successes are by no means irrelevant to promotion. An entering cohort will, indeed, find most of its members receiving their first promotions at about the same time. But those who demonstrate the greatest abilities will be given the slightly more prestigious posts; possibly they will be promoted slightly earlier. With each subsequent transfer progressively clearer graduations will appear, separating those marked for the highest achievement from the rest. The system of early retirement puts hard-working individuals in positions of authority at an early age and provides for a relatively continuous stream of talent through the halls of various ministries. It is not unusual for an official to head a regional office with a staff of over one hundred at the age of thirty to thirty-two.

With such a premium of "high flying," there is also a measure of security. Only the most blatantly scandalous behavior is enough to result in outright termination. A single failure is never enough to stifle a budding career. Risk-taking and creativity are encouraged within broad boundaries. Few if any individuals will be passed over for promotion for an embarrassing length of time. Rarely will any senior-level officials be in a position of direct subservience to those who entered the agency a few years later.

Along the way there are many opportunities for an individual to acquire additional skills. Various skill courses in foreign languages, economics, or computer skills are often given by an agency. The National Personnel Authority maintains a program for potential high fliers to be sent abroad for two years of advanced education. Individuals are often temporarily detached to another agency to gain needed skills. Diverse assignments serve to broaden one's perspective on the agency and its mission.

In all of these ways, therefore, the individual agency and the bureaucracy as a whole seek to identify the most talented individuals for positions, to test them on the job, to provide in-house training, to encourage responsibility, and to reward demonstrated success. As a consequence of all these factors, over time the higher civil service in Japan has consistently attracted individuals who would have to be classified as among the nation's most talented. Early retirements at the top, job training throughout the ranks, a mixture of security and challenge have all combined to provide opportunities, stimulation, and rewards for ambitious individuals.

The bureaucratic career continues to rank as among the nation's most esteemed.

At the same time, individual talent flourishes in a well-defined ideological and programmatic context. Loyalty to conservative political principles, to one's agency, its mission, and to one's immediate superiors are all taken for granted in the assessment and promotion of any individual bureaucrat. As noted, recruitment and promotion are the function of the individual agency. Peer evaluation plays a critical role in the personnel department's assessment of a civil servant's abilities while examples of lateral entry and of departure and subsequent reentry are almost nonexistent. Few important missions or memoranda are the work of a single individual; those few that are rarely carry individual attribution. Postbureaucratic careers are also highly dependent on the development and maintenance of close allies within one's agency and its client groups. The consensual aspects of Japanese organization and decision-making behavior and the deep socialization into a sense of national purpose also serve to constrain unbridled ambition and individuality. In all of these ways, collective checks are maintained against the temptation of an individual to advance either his career or his pet projects at the expense of the broader ends of his section or his agency. In short, the upper ranks of Japan's civil service are structured to minimize the likelihood of being staffed by Drones; but simultaneously there are rather few opportunities for Queen Bees to emerge.

BETWEEN GOVERNMENT AND SUBGOVERNMENT—AGENCY PRIMACY AND STRUCTURED COMPETITION

If there is a blend of security and competition in the recruitment and careers of individual civil servants, a good deal of autonomy is given to individual agencies within the Japanese bureaucracy. At times, particularly during the late 1920s and 1930s, this proved to be a major drawback to the effective functioning of the Japanese political system. In the postwar period it has also created interagency tensions and problems of coordination. Still, the overriding sense of national mission, the external threats faced during the prewar period, and the primacy given to economic recovery and high growth in the immediate postwar years all mitigated the tendencies toward subgovernmental disparateness to some degree. Moreover, structural and personal networks exist that reduce some of the centripetal force that agency autonomy would otherwise provide. As a result, Japan has "government" rather than "subgovernment." Furthermore, agency autonomy has resulted in a good deal of competition among agencies—competition to gain new functions, competition to outperform, and more recently, competition to avoid the personnel cuts that have become a part of the country's governmental reform efforts. Paradoxically, this competition has injected a healthy dynamism into the system as a whole. In the early years of Meiji, the bureaucracy was designed, not only with an eye toward attracting the nation's most talented individuals, but also with a sensitivity toward structuring the bureaucracy in ways that would provide leeway for expertise, clarity of responsibility, and a minimization of functional overlap and structural sprawl. When Japan was a relatively new nation-state, this was comparatively easy, at least in contrast to the earlier bureaucracies of Europe, where numerous functions and overlapping agencies had sprung up over time.

The key organizational unit was the ministry *(sho),* of which there were fewer than a dozen. Within the ministry, hierarchical lines of responsibility were clearly demarcated. Very few additional agencies, commissions, or other bureaucratic authorities stood outside the ministerial structures.

Equally striking is the fact that, for the most part, recruitment, socialization, and assignment of all members of a ministry were the exclusive function of that ministry. As noted above, the typical career of a top-level bureaucrat was centered in a single agency. The agency itself normally had highly specific arenas of power and reasonably clear-cut goals. A symbiotic intimacy thus developed between the career of an individual and the success of an agency. This in turn was highly conducive to the accomplishment of an agency's mission.

At the same time, interministerial, and often intraministerial competition was frequent (Imai, 1953; Fukumoto, 1959, among others). The story, perhaps apocryphal, is told of the individual within the prewar Ministry of Finance who needed various data that he knew had been collected by the section next door to his own. But upon requesting the data, he was told that if the material was so critical to his work, he and his section should collect it themselves.

Such solidarity among sections and ministries had a dual character. On the one hand, it built into the bureaucracy as a whole a high degree of competition. Could or would section A come up with a better solution to a problem than section B? If ministry X handled a mission poorly, would responsibility not revert to ministry Y? At the same time, the isolation of individual sections and ministries posed serious problems of coordination. The cabinet proved to be a poor device to cope with this. The civil and military portions of the national bureaucracy were completely separated, and both top-level civilian and military bureaucrats had a theoretically (and at times, practically) direct line of authority to the person of the Emperor, but no automatic ties to one another. Ministerial, not cabinet, responsibility prevailed. Cabinet coordination was difficult.

During the U.S. occupation, the structured competition of the prewar Japanese bureaucracy was exacerbated by the American tradition toward "interest group liberalism" in Lowi's words (1969) or toward the dominance of politics by "iron triangles" of functionally compatible legislative committees, bureaucratic agencies, and private interest associations (McConnell, 1964; Freeman, 1964).

Although the new cabinet was made constitutionally responsible as a body, the individual agency continued to reign supreme. In part this was because the U.S. military worked through the existing agencies with the result that the functional goals of various American reformers soon became congruent with those of their Japanese bureaucratic counterparts. Cross-national alliances soon developed around specific goals such as fiscal austerity, the introduction of civil liberties, improved local sanitation, highway construction, the democratization of the elementary or high school curricula, or the revitalization of newspapers. Achieving such specific goals frequently matched functionally responsible Japanese officials and American military personnel against their respective superiors in both the Japanese government and the American Occupation.

This pattern was particularly evident in response to various proposals such as those for decentralization of administration, for cuts in the size of the civil service, and for the testing of ranking civil servants.

The top levels of the Occupation, including the chief of staff and General MacArthur, rejected pleas for exceptional treatment in principle, contending that GHQ should not intervene to alter the details of Japanese government proposals except where some specific objective of the Occupation was jeopardized. Nevertheless, many of the protests proved successful, both within SCAP and the Japanese government; a series of cabinet decisions in 1949 and 1950, for example, exempted a number of agencies and divisions from all or part of the proposed personnel cuts.

In the period since the Occupation, the importance of the individual agency has remained extremly high. This is certainly true of recruitment and careers. Once an individual is appointed to a post, he typically remains with the same agency for the duration of his career. In a survey of civil servants holding top positions during the years 1949–1959, Kubota (1969) found approximately one-third had been with a single agency, one-third had served with one additional agency for a brief period and then returned to the agency of initial appointment, and only one-third had served in three or more ministries. More recent data show that fully two-thirds of those holding top posts in the early 1970s had served in only one ministry, while fewer than 9 percent had served in three or more ministries (Kubota and Tomita, 1977).

Because career patterns are dominated by service in a single ministry and because lateral entry is rare, loyalty to one's agency (or section within an agency) continues to be extremely high. This produces positive effects in terms of loyalty, work satisfaction, and the like, but it also exaggerates natural bureaucratic tendencies toward tunnel vision and compartmentalization. There is a tendency toward sectionalism, and agencies or even sections within the same agency frequently resist cooperation and coordination, each seeking to maximize a particular sphere of influence. Certain ministerial rivalries have achieved a degree of notoriety in Japanese politics, such as those between Finance and International Trade and Industry, for example, or between the so-called economic ministries and the so-called service ministries. Yet, in many instances, such competition has produced highly beneficent consequences. As one example, during the 1950s and 1960s new entrants to the Ministry of International Trade and Industry (MITI) were traditionally told that they would have to work twice as hard as that agency's rivals in the Ministry of Finance (MOF), since the residual prestige of the latter was higher (Honda, 1974). In fact, the implicit competition between the two agencies resulted in a highly efficient mix of the structural policies advocated by MITI and the solid fiscal conservatism promoted by the MOF (Johnson, 1982).

This positive dimension to intrabureaucratic competition is bolstered by a far greater attention to the coordination of the collective opinions of individual bureaus or agencies. Much of this coordination takes place in a variety of informal settings, such as study groups, alumni clubs, and other bodies. Moreover, political bodies, both at the party and governmental levels, exist to consolidate various bureaucratic differences. Within the bureaucracy itself some coordination of otherwise competing ministries is achieved through the informal but, nonetheless, powerful conference of administrative vice-ministers that meets weekly, just before cabinet meetings. Its primary function is to iron out organizational disputes and to resolve differences in the goals and programs of different government agencies. In addition, various interministry teams are often established to analyze and make policy recommendations on specific problems such as the reversion of Okinawa, the energy crisis, or the country's position in General Agreement on Tariffs and Trade (GATT) negotiations.

Coordination among such groups is helped considerably by the fact that most of the negotiating civil servants have been trained as general administrators rather than as narrow technical experts. In most agencies, as Suttmeier (1978) has shown, civil servants with highly technical backgrounds find it difficult to achieve top-level posts. Those trained as administrative generalists tend to hold a wide variety of posts and to predominate in most agencies. And as generalists, most have some breadth of experience and are committed less to rigid interpretations and to specific details. Where necessary, these can be compromised in the interest of a more broadly acceptable, although often abstract and amorphous, package deal.

Administrative reform as it has come to be defined in Japan has also become extremely important as a device to channel agency primacy and structured competition into directions beneficial to the government as a whole. Behind the reform is the commitment to small government taken as relatively sacrosanct by the political coalition which has governed Japan since 1955. The coalition has made a consistent effort to keep down the costs of government, and to reduce the tendency toward bureaucratic expansion and the creation of new governmental programs to deal with all manner of social ills. The bases for such goals and the manner of their implementation are far broader than can be analyzed in depth. What is most relevant at this point is the freezing of the number of posts within the national bureaucracy, and the reallocation of positions within this fixed number to meet changing social needs by cutting back on outmoded bureaucratic functions. It also rests heavily on "pushing down" to local governments or "hiving off" to the private sector, or to semipublic corporations, many functions that are dealt with by government bureaus in other countries.

Between 1931 and 1951, the size of the national government had jumped from 591,000 to 1,400,000 while prefectural and local government officials had skyrocketed from 90,000 to 1,300,000. Personnel costs had soared comparably just as economies in government were being demanded by the Americans and by Japanese conservatives. A series of cutbacks in 1949 and 1951 resulted in some damming of the tide. Still, during the 1950s and early 1960s, the Japanese national bureaucracy grew at the rate of approximately 10,000 new posts per year. And between 1952 and 1963, government expenditures as a percent of national income rose from 17 percent to 24 percent (*Nihon Kokusei Zue*, annual).

A number of unsuccessful proposals emerged for cutting back the size of government, but most foundered on unified opposition from the agencies. Government employee unions, fearful of the impact that cutbacks might have on job security and union activity, also opposed reductions. The eventual solution came in a manner designed to minimize the potential opposition of both groups. The first step came in August of 1964 with Prime Minister Ikeda's proposal to leave a portion of all existing vacancies unfilled. Cabinet approval during the next month led to a system in which a certain portion of all positions vacant as of that time would be frozen. Within three years, although some 7,000 of these were utilized to fulfill new needs, a net of 7,500 positions was left unfilled.

This relatively even-handed freeze on potential expansion involved few if any actual layoffs, yet led to reductions in the total number of authorized personnel; natural attrition rather than wholesale firings provided the cuts. This method reduced union opposition. More importantly, since all government agencies were rather uniformly affected, few could cry "foul" on grounds of partiality. Instead, all were forced to meet changing internal priorities through reorganization and reallocation of existing personnel, rather than through add-ons and unchecked expansion.

The principle behind this policy was expanded in 1967. Then a cabinet decision called for a cut of one bureau by each of the government's main ministries or agencies. Furthermore, it mandated a systematic 5 percent reduction in the number of fixed personnel within each agency, to take place over a three-year period, 1969–1971. The agency itself could determine which bureau and positions to cut. Most cuts were effected through natural attrition, followed by internal reorganization of the agency or ministry. Eliminated positions then went into a collective pool from which all agencies could request any supplements in their total personnel so as to meet new national needs or to create new programs. Individual agency requests were evaluated in comparison with one another, encouraging a dimension of creative competition among agencies. The agencies that proved unsuccessful in this competition were forced to determine their own priorities for personnel use within declining limits. In this way, sections or subsections that had outlived their original purposes were eliminated, and the personnel staffing such bodies were transferred within the agency to units deemed more essential.

The basic outlines of this 1968 plan were extended in 1972, 1975, and 1977. The result was a continuous freezing in the total number of national government personnel. Between 1957 and 1967, when the major programs aimed at reduction were begun, the number of government personnel (*teiin kanri* exclusive of the Self-Defense Forces, which were not affected by the reforms) had jumped from 377,000 to 507,000. Employees in the five major government enterprises (the Post Office, National Forestry, and the Printing, Alcohol, and Mint Monopolies) had risen from 288,000 to 373,000. The number of personnel staffing local branches of national government offices had more than doubled from 8,800 to 19,900. Twelve years later, in 1979, each of the figures had leveled off or was below these 1967 levels. Civilian government personnel stood at 504,000, those in the five enterprises had fallen by about 15,000, and staff in local branches were at 18,900.

The thrust of these efforts came to a much more publicized and politicized climax in November 1980, when the government established a blue ribbon commission to make comprehensive recommendations for administrative reform. The final report of the commission, issued in July 1982, called for sweeping cuts in the functions and size of a wide range of government operations, focusing particularly on public corporations and semigovernmental bodies which, it was contended, could readily be hived off to the private sector at great savings to the public treasury, and with a presumed increase in overall efficiency. Meanwhile, in September 1981, the Cabinet authorized a further 5 percent reduction in government personnel to be carried out between 1982 and 1986.

Curtailing absolute growth did not entail a freezing of all structures and expansions within the national government bureaucracy, however. Innovation and change continued to occur. Thus, for example, the government established an Environment Agency in 1971, a Price Bureau and a Natural Resources and Energy Agency in 1973, and a National Land Agency in 1974. There was an overall growth of about 18,000 in the number of government personnel assigned to national schools and hospitals, while in 1977 a new system of national medical colleges was created de novo. Initially staffed by 6,400 people, two years later it was employing over 11,000. But such expansions were paralleled by significant cuts in the number of authorized personnel in agencies such as the Ministry of Agriculture, Forestry and Fisheries, the Ministry of Construction, and the prime minister's office, where less valued functions were dropped. Reallocation rather than simple expansion was the guideline.

This constraint in the size of the national bureaucracy was balanced to some extent by expansion at lower levels of government. While the number of national government employees remained stable or declined following 1967, the number of local government officials grew steadily from 1.8 million in 1958 to 2.5 million in 1970 to nearly 3.2 million in 1980. In effect, local governments picked up much of the policy slack left by the stability in the national government's size. Yet from a different perspective, the entire policy of administrative reform allowed the national government to "push down" various of its less critical functions to local levels of government, while retaining the capacity to concentrate only on items of extremely high, and truly national, significance.

This growth in local government, however, has still left Japan with a much smaller proportion of government employees than any other major industrial state. Differences in administrative structure, institutional variation, and methods of calculation make accurate comparisons difficult, but government employees represent from 6 to 9 percent of the total populations in the United States, Britain, West Germany, and France and between 14 and 20 percent of the employed populations of these countries. In Japan the figures are 4.5 and 9 percent, respectively (Kato, 1977: 18). Thus, government is still much smaller in Japan than elsewhere.

This small size has added to the prestige associated with employment in the government, particularly in the senior ranks. Thus, as was noted, there has been a dramatic increase over the past two decades in the number of applicants for top-level civil service positions. Such figures in themselves say little about the quality of the individuals being hired, but it seems intuitively logical to conclude that the cuts in the size of the civil service did little to impair the quality of personnel being hired. In all probability the quality level rose, increased exclusiveness attracting more exceptional candidates. Furthermore, improvements in quality appear to have been felt at the local level as well. There, unsuccessful candidates for the national civil service have found an expanding arena with increased responsibilities, and the consensus in Japan seems to be that there has been a dramatic improvement in the quality of local government bureaucrats since the mid-1960s.

Most importantly, relatively smaller national government with high-quality personnel has meant a government capable of setting priorities. Particularly impressive in Japan is the apparent ability of the government to develop a relatively coherent and consistent set of policy objectives and then to devote high levels of attention and energy toward their achievement. This would have been far more difficult were each government agency allowed to follow its own narrowly defined priorities and interests. By forcing cutbacks in all agencies, the government required agencies to set internal priorities for actions. And by allocating new positions only insofar as demands from one agency could be made to appear more necessary than those of another agency, each agency was forced to remain sensitive to overall national priorities, and to develop programs designed to meet them. The organizational success of individual agencies in Japan has thus come to depend on their willingness and ability to adapt to changing national priorities.

EVALUATING EFFICIENCY

Though far from perfect, the Japanese bureaucracy functions with a high degree of efficiency for the many reasons already noted. The civil service, especially in its top ranks, is staffed by individuals who clearly would rank among the most talented the country has. These individuals simultaneously have a strong sense of service and duty; they are intimately involved with the mission of their agency, and with what they see to be the needs of the country. Agencies compete vigorously with one another, and against a variety of domestic and international obstacles, to achieve their relative missions. Through it all, they are checked in only the broadest ways by electoral and party politics. The close intimacy they enjoy with the dominant LDP gives them great discretion in the means by which they pursue the broad policy ends sought by the nation's dominant conservative coalition.

In all of these ways, the Japanese bureaucracy seems balanced between the negative extremes of incompetent and overly ambitious personel, between subgovernment and government, and between "red" and "expert." Tendencies in one direction or another are typically checked by contrary pulls.

Such a focus on efficiency may convey too rosy a picture, however. It would be well briefly to consider some of the pitfalls otherwise ignored. First of all, with conservative political ends so pervasively accepted, it is typically the function of the individual agency to determine the most suitable means to achieve these ends. The classical "ends-means" problem emerges with acuity in the Japanese bureaucracy, because there is little incentive for anyone to question the legitimacy of "necessary" means.

Agency togetherness and loyalty are pervasive; it becomes extremely difficult for the isolated or skeptical individual to speak out against means that may appear tainted. The agency into which he has been socialized has in all likelihood "done things this way for decades." Protest is usually futile, if it is even considered.

The need to work closely with outside groups and with politicians poses a related problem. It becomes difficult to isolate oneself or one's agency from potential corruption. The electoral success of a helpful politician; the securing of an international contract by a closely related firm; gaining access to foreign sources of raw materials—all these things easily become the ends of the agency itself, or at least the means to achieving the agency's ends. The persistent emergence in Japan of financial scandals and political corruption implicating high civil servants is a reminder of this hazard (e.g., *Economist,* Dec. 8, 1979; *Japan Quarterly,* April–June, 1980; Ouchi, 1977).

Beyond this, the hegemonic position enjoyed by the LDP removes one of the major potential checks on bureaucratic corruption and arrogance present in most democracies. There is no threat that a new government and new ministers will disagree sufficiently with the ends of a previous administration to change them, and in the process to examine the means by which they were achieved. No one is looking for the closet's skeletons.

Alteration of government by no means guarantees that political ends and means will be consistently reevaluated. Indeed, Japan's opposition parties have themselves been tainted by suspicion in many of the political scandals that have emerged, and their own organizations appear as susceptible to self-righteous arrogance as that of the government party. At the same time, given their official hostility toward, say, the closeness of Japan's relations with the United States, there is little doubt but that they would explore all facets of U.S. arms sales in Japan, were they to have access to bureaucratic records. They would also undoubtedly be quite interested in domestic construction projects carried out by large Japanese firms and in the entertainment budgets used by supervising officials and, more importantly, members of the ruling party. In such ways, some checks on certain problem areas would be likely.

The important question, however, is not whether a change in government would eliminate some few remaining flaws in an otherwise highly efficient civil service. The likelihood is that an occasional ignoring of the means used to reach one's ends, the injection of periodic corruption scandals into the civil service, or the manifestation of arrogant self-righteousness will be inevitable concomitants of any organizational behavior, in Japan or elsewhere. The more significant question, perhaps, is whether efficiency should automatically be accorded the highest priority in a national bureaucracy. Openness to citizen influence, capacity to reevaluate broad goals on a regular basis, sensitivity to changing socioeconomic needs, provision of a humane work environment, and a host of other values are surely desirable as well. But the unflinching worship of efficiency can easily cause them to be ignored. Though the implications of such a perspective are surely vague at best, it would be unwise to forget it totally in any assessment of Japan's higher civil service.

BIBLIOGRAPHY

Ari, R. et al. (1974) *Gendai Gyōsei to Kanryōsei.* Tōkyō Daigaku, Shuppankai.
Armstrong, John A. (1973) *The European Administrative Elite.* Princeton: Princeton University Press.
Asahi Nenkan (annual).
Ashford, Douglas (1981) *Policy and Politics in Britain.* Philadelphia: Temple University Press.
Banfield, Edward, and James Q. Wilson (1963) *City Politics.* Cambridge: Harvard University Press.
Beer, Samuel H. (1965) *British Politics in the Collectivist Age.* New York: Knopf.
Campbell, John C. (1979). "The Old People Boom and Japanese Policymaking," *Journal of Japanese Studies.* 5, no. 2: 321–357.
Crozier, Michel (1963) *The Bureaucratic Phenomenon.* Chicago: University of Chicago Press.
Donnelly, Michael (1977) "Setting the Price of Rice: A Study in Political Decision-

making," in T. J. Pempel (ed.) *Policymaking in Contemporary Japan.* Ithaca: Cornell University Press.

Economist.

Esman, Milton J. (1946) "Memorandum for Chief, Government Section," 30 Jan. 1946, reprinted in SCAP, *Political Reorientation of Japan.* Washington: U.S. Government Printing Office.

Freeman, J. Leiper (1966) *The Political Process.* New York: Random House.

Fukumoto, Kunio (1959) *Kanryō.* Tokyo: Kobundo.

Granick, David (1954) *Management of the Industrial Firm in the USSR.* New York: Columbia University Press.

Graziano, Luigi (1978) "Center Periphery Relations and the Italian Crisis: The Problem of Clientelism," in S. Tarrow et al., *Territorial Politics in Industrial Nations.* New York: Praeger.

Heclo, Hugh (1977) *A Government of Strangers.* Washington: Brookings.

Honda, Y. (1974) *Nihon Neokanryō Ron.* Kōdansha.

Imai, Kazuo (1953) *Kanryō.* Tokyo: Yomiuri Shimbun.

Inoki, M. (1964) "The Civil Bureaucracy: Japan" in R. Ward and D. Rustow (eds.), *Political Modernization in Japan and Turkey.* Princeton: Princeton University Press, 283–300.

Isomura, E., and M. Kuronuma. (1974) *Gendai Nihon No Gyōsei.* Chihō Gyōsei Gakkai.

Japan Quarterly.

Jinjiin (annual) *Nenji Hōkokusho* (Tokyo: Ōkurashō Insatsukyoku).

Johnson, C. (1975) "Japan: Who Governs? An Essay on Official Bureaucracy." *Journal of Japanese Studies* 2, no. 1: 1–28.

——— (1978) *Japan's Public Policy Companies.* Washington, D.C.: American Enterprise Institute.

——— (1982) *MITI and the Japanese Miracle.* Stanford: Stanford University Press.

——— (1974) "The Reemployment of Retired Government Bureaucrats in Japanese Business." *Asian Survey* 14: 953–965.

Kato, Tomiko (1977) "Present Problems Concerning Managerial Personnel in the Public Sector." *Local Government Review* 5: 17–35.

Kaufman, Herbert (1956) "Emerging Conflicts in the Doctrines of Public Administration." *American Political Science Review* 50, no. 4 (December): 1057–1073.

Kawai, Kazuo (1960) *Japan's American Interlude.* Chicago: University of Chicago Press.

Kosaka, Masataka (1981) *Kōdōsangyō Kokka no Rieki Seiji Katei to Seisaku—Nihon.* Toyota Zaidan Josei Kenkyū Hōkokusho.

Kubota, A. (1969) *Higher Civil Servants in Postwar Japan: Their Social Origins, Educational Backgrounds and Career Patterns.* Princeton: Princeton University Press.

Kubota, A., and Tomita, N. (1977) "Nihon Seifu Kōkan no Ishiki Kōzō." *Chūō Kōron* 1079 (February): 190–196.

Kusayanagi, D. (1975) *Kanryō Ōkokuron.* Bungei Shūnjusha.

Lorwin, Val (1971) "Segmented Pluralism: Ideological and Political Cohesion in the Small European Democracies." *Comparative Politics*, January, pp. 142–155.

Lowi, Theodore J. (1969) *The End of Liberalism.* New York: Norton.

Maki, John M. (1947) "The Role of the Bureaucracy in Japan." *Pacific Affairs* 20 (December), pp. 391–406.

Masumi, Junnosuke (1965–1968) *Nihon Seitōshiron.* Tokyo: Tōkyō Daigaku Shuppankai.

McConnell, Grant (1966) *Private Power and American Democracy.* New York: Vintage.

Moore, Barrington, Jr. (1963) *Soviet Politics—The Dilemma of Power.* New York: Harper.

Moulin, Lee (1975) "The Politicization of the Administration in Belgium," in Mattei Dogan (ed.), *The Mandarins of Western Europe.* Beverly Hills: Sage.

Muramatsu, Michio (1978) "Gyōsei Kanryō no Katsudō Taishu." *Kikan Gyōsei Kanri Kenkyū* 12, no. 4: 10–23.

———— (1981) *Sengo Nihon no Kanryōsei.* Tōyō Keizai.

Ouchi, Minoru (1977) *Fuhai no Kōzō.* Tokyo: Daiyamonde.

Pempel, T. J. (1974) "The Bureaucratization of Policymaking in Postwar Japan." *Amer. J. of Pol. Sci.* 18, no. 4 (November): 647–664.

———— (1978) "Political Parties and Social Change: The Japanese Experience," in L. Maisel and J. Cooper (eds.), *Political Parties: Development and Decay.* Beverly Hills, Sage, 309–341.

———— (1982) *Policy and Politics in Japan: Creative Conservatism.* Philadelphia: Temple University Press.

———— (1984) "The Tar Baby Target: 'Reform' of the Japanese Bureaucracy under the U.S. Occupation," in Robert E. Ward and Yoshikazu Sakamoto (eds.), Democracy and Planned Political Change. Honolulu: University of Hawaii Press.

Putnam, Robert D. (1976) *The Comparative Study of Political Elites.* Englewood Cliffs, N.J.: Prentice-Hall.

Rosenberg, Hans (1958) *Bureaucracy, Aristocracy, and Autocracy.* Boston: Beacon.

Scalapino, Robert A. (1962) *Democracy and the Party Movement in Prewar Japan.* Berkeley: University of California Press.

Shefter, Martin (1977) "Patronage and Its Opponents: A Theory and Some European Cases." Cornell University Western Society Program. *Occasional Papers.*

———— (1978a) "The Electoral Foundations of the Political Machine: New York City, 1884–1897," in Joel Silbey et al. (eds.), *American Electoral History: Quantitative Studies in Popular Voting Behavior.* Princeton: Princeton University Press.

———— (1978b) "Party, Bureaucracy, and Political Change in the United States," in *The Development of Political Parties: Patterns of Evolution and Decay.* Louis Maisel and Joseph Cooper (eds.), Beverly Hills: Sage.

Shirven, Maynard N., and Joseph L. Soeicher (1951) "Examination of Japan's Upper Bureaucracy." *Personnel Administration* 14, 4 July: 48–49.

Silberman, B. (1974) "The Bureaucratic Role in Japan, 1900–1945: The Bureaucrat as Politician," in B. Silberman and H. Harootunian (eds.), *Japan in Crisis:* 183–216. Princeton: Princeton University Press.

Spaulding, Robert M. (1967) *Imperial Japan's Higher Civil Service Examination.* Princeton: Princeton University Press.

Steslicke, William (1973) *The Political Life of the Japan Medical Association.* New York: Praeger.

Suttmeier, Richard P. (1978) "The 'Gikan' Question in Japanese Government: Bureaucratic Curiosity or Institutional Failure." *Asian Survey* 18, 10 October. pp. 1046–1066.

Watanabe, Tatsuo (1974) *Kōkyō Komuin no Ishiki,* in Ari et al.

Watanabe, Tsuneo (1958) *Habatsu.* Tokyo: Kōbundō.

FROM RIGHT TO LEFT
Bureaucracy and Politics in France

Ezra N. Suleiman

It is customary and generally useful to begin a discussion of the relation-ship between politics and administration by invoking Max Weber's classic distinction between the two domains. At the heart of this distinction lay a larger conception of the democratic process that guided Weber's writings on the subject. The election of the politician endowed him with legitimacy and forced on him a sense of responsibility because he would be held accountable for his actions; the appointment of the civil servant conferred no national legitimacy because it required no accountability. "According to his proper vocation," wrote Weber, "the genuine official will not engage in politics. Rather, he should not do precisely what the politician, the leader as well as his following, must always and necessarily do, namely, fight."[1]

The distinction between the professional politician and the profes-sional bureaucrat remains important partly on normative grounds and partly as a framework for approaching the study of the relationship be-tween politics and administration in specific contexts. At no point did Weber claim that he was describing reality. "Every problem," he noted, "no matter how technical it might seem, can assume political significance and its solution can be decisively influenced by political considerations."[2] Weber recognized that "engaging in politics" can be done by a variety of means. Politics, in other words, involves more than getting elected. When we speak of "policy," says Brian Chapman, we are, in effect, "describing what civil servants do when they play a part in determining ends, choosing means and fixing priorities." Policy, says Chapman, means "no more than the political activity of civil servants."[3] Taking into account that bureaucrats often intervene in "politics," or in the policy-making process as much as do politicians, one recent study observes that "the last quarter of this century is witnessing the virtual disappearance of the Weberian distinction between the roles of politician and bureaucrat, producing what we might call a 'pure hybrid.' "[4]

The politico-administrative hybrid exists in different degrees of perfection in different societies, and has different origins. This chapter deals with the French politico-administrative system, and it will be largely concerned with the ways in which the French social and political system encouraged the incursion into politics by civil servants. It will become evident in the course of our argument that it is not primarily the increasing role of the French state in the society and in the economy (for what industrial society has not seen its social and economic responsibilities increase markedly in the post–World War II period?) that accounts for the facility with which civil servants move into political roles. Rather, this is accounted for by a commitment on the part of the state to a particular training system which seeks to create a highly selective cadre of experts and to endow this small group with remarkable advantages, as well as by a political culture that rationalizes, and hence legitimizes, the simultaneous holding of administrative and political posts. The change in government that occurred in May–June 1981 has not affected either the state's commitment to training an administrative elite or the particular practice of encouraging civil servants to occupy political offices. For a long time it was possible to impute the politico-administrative system of the Fifth Republic to the control of the state apparatus by governments of the Right. Certainly, this argument was made by some of the more influential members of today's left-wing government when they were in the opposition.[5] The association of France's politico-administrative system with the Right is no longer tenable for the principles which guided this system in the past continue to do so today. As we shall see, the reforms that the Mitterrand-Mauroy government have proposed in no way constitute a break with past practices. Indeed, the Left has been generally less hostile to the bureaucracy than was the Right at various stages during the years of the Fifth Republic. The Left has sought to make some changes in recruitment procedures, and it has sought to ensure that the administrative machine adapts itself to Socialist goals. But it has not attempted to undo an administrative structure that has been able to serve both the state and the party in power. The peculiar relationship that obtains between politics and administration in France serves to oil the policy-making process. Once this was acknowledged by the Left, all attempts at structural reforms evaporated. And yet, as we shall see, the Socialists are likely to bring about changes in the administrative structure in spite of themselves, or despite the maintenance of the inherited structures.

The Role of the State

The recruitment system, itself a reflection of the general social system, seeks to create an elite, to nurture it, to guarantee it rapid promotion, and even to subsidize its entry into politics. This system is, as we shall see, not without its effects on the policy-making process. One needs to note a paradox in this system. In the United States, as Heclo shows, there has always existed in the very nature of the personnel system an ambiguity with respect to administrative and political roles. "Founded well before any concern with modern bureaucracy had developed, the American constitutional structure left the question of the national bureaucracy open, which is to say, vulnerable to fits of improvisation and neglect. To the jagged and variable contours of the formal structure, informal arrangements have added their own considerable ambiguity, blurring demarcations and mutual obligations between political executives and civil servants."[6] In France, on the other hand, the recruitment system leaves little room for the ambiguities that obtain in the American bureaucracy. In fact, the existence of a National School of Administration (ENA) ought to have given rise to the kind of neat separation between politics and administration that Weber had in mind. The result has been the reverse. This is because ENA is both a school that trains the future higher civil servants and that trains an elite. In other words, the status it accords the higher civil servants is such that it can be used just as easily outside the confines of the administration proper.

To understand the particular importance of higher civil servants in the French politico-administrative system, it is necessary to understand the general system of elite recruitment that the French state has devised. In this respect, the French model is probably closer to the Soviet model than it is to the German or British systems. The creation and growing importance of specialized schools over the past century and a half distinguishes the French system of elite training. It is in this sense that we can properly speak of "state-created elites" in France.[7] Thus we can read in the opening lines of a pamphlet, issued by the *Conférence des Grandes Ecoles:*

> Among the one hundred largest French firms, two-thirds are headed by graduates of the grandes écoles. An even higher larger proportion are found at the highest levels of government administration. Finally, the

grandes écoles provide France with most of its engineers, managers, researchers in industry, and administrators.

This means that whoever has occasion to come into contact with the decision-makers in the private or public sectors in France inevitably finds himself face to face with men whose mind and manners and attitudes have been profoundly marked by a training which, despite any differences in specialization, manifests a number of common traits.[8]

Societies devise different means for preparing their leaders. In England and the United States a few schools have usually trained a disproportionate number of the political, economic, and administrative elites. These schools have been credited with the creation of networks among the different elites that are said to be linked by the so-called old school tie.[9] The French system of elite recruitment differs from that of other societies in one important respect: it is characterized by the existence of institutions whose avowed task is to select competent elites. There is no attempt to disguise or be defensive about the essential purpose of these institutions. In short, the recruitment of elites in France is not left up to chance: it is a highly institutionalized system that depends on competitive examinations into professional schools that serve as the gateway to the elite. France has been able to devise a system that differs in another important way from the systems of the Anglo-Saxon countries: it has been able to create a system of elite recruitment that combines a class-based elite with merit.

The different regimes that have governed France over the past two centuries, whether Monarchical or Republican, Left or Right, have generally adopted similar policies with respect to the recruitment of elites. All have sought to create or maintain the *grandes écoles.* The *ancien régime* created the school known today as the *Ecole Nationale des Ponts et Chaussées;* the Convention created the *Ecole Normale Supérieure;* Napoleon consolidated the existing grandes écoles and created others; the Third Republic supported the creation of the *Ecole Libre des Sciences Politiques;*[10] the Popular Front sought to create an *Ecole Nationale d'Administration;* and, finally, the major political forces that shared power at the Liberation created the *Ecole Nationale d'Administration.*

The partiality that different regimes have shown for the professional schools suggests that these schools could perform similar functions for different governments. I shall return to the question of how the higher civil service, long associated with the Right, has adapted itself to the left-wing government in power today. It has been argued, for example, that the failure of Blum's Popular Front government (1936–1937) was due as much to the conservatism of the higher civil service as to the failure of the Blum government to stick by a strong anti-Fascist foreign policy. Irwin

Wall has argued that "a root cause of Blum's failure, and an explanation for the cautious conservatism of his government's actions, stems from the inherent resistance to innovation of the conservatively biased career civil service which the Socialist government proved unable to counter by the one means available to it—finding the personnel appropriate to its policies."[11] The Popular Front government was in fact laying the ground-work for the creation of the Ecole Nationale d'Administration that was to be created in 1945. This suggests that there has been a general agreement among French political forces to fall back on elite-forming institutions. The creation of a grande école, it should be remembered, generally oc-curred in response to a pressing need, whether for engineers, military officers, teachers, diplomats, or civil servants. As a result, they quickly became indispensable in their specific areas and were, as a consequence, seen as bulwarks against political instability.[12]

When General de Gaulle and Michel Debré created the Ecole Nationale d'Administration in 1945, they were above all preoccupied with the restoration of the state apparatus. Debré noted recently that before the war he had recognized that "it was necessary to refashion an Adminis-tration whose importance had been underestimated for too long. . . . I insisted on the need for training men who would serve the State intelli-gently and with daring."[13] The creation of ENA was based on a tried model (the Ecole Polytechnique) that, from the standpoint of the state's interest, had been judged a success.[14] Its purpose was to ensure the con-tinuity of the state at all times. In a society known for its periodic upheav-als, whether caused by wars or by domestic dissension, this purpose has a strong resonance across the political spectrum. While the Right has been more prepared to avow the importance of the preservation of the state, the Left has, by its actions, appeared to share both the goal and the means of achieving it.

> The ultimate responsibility [noted Michel Debré] lies undeniably with the political authorities. But we must be honest about the principles of democracy and suffrage. Power is not a permanent entity. The legiti-macy of a Republic is not only, as is often stated, based on alternation; it also resides in the fundamental fact that power cannot be appropriated by a single man, family, or professional or social category. The rule of democracy requires a regular return of power to the electorate. Whereas the Nation is permanent, like the State which is its necessary expression, the highest authority is constrained by shifting circumstances which give it a temporary character.[15]

Because the electorate is volatile and unpredictable and because gov-ernments tend to change rather frequently, an administration dedicated to the higher aims of the state was critically needed. This has always been the view of men like Debré who were embarrassed by and fearful of the unstable governmental system of the Third and Fourth Republics. The higher civil service, in effect, benefited from these years of political instability. It "seemed to be a model of competence and solidity, in contrast to a political class that was unstable and soon devalued. A myth was born and spread quickly in the mind of the public: if France was able to undertake reforms and to make brilliant economic progress, it was because of its *grands commis,* who brought in new ideas and a taste for innovation, and assured a genuine stability for the country behind the smokescreen of ministerial crises."[16]

The Socialist government sent tremors through the administration even before it took power. Its plans for large-scale reforms were not insignificant, though over the years they gradually got scaled down. Nonetheless, it was generally assumed that a Socialist government could not accept to work in and with an administrative structure that had long served the Right. Louis Mermaz, one of President Mitterrand's closest allies and currently president of the National Assembly, expressed a widespread view when he noted in an interview with *Le Monde:* "It is necessary to make changes at certain levels of the state administration, whether for political or economic reasons. There is no longer any doubt that the administration mobilized for the construction of a socialist society cannot have the same behavior as an administration which had the responsibility of managing a strictly capitalist France."[17] Two Socialist projects to bring about a new administration received the greatest attention: changing the personnel at the highest levels of the civil service, and reforming the recruitment procedure into the higher civil service.

With respect to the personnel changes, the purge that was anticipated, and called for by a number of Socialists,[18] did not take place. To be sure, there were changes in personnel. Out of 139 directors of the central administration, 59 (42 percent) were kept in their posts, 6 (4 percent) were transferred to other directional posts, 64 (46 percent) were changed, and 10 new posts were created. Thus, over half of the directors of the central administration were changed in the first year of socialist government. But, as Yves Agnès notes, "it is utterly wrong to maintain, with respect to changes in the state apparatus, that there was a systematic witch hunt. But it is plausible to maintain that a certain number of people who belonged to the 'phalanges de Giscard' were cast aside."[19] Despite the important number of changes of personnel in the administration proper and in the semipublic and nationalized sectors, there was clearly no purge. Indeed, we will have to offer an explanation of why the changes were not greater and more systematic than the Socialists led one to expect they would be. Ultimately, the personnel changes were of the order of magnitude of those that took place when Giscard d'Estaing became president.

In the area of recruitment much was expected to change, particularly in view of the fact that Mitterrand himself was known to be hostile to the elitist nature of ENA and to the grands corps structure. Once it became clear that the socialists had no intention of abolishing ENA, despite the naming of a Communist as minister of the civil service, there remained the expectation that some structural reforms would be introduced. The reform prepared by the minister in charge of the civil service, Anicet Le Pors, and discussed in parliament on October 5, 1982, aims to do little more than widen the recruitment of higher civil servants. At the time of preparing the reform, Le Pors had said that its main aim would be to ensure that "the higher civil service reflects the social reality of the nation."[20]

The principal innovation of the reform is the introduction of a "third avenue" of entry into ENA. Since 1945 there have been two paths into ENA: the *concours d'étudiants* and the *concours des fonctionnaires*. The first is reserved for students who have had a normal (privileged) educational background, while the second is reserved for civil servants who have the desire to move up the bureaucratic ladder but who have lacked the educational advantages of the first concours entrants or, as has become more and more the case, who failed to enter the school through the terribly competitive *concours d'étudiants*.

The idea of creating yet a third avenue was one that Mitterrand himself held very dear, and the new reform will largely be remembered for this innovation. The purpose is to allow trade union officials, local elected officials, and members of various associations to enter the higher civil service and to alter the Parisian, bourgeois character of the group that administers the affairs of the country. As Mr. Le Pors put it during the parliamentary debate, there is a need "to develop a new kind of civil service."[21] The aim, or hope, of this reform is to transform the higher civil service from an elitist institution into one that is connected socially to the society.

This ambition is not new. It has been proclaimed repeatedly by all governments since the creation of ENA. While presenting this as a major reform, the government appears to recognize that its net effects are likely to be modest. Like previous governments, it has fallen back on the argument that ENA is only a cog in a large educational machine and that the machine itself must first be overhauled. Mr. Le Pors used almost the same words that a number of previous conservative ministers have used to indicate that ENA is the prisoner of the educational system. "There can be no good reform of ENA, of a real democratization of the recruitment of higher civil servants as long as the educational system cannot guarantee a genuine equality of opportunity and assure an accurate reflection of the social realities of the nation."[22]

The government, following its predecessors of the Right, chose to concentrate on tinkering with access to ENA. Like its predecessors, it chose not to tamper with the administrative structure, not to alter the structure of the corps, or the class ranking of ENA, which determines who will enter into the grands corps, or to reduce the number of corps. The early hopes of a serious reform were quickly dissipated. As André Passeron noted at the time the government was preparing the reform of ENA: "The attitude of the new rulers toward ENA has considerably evolved, not only compared to what it was prior to May 10 [1981], but even since this date. The 'énarques' are as numerous in the ministerial cabinets of the Mauroy government as they were in the preceding governments."[23] Yet, recruitment into ministerial cabinets has changed, and certain of the grands corps (the *Inspection des Finances,* for example) have a considerably diminished role, while other corps (the *administrateurs civils*) have a far greater presence than in the past.[24]

Unity, Cooperation, and Promotion

Whatever aspirations the reformers of the Liberation period had, one goal stood out:[25] to create a group of dedicated higher civil servants. The arguments used to support the creation of ENA were not all believed in with equal force by those who made them. What mattered, above all, was the creation of an administrative elite. As Debré noted, recalling that he did make a long speech to De Gaulle, "I simply explained the simplest reason: the State, which took great care in the training of its officers and engineers, had neglected the training of its administrators."[26] If ENA "was given the impossible task of combining democratization with intellectual elitism,"[27] there was, nonetheless, a clear sense of priority, and this placed elitism above democratization.[28] This is why we were able to conclude some years ago that "the reform of 1945 contained no radical elements. None of the hallmarks of the administrative system were questioned: the concours, the corps, the assignment to posts based on rank. Indeed, the reform was negative in one very important sense: it made no allowance for, and in fact denied the virtues of lateral entry into the upper ranks of the civil service. . . ."[29]

Those responsible for the creation of ENA believed that the state could only be served loyally by civil servants who recognized that they were part of an elite dedicated to state service. In order for them to arrive at this recognition, it was necessary to see state service as being a privilege because of the rewards that come with the exercise of this métier. Hence, it was necessary to compete for entry into the elite and to cooperate with one's colleagues once entry was attained. Severe competition followed by rewards to the winners was an old Napoleonic custom that remains ingrained in French culture. In the higher civil service, competition takes place when entry into ENA is at stake; cooperation occurs when the most successful join one of the grands corps. The corps constitute the basis of the French administrative system, without which it is not possible to understand the relationship between politics and administration.

The technical and administrative elite trained by the Ecole Polytechnique and ENA is selected by a strenuous process that entails long preparation for an entrance examination into these schools. The costs (mostly emotional) of entering the elite, the socialization into the elite, and the taste of the rewards of entry into the elite are all experienced during the years spent between graduation from the *lycées* and entry into the school. The students spend these years (usually two) in the *classes préparatoires,* which are special preparatory classes for entrance into the grandes écoles. Even entry into the classes préparatoires is on a severely competitive basis. The competitive element does not subside once entry into the school is attained, for one's entire career will depend on one's rank in the graduating class. Upon graduation one chooses a career on the basis of one's rank. The most prestigious posts are those of the *Grands Corps de l'Etat*—the *Inspection des Finances,* the *Cour des Comptes,* the *Conseil d'Etat*—and these go to those who have graduated at the top. Indeed, the main line of demarcation in careers is drawn at the cut-off point between the grands corps and the rest.[30] This is also true outside of the public sector proper; the directorial posts in the nationalized sector, in the industrial sector, and in the banking sector are more likely to be occupied by a member of the grands corps.

The division of the administration into corps is now a generally accepted part of the French administrative system, notwithstanding the vehement criticism to which it is periodically subject. No political force can any longer challenge the corps, and certainly not the grands corps. We have already seen that the Socialist government has been as reluctant to challenge the grands corps as were its predecessors. Hence, we need to try to understand in what ways they determine or shape politico-administrative relations and in what ways such a structure determines or shapes the political context within which decisions are made. Marceau Long, a former director general of the civil service and until recently secretary general of the government, notes that, while the corps phenomenon is not without advantages, it clearly does not favor unity and uniformity within the administration as a whole:

> One must recall here the profound reality of the corps of civil servants, heirs to a long tradition of professional particularism; they are

united by common interests, are passionately in favor of equality, but are also intransigent about the preservation of their particular status. A corps is not unlike the guilds of the past; like them, it has its strict rules codified in a specific statute, it submits its new members to an initiation involving an entrance test and an apprenticeship, it even enjoys privileges such as job monopolies, working conditions and special allowances. It constitutes a closed little society, a fact which does not have only negative consequences, for it reinforces, without any doubt, the level of competence and the sense of public service. This particularity of the corps has persisted despite the common statutory structure. Within an apparently rigid framework, the corps have succeeded in preserving their identity.[31]

One of the main aims of the professional schools is to create a bond among the future servants of the state. But the schools could not do this effectively if all the members were dispersed after their training and if they met only in social clubs. To foster an *esprit de corps,* a genuine network, a system was designed whereby the training and the future career of the civil servants were linked. The students who are admitted to ENA and Polytechnique become civil servants, and paid as such, from the moment of their admittance to the schools. The training becomes, in effect, the beginning of one's career. The top graduates of ENA and the Ecole Polytechnique all go into one of the prestigious corps (mines, ponts et chaussées, Inspection des Finances, Conseil d'Etat, Cour des Comptes). This serves not only to link the graduates of the schools, to make them feel part of a club or a society whose members continually support one another, but it also establishes an institutional link between the schools and the corps.

The link between the schools that provide the training for the civil servants and the corps with which they come to be associated reinforces the prestige of each. The top graduates choose certain corps, which are the most prestigious corps in part because they are chosen by the graduates of the top schools. Similarly, ENA and the Ecole Polytechnique remain the most prestigious schools because they provide the key corps with their ablest graduates.[32]

For this symbiotic relationship to endure successfully, the future higher civil servants who demonstrate the highest level of competence at Polytechnique and ENA have to be assured of three things: rapid promotion, prestigious posts, and a varied career. In other words, the members of the grands corps (that is, the top graduates) have to enjoy greater career mobility and success than do graduates of other schools and members of other corps. This implies, above all, that the top graduates *choose* to enter the grands corps and that the latter offer their members interesting careers outside of the narrow functions of the corps, relatively high salaries, and good occupational prospects beyond their administrative careers. There is thus created a situation in which the grandes écoles come to have strong ties throughout the society as a result of the organizational structures that their graduates enter. Their graduates gain legitimacy in the posts they come to occupy because they are graduates of the grandes écoles, and the grandes écoles reinforce their position because of the success of their graduates.[33]

In no other country does a set of institutions exist for the purpose of creating a higher civil service elite in quite the same way as in France. For civil servants are not simply trained in France. From the beginning of the recruitment process to the way in which the politico-administrative system functions, the entire world of the civil servant is fashioned and shaped by institutions set up for this task. It is this that allows civil servants to move into political careers with the greatest ease and with little cost. In other words, it is not the extension of the state's role nor the growing complexity of issues that compels civil servants to move into positions that are, or were, the domain of the professional politician. Rather, once an elite is created and recognized as such, it can legitimately come to expect privileges. One of the privileges that the French administrative elite comes to expect is the possibility of making forays into other sectors in order to escape the confines of the administrative career.

It is not an accident that the Socialist government has preferred to keep intact the administrative structure that provides important privileges to those who reach the top of the administrative structure. The Socialists have been able to appoint civil servants who share an affinity with the Left's ideology. More important, they have been able over the years to draw on civil servants who could provide the party with time and expert advice. The higher civil service is a pool from which all parties can draw freely. To tamper with this is to risk inflicting wounds on one's own organization. That is why all parties prefer to preserve the administrative structure. Passeron touched on this when he tried to explain the moderation of the Socialist government in this area of administrative reform.

> Thus the higher civil service, and particularly E.N.A., constitutes the pool from which the new authorities plucked more than half of the chiefs of the newly nationalized sector. How could it be otherwise, when what was required were general administrators and E.N.A. has, since the Liberation, had the monopoly of this training. This, despite the fact that the Left, before coming to power, accused E.N.A. of all the horrors of "technocracy."[34]

The ties of the administrative system to the political structures are such as to practically preclude any major reforms. The attack against the elitism of the higher civil service is a sport that all political parties engage in, and it serves to distract from the underlying realities of the system that benefits both the administrative elite and the political structures.

The Dispensability of an Elite

Because the state consciously nurtures its own elite and because it has established a system that is designed to reward, rapidly and generously, this public service elite, it accords the kind of treatment to its higher civil servants that separates them from other civil servants and from the rest of society. If the state does not encourage the entry of its higher civil servants into the political arena, it at any rate subsidizes this entry, for it allows them the kind of freedom that it does not allow its other civil servants. This occurs in large part because the first privilege that is accorded to the administrative elite is that of being considered "dispensable" in Max Weber's sense of the term. For Weber, "economic dispensability" was one of the factors that allowed one to become a professional politician. "Neither the worker nor . . . the entrepreneur . . . is economically dispensable. For it is precisely the entrepreneur who is tied to his enterprise and is therefore *not* dispensable. . . . For purely organizational reasons, it is easier for the lawyer to be dispensable; and therefore the lawyer has played an incomparably greater, and often even a dominant, role as a professional politician."[35] Now these "organizational reasons" are applicable to and explain the greater freedom to pursue a political career by a certain group of civil servants as compared to other civil servants and to other groups in the society. Were it not for this dispensability, which is inherent in the French administrative system at its uppermost reaches, far fewer higher civil servants would venture into the political arena. What explains the increasing entry into politics of higher civil servants over the past two decades are the propitious conditions provided by the regime of the Fifth Republic.

There is no doubt that the administrative structure, coupled with the kind of regime now in existence, works to the advantage of a small group of civil servants whose rapid success in the public sector enables them to move with relative ease into the political sector. The Ecole Nationale d'Administration has become over the past twenty years more and more a school of elite selection and less and less a school that aims to give a technical training to the state's future administrators. As François Bloch-Lainé put it: ENA is a machine for ranking; "it is hardly a machine for teaching."[36] Today, far more than in the past, ENA is seen by those who succeed in gaining entry into it as a gateway to a political career. As a stepping stone to politics, it offers distinct advantages over the "apprenticeship" career pattern of the Third Republic.

Foremost among these advantages is the rapidity with which one can win a mayorship, a seat in the National Assembly, or a ministerial portfolio. It is possible to attain these political heights without spending many years developing a constituency in the provinces. Indeed, the political career pattern is gradually coming to be overturned: success at the national level (becoming a minister or secretary of state, for example) leads to success at the local level. Prior to the Fifth Republic, the progress of a political career developed from the local to the national level.

The law in France poses no hindrance to the civil servant who wishes to enter politics. He need not resign from the civil service either while he is a candidate for office or when he is elected. While he is a candidate for an elective office, he neither resigns nor takes a leave of absence. He continues to draw his salary exactly as if he were performing his normal duties. When he is elected to a local office, he continues to exercise his function as a civil servant.[37] The *cumul* of two positions—administrative and political—legally inadmissible in other Western countries, is sanctioned by law in France.[38] Noting the phenomenon that in France it is possible "for a member of a grand corps to be at the same time an active politician, a member of a *cabinet* and a Mayor (roles which place him in some kind of political and administrative no-man's land)," Vincent Wright concludes:

> It is perhaps paradoxical that a country which prides itself on its love of logic and order should have evolved a politico-administrative system which appears to evoke more readily the surrealism of the Wonderland of Alice than the intellectual order of the universe of Descartes. It is a world composed of entrenched traditions, half remembered rules and conveniently forgotten stipulations . . .[39]

What Wright is referring to is the contradiction between the proclaimed ideal of the separation of functions and the practice that allows the neglect of this ideal. For the consequence of this form of *cumul* is, not only that it does little to separate the political from the administrative domain, but that it allows the state to subsidize, in different ways, the political career (or the attempt at such a career) of its privileged civil servants. Notwithstanding the fact that the state devised specific institutions, and expends considerable sums of money, to train its officials, it at the same time facilitates their move out of state service and into politics.[40] There are numerous ways in which the higher civil servants, and most particularly those who belong to the Grands Corps de l'Etat, benefit from a state subsidy.

Ministerial Cabinets

Every minister gathers around him a staff of loyal advisors, who today are almost all civil servants. Service in a ministerial cabinet clearly helps to propel a civil servant's career and increase his (political or administrative) options.[41] In serving in a ministerial cabinet, an official acts as an advisor to a minister and as the minister's watchdog in the ministry.[42] Some students of the French administration have maintained that a civil servant who serves in a ministerial cabinet continues to fulfill a technical role and eschews any political involvement.[43] This is a view that can scarcely be applied any longer to any higher civil servant (let alone to one who acts as the "eyes and ears" of a minister) unless one adopts an overly restrictive definition of what constitutes a political activity.

The important point that bears emphasizing is that civil servants who enter a ministerial cabinet—who are, in other words, serving a minister who belongs to a government and, almost always, a political party—continue to get paid by the corps or administration to which they belong. What occurs, in effect, is that a public institution continues to pay the salary of a civil servant who no longer works for it and who is doing some form of political apprenticeship. That this practice may be rendered necessary by the fact that ministerial cabinets have no real budgetary allocations in no way explains why a public service agency needs to subsidize ministerial cabinets. A member of the Conseil d'Etat noted (in a juridical study of the French presidency) with respect to the president's advisors: "The state of these collaborators is precisely that of members of ministerial cabinets: (1) they remain, administratively, in a position of active service to their corps, which is evidently a pure fiction, but which allows for their remuneration by their corps; (2) they are chosen freely by the President of the Republic who names them by decree bearing only his signature."[44]

As a consequence of allowing civil servants to be paid out of the budget of the corps or administration to which they belong while serving in ministerial cabinets, ministers feel no need to reduce the size of their cabinets (since they are not paying their advisors) and civil servants are not required to make any sacrifices. Given the ease with which civil servants can serve in ministerial cabinets, it is not surprising that their numbers have reached rather extraordinary proportions. A recent study of the cabinets of the presidents and of the prime ministers in the Fifth Republic concluded:

> One has the impression that the sample analyzed . . . is, on the whole, not very different from the other ministerial cabinets during the same period: predominance of the grands corps and of civil servants in general, well-to-do social background, a more or less spectacular promotion upon leaving the ministerial cabinet, loyalty to a limited number of ministers, participation in a limited number of cabinets.[45]

The extent to which civil servants in general, and members of the grands corps in particular, dominate ministerial cabinets, can be seen more precisely by looking at the cabinets of the three former presidents of

TABLE 1. Professional Background of Presidential Staffs

CORPS OF ORIGIN	DE GAULLE		POMPIDOU		GISCARD D'ESTAING	
	no.	%	no.	%	no.	%
Diplomacy	17	24	6	14	8	20
Conseil d'Etat	7	10	2	4	3	7
Inspection des Finances	4	6	3	7	4	10
Cour des Comptes	2	3	3	7	3	7
Prefectoral Corps	8	11	6	14	4	10
Ingénieurs des Mines	3	4	4	9	1	2
Magistrats	3	4	2	4	1	2
Academics	4	6	3	7	1	2
Other Corps	15	21	3	7	11	27
Non Civil Servants	7	10	12	27	5	12
Total	70	99	44	100	41	99

Note: Reprinted from Samy Cohen, "Le Rôle du Secrétaire Général de la Présidence de la République," paper presented at the conference on L'Administration et la Politique en France sous la Ve République, November 30–December 1, 1979, Paris, page 31.

Because of rounding off, the total in two percentage columns does not add up to 100 percent.

the Fifth Republic. In fact, as Mme Coutrot observes, ministerial cabinets tend to follow the same pattern of composition as the cabinets of the prime minister and the president of the Republic. There is, in fact, reason to suppose that the pattern is established by the heads of the government, so that it would be unlikely for ministers to deviate in any significant way from their superiors when forming their personal staffs.

As one would expect, higher civil servants predominated in the cabinets of de Gaulle, Pompidou, and Giscard d'Estaing. They accounted for 83 percent in de Gaulle's cabinet, 66 percent in Pompidou's cabinet, and 80 percent in Giscard's cabinet. The total number of civil servants was somewhat higher in the cabinets of all three presidents.[46] Although no one corps is overly represented (table 1), there nonetheless emerges a dominance of the grands corps, which is the same pattern found in all ministerial cabinets. As Samy Cohen summarizes the representation in the cabinets of the presidents:

No single corps clearly dominates the others in its representation. . . . One must above all point out that a kind of "oligarchy"
was formed each time, including members of the three grands corps

(Conseil d'Etat, Inspection des Finances, Cour des Comptes), diplomats and members of the Prefectoral corps, representing more than 60% of each president's entourage and occupying the highest positions in the hierarchy: secretary general and associate secretary general, cabinet director under de Gaulle and cabinet chief under the present head of state, as well as several "special representatives" *(chargés de mission)* appointed by Giscard d'Estaing.[47]

Ministers, too, tend to turn more toward members of the grands corps than to other civil servants when composing their cabinets. They do so largely because they wish to insert themselves into an on-going network that they believe will facilitate their task of governing a ministry. Bodiguel has conducted an extensive study of the composition of ministerial cabinets. He notes:

> We can derive a rather clear conclusion: the members of cabinets graduating from E.N.A. are, to a greater proportion than is the case for their colleagues who have not gone through this school, recruited through the *concours étudiant,* come from the Paris region, graduated from the Institut d'Etudes Politiques of Paris and belong to the highest social categories. This portrait is, in fact, that of the members of the grands corps whose characteristics are always superior to that of other civil servants.[48]

The proportion of civil servants and of members of the grands corps in ministerial cabinets has declined under socialism. Former *énarques* account for 94 members of ministerial cabinets in the second Mauroy government, whereas they accounted for 103 in the Barre government. There were 25 polytechniciens in the ministerial cabinets of the second Mauroy government, whereas there were 36 in the Barre government. The grands corps are not as strongly represented in the present government as they were in the preceding one. One important difference between the Mauroy government's ministerial cabinets and those of preceding governments is that a much larger place has been made for civil servants who did not graduate from ENA and who are not members of the grands corps. The modest fonctionnaire, and particularly the school teacher, has found a place in the politico-administrative structure. To be sure, the schoolteacher is now well represented in elective assemblies and, since June 1981, especially in the National Assembly.[49]

Despite the important role that higher civil servants continue to play in the upper reaches of the politico-administrative system, it is already evident that they do not play the same role as they played in the previous governments. The representation of higher civil servants in François Mitterrand's entourage at the Elysée is half of what it was in the entourages of the previous presidents. Similarly, the representation of the grands corps in Mitterrand's Elysée cabinet declined by two-thirds.[50]

Party Politics

In addition to the initiation into politics that civil servants get from entering ministerial cabinets, they have come to play a more direct political role by joining various political movements and political parties. They carry out their political activity while continuing to exercise their functions as civil servants. Jean-Louis Quermonne notes that there has not only been a growing intensity in the relationship between politicians and civil servants, but also the gradual effacement of any separation between the political class and the administration. He maintains that, until 1968, higher civil servants were content merely to collaborate with politicians in power, whereas "more recently they have cheerfully crossed the border and entered the political class, more often than not with an electoral mandate. Coming into direct competition with the full-time politicians and the provincial notables, a respectable number of them have chosen to run for office and to occupy posts in municipal councils, general councils, and parliamentary assemblies. The technician-ministers have been succeeded by civil servants who became deputies in order to remain ministers."[51]

Now it is clear from the available historical data that the entry of civil servants into the political arena is not a new phenomenon. The July Monarchy, for example, witnessed a massive entry of civil servants into the Chamber of Deputies, whereas the number was rather small in the legislatures of the Third Republic.[52] The Fifth Republic unquestionably increased the number of civil servants in Parliament; there were three times as many civil servants in the legislature of the Fifth Republic as there were under the Fourth Republic.[53] It is interesting to see the growing progression of civil servants attracted to an elective office. Table 2 shows that the number of civil servants sitting in Parliament saw a sharp increase between 1956 and 1967. This trend has continued, for the number of civil servants elected to Parliament in 1978 (the National Assembly) was 186, excluding teachers, who are all civil servants. The number of deputies elected in 1978 who were members of the grands corps amounted to 10.8 percent of the National Assembly.

Although the number of civil servants elected to Parliament has been consistently on the increase, it does not give an accurate picture of the involvement of civil servants in electoral politics. The number of civil servants who present themselves as candidates is considerably higher (see table 3).

In the 1978 legislative elections, higher civil servants alone represented 10 percent of the candidates in the Republican party, 7.2 percent in

TABLE 2.   Civil Servants or Former Civil Servants Elected Deputies

	1956	1958	1962	1967
Judges	3	—	2	2
Grands Corps	16	31	40	53
Other	16	12	11	8
Cabinets	—	—	3	—

Note: Reprinted from Vincent Wright, "Politics and Administration under the Fifth Republic," *Political Studies* 22, No. 1 (March 1974), p. 48

the RPR (Rassemblement pour la République), 6.9 percent in the MRG (Left Radicals), 5.2 percent in the Socialist party, and 1.6 percent in the Communist party.[54] Of the 491 deputies elected, 186 were civil servants.[55] At the local level, a similar involvement by civil servants can be seen. Approximately 10 percent of mayors and 23 percent of general councilors are civil servants.[56]

The election of the Socialists to power in 1981 merely reinforced the trend that had seen civil servants moving increasingly into the political arena. Table 4 shows that close to 40 percent of the deputies elected to the National Assembly in 1981 were civil servants. The majority of these civil servants were schoolteachers. The Socialists have thus benefited over the years in opposition from a state subsidy both at the higher reaches of the administration and at less exalted levels.

Quite apart from the attraction that elections have for civil servants, it has become customary under the Fifth Republic to elicit the support of civil servants for political movements and to use civil servants as political advisors in political parties and in a variety of movements. There are numerous examples of civil servants belonging to the grands corps whose principal activities consist in running for office, in advising political lead-

TABLE 3.   Civil Servants or Former Civil Servants Standing in General Elections

	1956	1958	1962	1967
Judges	6	5	1	6
Grands Corps	48	68	94	109
Others	109	114	68	72
Cabinets	5	6	8	1

Note: Reprinted from Vincent Wright, "Politics and Administration under the Fifth Republic," *Political Studies* 22, No. 1 (March 1974), p. 48.

TABLE 4.   Socio-Professional Composition of National Assembly, 1981

PROFESSION	PC	PS	RPR	UDF	TOTAL
Higher Civil Servants	0	4.1	18.2	17.2	8.1
Corporate Presidents	2.3	3.0	17.1	10.4	6.5
Upper-level Management	0	11.1	23.1	13.8	13.2
Liberal Professions	2.3	15.0	17.1	24.1	15.5
Lawyers	—	(6.3)	(2.4)	(10.4)	
Doctors	(2.3)	(5.2)	(6.1)	(6.9)	
Engineers	0	3.4	3.7	5.2	3.4
Middle-level Management	7	15.8	8.5	8.6	12.3
Teachers	27.9	43.0	3.7	8.6	30.2
Professors	(9.3)	(36.9)	(3.7)	(8.6)	
Schoolteachers	(18.6)	(4.9)	(0)	(0)	
Small Businessmen & Artisans	2.3	0	0	0	0.2
Farmers	7	0.4	3.7	8.6	2.7
Employees	9.3	1.9	0	0	2.0
Workers	39.6	0.7	0	0	4.3
Others	7	1.9	1	3.5	1.6

Note: *Le Matin*, July 6, 1981.

ers, in politicking within political parties, and who are paid by the state while they engage in these activities.

The question can be raised as to how it is possible for civil servants to engage in an activity that is so overtly political while exercising, or purporting to exercise, their functions as civil servants. Clearly, there is an evident incompatibility, for either the civil servants are devoting their time to political activities, in which case the state is simply providing an indirect subsidy to political movements; or they attempt to continue to exercise their function as civil servants, in which case there is no longer even a semblance of adherence to the principle of administrative neutrality.

It is especially in electoral periods that the contradictions in the administrative system, and the benefits that higher civil servants derive from these contradictions, become most evident. The civil servants enter the political arena with great alacrity, forgetting the noble principles on which they were raised (neutrality, *"obligations de réserve"*). Nor is the law requiring their neutrality observed or applied to them, though it has often been applied to civil servants low down in the hierarchy. They devote full time to their political activity all the while receiving their salaries as civil servants. There is no clearer example of the way in which the state sub-sidizes the political activity of its administrative elite than the way it pays the salary of members of this elite while asking for little in return. Engaging in politics becomes simply one of the rewards of belonging to the elite.[57]

Ministers

It is only when higher civil servants become cabinet ministers that they recognize themselves as having moved into the political arena. They no longer draw their salaries from their corps and are paid as members of the government. Because, however, they are regarded as being in state service, they can return to their corps when they choose. The phenomenon of the civil servant–minister has been one of the characteristic features of the Fifth Republic. It received an impetus from the outset of the Fifth Republic when de Gaulle began to call on civil servants to run the government. At that time, there were not many civil servants who resisted the temptation. Today, it is the ambition of most. The notion of serving the state and the "general interest," irrespective of regime, has fallen on hard times in France. François Bloch-Lainé's account of why he turned down on two occasions offers by de Gaulle to become minister of finance reveal the ethic with which an older generation of civil servants was imbued:

> Among the reasons I had for declining his offer, I only mentioned two to him, both of an ethical nature. Primo: I had chosen always and fully to belong to the civil service, refusing to become a deputy in 1946, refusing to become a banker in 1954. At a time when many *grands commis* were being led astray by events, at least a few, both civilian and military, had to remain in their category. Secundo: except in a purely presidential regime, which was not, or not yet, in effect, every member of the government shared responsibility for the political acts of his chief. . . . As a civil servant, I would be, whatever my own preferences, wholly devoted to his legitimate authority and to his orders, whatever they might be; as a minister, I would be constantly exposing myself to an ethically uncomfortable position.[58]

The generation of civil servants that ENA has produced no longer feels a moral dilemma when confronted with the possibility of a ministerial career. The number of civil servants who served in the various governments of the Fifth Republic attests to this. The proportion has varied "between a minimum of 41% in the first Pompidou government in 1962, and maximum of 65.5% in the last Messmer government in 1974. As for the third Barre government, the percentage is . . . 57.5%."[59] The role of higher civil servants in the political arena becomes more important in the more critical decision-making structures. As M. Quermonne observes:

> Thus one could schematize the hierarchical pyramid of the political class by the increase in the percentage of members of the administration as one moves up in the hierarchy: from 34%–41% in the National Assembly, from 41%–65% in the government, the proportion of civil servants would rise to 100% at the top of the government and of the State.[60]

Becoming a minister has come to be considered as the summit of both a political and an administrative career. Giscard d'Estaing himself claimed shortly after his election to the presidency in 1974 that his administrative career had been but "an apprenticeship for a political career."[61] Now, not all higher civil servants seek to enter politics and not all who enter are equally successful. The important point is that the growing number of those who are involved in politics or who attempt to seek elective office are able to do so because they need render little if any service to their corps.

The Phenomenon of State Subsidy

A civil servant who is able to engage in politics without losing his permanent position in the civil service and, as we have seen, without losing his salary, is clearly "dispensable" in Weber's sense of the term. This practice, however, has to be seen for what it is: first, it involves the granting of a subsidy by the state to a privileged group that is involved, in one manner or another, in politics; second, it introduces a novel way of conceiving of the political career since it eliminates the element of risk; and third, it contributes to inequality both within the administration and within the society.

The manner in which the administrative elite is recruited and the way in which a career that knows little downward mobility is guaranteed give the administrative elite an extraordinary degree of liberty. The civil servants who belong to this elite need scarcely account for their activities. The "obligation de réserve et de neutralité" applies in practice only to those officials who find themselves on the lower levels of the administrative hierarchy. The work the privileged civil servants do and the amount of time they devote to it are matters that are left up to them.

The Fifth Republic has been largely responsible for this state of affairs, even though the practices I am describing are the logical consequence of the French system of elite training. Nonetheless, the past twenty years have witnessed an expansion of what might be called state subsidies for an elite desiring to enter politics. Several factors have contributed to an acceleration of this process: the entry of civil servants into ministerial posts and into ministerial cabinets; the increasing number of ENA graduates; the spectacular political success of some former civil servants; the imperialism of the grands corps who are forever on the lookout for additional sectors to conquer so as to prevent rivals from getting there first; the rapid success of members of the grands corps within the administrative sector, which leads them to seek outlets beyond the administration; finally, the easy success which they often attain in politics (within political party hierarchies, in ministerial cabinets, in elective posts), which makes the political career more attractive. There are thus factors inherent in the administrative structure (and in the political arena) that lead civil servants to opt for political careers.

The second consequence of the extension of the state subsidies for entry into a political career is that the subsidies alter considerably the way in which such a career is conceived. Risk is undoubtedly the main ingredient of a political career. Its insecurity is enormous, for even serving one's constituency with great devotion does not guarantee success.

Yet, the French civil servants have essentially succeeded in taking out the element of risk associated with the political career. The extraordinary facility with which they are able to move into and out of politics, the possibility of campaigning without resigning their positions, the liberty of testing the terrain, of joining political movements—all this they can do as easily as entering a ministerial cabinet. If they do not succeed they can simply return to their corps. Their post, being a permanent one, has been kept warm for them and they have not even had to accept a loss in salary in their attempt to break into the political profession.

The third consequence of this system is the extreme inequality that it introduces. It is evident that the inequality has nothing to do with the Left-Right division of the society. It cannot be claimed that it is only those who are associated with the governing majority that benefit from this system. On the contrary, the system is designed for the advantage of an elite and it makes no distinction regarding the political coloration of the members of this elite. Hence both the opposition and those in power benefit from the subsidy. The inequalities that exist concern the strata *within* the administration. It is clear that only a very privileged group within the administration is able to profit from the subsidy. This group is made up of those who belong to the grands corps.

The spectacular successes of a number of former civil servants in political and other careers have become a model for the younger generation, for whom *le sens de l'Etat* means something very different from what it meant to the previous generation of civil servants. When Michel Debré created the Ecole Nationale d'Administration, he noted: "The training—one need not hide this—also has a moral objective. It is not one of the missions of the school to play politics or to impose a particular doctrine. But the school must also teach the future civil servants 'le sens de l'Etat,' it must make them understand the responsibilities of the Administration, make them taste the grandeur and accept the servitudes of the métier."[62] Thirty years ago, this aim did not appear outmoded, and it was the expression of a generally accepted principle. Today, members of the administrative elite are no longer content to remain confined to the administration. They continue to believe that they are imbued with a *sens de l'état*. Their conception of what constitutes *l'état* has, however, drastically changed.

All this does not mean that the old administrative ethic has been totally abandoned. It means that the French administrative system, which depended on a separation of responsibilities and those who bore them, is gradually giving way to a new system. The edging toward this new system was seen over thirty years ago by Michel Debré, who wrote:

> "Our Republic is meeting its most painful failure today in the area of political independence . . . the independence of the State has to require an abstention from political activity, at least from activist politics. . . . We are engaged on the most dangerous road possible for a Republican state. . . . Politics is no less ardent than unionism: it is entering in full swing into the administration. In a period of a few months, the danger point has been passed.[63]

It may be that Debré had a rather idealized view of state service and state independence. The alarm he was ringing in the late 1940s, which was signaled by the era of *tripartisme* and particularly by the Communist party's colonization of certain ministries, was the expression of a fear about the evolution of the administrative system as it had functioned until the end of the Third Republic. It is perhaps not a minor irony that the entry of politics into administration and of administrators into politics—"the most painful failure," as Debré called it—owes its most rapid development to the Fifth Republic. If an irreversible trend has been created, part of the responsibility for this lies with the Gaullist regime.

The question this raises is why an administrative system that gives such large privileges to a small group of civil servants and that allows them to use their positions within the state apparatus as mere ports of embarkment for political careers enjoys such a general consensus, if not in society—which remains largely ignorant of this system—at least among the various political forces. The answer is that the spoils that are offered by the system are shared by all the parties. Political party involvement—with the possible exception of membership in the Communist party—is no hindrance to benefiting from the system. For about the year preceding the 1978 legislative elections, many members of the grands corps were so busy with their various political activities that they did not treat a single dossier. Yet, except for a few private utterances, not a single corps found this situation sufficiently irregular to warrant putting it into question. Nor did any political party propose to do away with this abuse of state service. The reason is that the state becomes likened to a kitty into which Gaullists, Socialists, Republicans, Centrists, and others can dip. Besides, putting into question the liberty to engage in politics is to put into question all other liberties that members of the grands corps enjoy. To deny the grands corps the liberties that their members enjoy would be, in effect, tantamount to advocating their abolition for they can exist only insofar as they can offer privileges to their members. In short, a consensus exists among the various political forces for maintaining a system that provides privileges to members of the administrative elite regardless of political affiliation. The entry into the political arena by higher civil servants is, therefore, a consequence of the elitist system of recruitment. The important change that has come about in recent years is that it is not only the members of the grands corps who now benefit from this system. In fact, the reason that so many schoolteachers were elected to the 1981 Assembly was because they enjoyed sufficient liberty in their work to be able to combine it with party activism.

Conclusion

In 1967, Jean-Pierre Chévènement, who served as minister of industry, technology, and research in the first and second Mauroy governments, wrote that "the abolition of the ranking system is the principal reform that has to be envisaged in order to give the School [ENA] its veritable function. This can be made possible by a reform of the Administration."[64] It is now clear that the Socialist government has abandoned any intention of altering the ranking system or to effect any major structural changes within the administration.

There are a number of reasons for the Socialist government's reluctance to undertake a major reform of the administrative system. First, in view of the priorities that the government has established for itself, the reform of the administration is not considered to be politically feasible or socially urgent.

Second, the Socialist government has faced one crisis or another from the outset, and it relied on those grands commis who had loyally served the Fifth Republic to help resolve these crises. When the Mauroy government rewarded Jean-Yves Habrer with the presidency of the Paribas bank, this was largely in recognition of the help he had rendered in sustaining the franc after May 1981. Habrer had been at the service of previous governments for twenty years. Indeed, it is striking how ready the Socialist government was to use the help of those distinguished civil servants of the previous regime. Habrer is only one such example. André Chadeau was one of those politically committed grands commis of the Gaullist-Giscardian era. A prefect, directeur de cabinet of Prime Minister Chaban-Delmas, director of DATAR, Chadeau became an advisor of Prime Minister Pierre Mauroy in June 1981. He held this position for a short while before being named president of the SNCF (the French railroad company). There were indications that Mauroy had wanted to name him as his directeur de cabinet, but this was apparently opposed by the Elysée. Indeed, it was the use of men like Chadeau that led to the fiery speeches at the Socialist party's congress in Valence in October 1981.

Tempers have now calmed, though little has changed. The reform of ENA is a mild one that leaves all the essentials intact. All the reform projects having to do with the grands corps, the ranking system, the examinations, the inequalities in career prospects and incomes, have been shelved. The socialist government quickly came to realize that so strong had become the link between ENA and the state that to attack ENA was tantamount to inflicting a wound on itself. In other words, the Socialist government would strengthen its own legitimacy by securing the adhesion of the civil service. Since the question of legitimacy was important for the new rulers in June 1981, the help offered by the Chadeaus and the Marceau Longs (secretary general of the government who stayed in his post to guide the new government in its attempts to get established) was quickly accepted and was judged crucial in preventing sabotage by the civil service.

The new rulers, many of whom are civil servants and members of the grands corps, realized that it is not possible to govern without an administrative machine and that governing is facilitated by having an administrative machine based on an extensive network system.[65] Ultimately, this is the distinctive feature of the French administrative system,[66] and the Socialists decided that they could only govern by preserving it even though its social effects do not conform to the Socialist vision of equality.

Nonetheless, in the long run the Socialists will have effected important changes in the administrative machine without having had to transform the structure. The transformation of the party structure and the rise of mass, organized parties has created, on both sides of the political spectrum, a growing group of party militants. The Socialists have not been averse to rewarding their militants, and the Right will not be either when it returns to power. The true politicization of the administration has now begun, for politicization occurs not when civil servants decide to become politicians. It occurs when, as civil servants, they *avow* political commitments. Just as today a majority of members of ministerial cabinets openly admit to their closeness to the Socialist party,[67] an entirely new phenomenon, so tomorrow only those committed to the Right will be taken into these critical circles. The Right, in all likelihood, will proceed to "clean up" the administration more systematically when it returns to power, for it will be reacting to what it perceives has been a massive Socialist and Communist infiltration. Important changes have been set in motion without dismantling a single institution.

NOTES

1. Max Weber, "Politics as a Vocation," in H. H. Gerth and C. Wright Mills, eds., *From Max Weber: Essays in Sociology* (New York: Oxford University Press, 1958), p. 95.

2. Cited in J. Aberbach, R. Putnam, and B. Rockman, *Bureaucrats and Politicians in Western Democracies* (Cambridge, Mass.: Harvard University Press, 1981), p. 5.

3. Brian Chapman, *The Profession of Government* (London: Unwin University Books, 1959), p. 275.

4. Aberbach, Putnam, and Rockman, *Bureaucrats and Politicians,* p. 16. See also B. Guy Peters, *The Politics of Bureaucracy: A Comparative Perspective* (New York and London: Longman Inc., 1978), pp. 137–166.

5. See François Mitterrand, *Le Coup d'Etat Permanent* (Paris: 1965), and Jacques Mandrin, *L'Anarchie ou les mandarins de la société bourgeoise* (Paris: La Table Ronde de Combat, 1967).

6. Hugh Heclo, *A Government of Strangers: Executive Politics in Washington* (Washington, D.C.: The Brookings Institution, 1977), p. 82.

7. See Ezra N. Suleiman, *Elites in French Society: The Politics of Survival* (Princeton: Princeton University Press, 1978), pp. 17–30.

8. *Les Grandes Ecoles Françaises: une introduction à un système original de formation* (Paris), p. 1.

9. See Philip Stanworth and Anthony Giddens, eds., *Elites and Power in British Society* (Cambridge: Cambridge University Press, 1974); Dean E. Mann, *The Assistant Secretaries* (Washington, D.C.: The Brookings Institution, 1965); David Stanley, Dean E. Mann, and Jameson W. Doig, *Men Who Govern* (Washington, D.C.: The Brookings Institution, 1967); and C. Wright Mills, *The Power Elite* (New York: Oxford University Press, 1959).

10. This school was initially created by private funds, though throughout the Third Republic it trained over 80 percent of the entrants to the grands corps.

11. Irwin M. Wall, "Socialists and Bureaucrats: The Blum Government and the French Administration, 1936–1937," *International Review of Social History* 19, No. 3 (1974): 326.

12. Ezra N. Suleiman, "La Gauche et la haute administration," *Promotions,* No. 100 (November 1976).

13. Michel Debré, Preface in Marie-Christine Kessler, *La Politique de la*

haute fonction publique (Paris: Presses de la Fondation Nationale des Sciences Politiques, 1978), p. xiv.

14. See Terry Shinn, *Savoir scientifique et pouvoir social: L'école Polytechnique, 1794–1914* (Paris: Presses de la Fondation Nationale des Sciences Politiques, 1980), pp. 101–140.

15. Debré, Preface, in Kessler, *La Politique de la haute fonction publique,* p. xv.

16. Jean Legrès, "Une certaine idée de l'Etat," *Etudes,* January 1975, p. 7.

17. *Le Monde,* June 30, 1982.

18. At the Socialist party congress in Valence in October 1981, certain fiery speeches were made claiming that the Socialist party's program could not be implemented by those who had served the former government. Paul Quilès, among others, cried: "Heads must roll."

19. Yves Agnès, "L'Administration et le changement: I. Vers l'Etat-P.S.?" *Le Monde,* June 29, 1982, p. 7. See the series of articles by Agnès that includes those published in *Le Monde,* June 30 and June 31, 1982.

20. Cited in Eric Rohde, "L'ENA a-t-elle échoué?," *Le Monde de l'Education,* April 1982, p. 55.

21. *Le Monde,* October 7, 1982.

22. Ibid.

23. André Passeron, "Ni 'chasse aux sorcières' ni sabotage," *Le Monde,* February 23, 1982.

24. M. Dagnaud and D. Mehl, *L'Elite Rose* (Paris: Editions Ramsay, 1982), pp. 23–32.

25. For the debates and arguments surrounding the creation of ENA, see Ezra N. Suleiman, *Politics, Power and Bureaucracy in France* (Princeton: Princeton University Press, 1974), pp. 42–62.

26. Debré, Preface, in Kessler, *La Politique de la haute fonction publique,* p. xiii.

27. Michalina Vaughan, Martin Kolinsky, and Peta Sheriff, *Social Change in France* (New York: St. Martin's Press, 1980), p. 73.

28. For a discussion of the contradictory goals with which ENA was charged, see Kessler, *La Politique de la haute fonction publique,* pp. 57–66.

29. Suleiman, *Politics, Power and Bureaucracy in France,* p. 95.

30. For a comparison of the careers in the public sector of those who belong to the grands corps and those who do not, see Jean-Luc Bodiguel, *Les Anciens élèves de l'E.N.A.* (Paris: Presses de la Fondation Nationale des Sciences Politicques, 1978), pp. 82–116.

31. Marceau Long, "Les corps," *Cahiers Français,* no. 194 (January–February 1980), p. 44.

32. This is explored in greater detail in Suleiman, *Elites in French Society,* pp. 196–223.

33. Not all those who become higher civil servants enter the elite proper. On this point see, Catherine Grémoin, *Profession décideurs: pouvoir des hauts fonctionnaires et réforme de l'Etat* (Paris: Gauthier-Villars, 1979), pp. 341–406.

34. Passeron, "Ni 'chasse aux sorcières' ni sabotage," p. 8.

35. Weber, "Politics as a Vocation," p. 85.

36. François Bloch-Lainé, *Profession: Fonctionnaire* (Paris: Editions du Seuil, 1976), p. 236.

37. The only exception to this rule is that one cannot be a civil servant in the same *département* in which one holds an elective office. For more details on the phenomenon of *cumul*, see J. Brinton Rowdybush, "The Cumul de Mandats Phenomenon and the Renewal of French Political Elites," paper presented at Annual Meeting of American Political Science Association, Washington, D.C., August 27, 1980.

38. On the ways in which parties benefit from the "cumul des mandats" phenomenon, see Ezra N. Suleiman, "Toward the Disciplining of Parties and Legislators: The French Parliamentarian in the Fifth Republic," in Suleiman, ed., *Parliament and Parliamentarians in Democratic Politics* (forthcoming).

39. Vincent Wright, "Politics and Administration under the Fifth Republic," *Political Studies* 22, No. 1 (March 1974): 65.

40. It has been argued that the blurring of the distinction between politics and administration in France is in part due to the nature of the Constitution, which makes the bureaucracy part of the executive, which itself is not responsible to Parliament. Hence, naming civil servants to ministerial posts, as De Gaulle started doing, was seen as merely changing posts within the same domain. See Francis de Baecque, "L'Interpénétration des personnels administratifs et politiques" in F. de Baecque and J.-L. Quermonne, *Administration et politiques sous la Ve République* (Paris: Presses de la Fondation Nationale des Sciences Politiques, 1981), p. 19.

41. See Jean-Luc Bodiguel, *Les Anciens élèves de l'E.N.A.,* chap. 4.

42. See Suleiman, *Politics, Power and Bureaucracy in France,* pp. 209–238.

43. Marie-Christine Kessler, *Le Conseil d'Etat* (Paris: Armand Colin, 1968), p. 242.

44. Jean Massot, *La Présidence de la République en France* (Paris: La Documentation Française, 1977), p. 167.

45. Aline Coutrot, "Les Membres des cabinets des Présidents de la République et des Premiers Ministres," paper presented at the conference on L'Administration et la Politique en France sous la Ve République, November 30–December 1, 1979, Paris, p. 44. Reprinted in De Baecque and Quermonne, *Administration et Politiques,* pp. 61–67.

46. Samy Cohen, "Le Rôle du Secrétaire Général de la Présidence de la République," paper presented at the conference on L'Administration et la Politique en France sous la Ve République, November 30–December 1, 1979, Paris, p. 10. Reprinted in De Baecque and Quermonne, *Administration et Politiques,* pp. 104–128.

47. Ibid., pp.10–11.

48. Jean-Luc Bodiguel, "Les Anciens élèves de l'E.N.A. et les cabinets ministeriels," *Annuaire International de la Fonction Publique,* 1973–1974, p. 369.

49. See the lists of ministerial cabinets in *Le Monde,* November 17, 1982, p. 10.

50. Dagnaud and Mehl, *L'Elite Rose,* pp. 243–250.

51. Jean-Louis Quermonne, "Politisation de l'administration ou fonctionnarisation de la politique," paper presented at the conference on L'Administration et la Politique en France sous la Vᵉ Republique, November 30–December 1, 1979, Paris, p. 3. Reprinted in De Baecque and Quermonne, *Administration et politiques.*

52. Pierre Birnbaum, *Les Sommets de l'Etat* (Paris: Editions du Seuil, 1977), p. 28.

53. Ibid., p. 71.

54. G. Fabre-Rosane and A. Guéde, "Une Sociologie des candidats des grandes formations," *Le Monde,* 17 March 1978, and "Sociologie des candidats aux elections legislatives de mars 1978," *Revue Française de Science Politique* 28, No. 5 (October 1978): 852–855.

55. See table 3. See also G. Fabre and A. Guéde, "Portrait robot du député 1978," *Le Matin,* 19 April 1978.

56. Quermonne, "Politisation de l'administration ou fonctionnarisation de la politique," p. 14.

57. The above was first argued briefly in Ezra N. Suleiman, "Fonction publique et politique," *Le Monde,* 20 July 1979, and developed in my essay, "Administrative Reform and the Problem of Decentralization," in William G. Andrews and Stanley Hoffmann, eds., *The Impact of the Fifth Republic on France* (New York: State University of New York, 1981, pp. 69–79). Numerous examples of civil servants joining or advising political movements are given in this essay.

58. Bloch-Lainé, *Profession: Fonctionnaire,* pp. 144–145.

59. Quermonne, "Politisation de l'administration ou fonctionnarisation de la politique," p. 14. For further details, see Pascale Antoni and Jean-Dominique Antoni, *Les Ministres de la Vᵉ République* (Paris: Presses Universitaires de France, 1976), pp. 27–29.

60. Quermonne, "Politisation de l'administration ou fonctionnarisation de la politique," p. 16.

61. Interview with President Giscard d'Estaing, *The Observer,* 13 June 1976, p. 11.

62. Michel Debré, *Réforme de la Fonction publique* (Paris: Imprimerie Nationale, 1946), pp. 24–25.

63. Michel Debré, *La Mort de l'Etat Républicain* (Paris: Gallimard, 1947), pp. 115–116.

64. Mandrin, *L'Enarchie,* p. 141.

65. For an example of how one of the grands corps has maintained its hold over all the sectors it has been accustomed to dominating, see Daniel Schneider, "Une caste tranquille: L'Inspection des Finances," *Le Monde,* October 17, 1982.

66. I have described this system in detail and contrasted it with the American system and its absence of networks. See my "Presidential Government in France," in Richard Rose and Ezra N. Suleiman, eds., *Presidents and Prime Ministers* (Washington, D.C.: A.E.I. 1980), pp. 94–138.

67. Dagnaud and Mehl, *L'Elite Rose,* p. 43.

THE POLITICAL STATUS OF HIGHER CIVIL SERVANTS IN BRITAIN*

Richard Rose

Higher civil servants embody continuity in the direction of British government. Whereas politicians and parties come and go from office with considerable frequency, civil servants are secure for nearly forty years. This is long enough to see the party in power change six to ten times, and the particular minister they serve change fifteen to twenty times. The outlook and actions of higher civil servants express the institutionalized understanding of generations of predecessors. For example, the present head of the civil service, Sir Ian Bancroft, entered government in 1947 as private secretary to Sir Henry Wilson Smith, who had entered government in 1927 to be trained under persons who in turn had entered the civil service in Queen Victoria's reign.

Whilst the British civil service is in many respects traditionalistic, it is *not* a traditional institution of government; it is a Victorian innovation.

*The research reported herein is part of a study of the growth of government in the United Kingdom since 1945, sponsored by programme grant HR 7849/1 of the British Economic and Social Research Council to the author.

Britain is unusual in that the power of representative institutions was established *before* a civil service. When the modernization and democratization of British government commenced in the early nineteenth century, there were no administrative cadres that could be called permanent, civil, or a service. Administration was in the hands of political appointees, and ministers themselves discharged much of the work of government.[1] The peaceful revolution adapting government to the challenges of urbanization and industrialization owed much to the efforts of these political appointees. In today's terms, the great nineteenth-century utilitarian reformers appear as radicals and enthusiasts; certainly they would have had trouble entering the modern civil service or exercising influence today as they did then.[2]

The foundations of the contemporary higher civil service in Britain were laid in 1854 by the Northcote-Trevelyan Commission, which recommended the creation of a civil service recruited and promoted on the basis of merit rather than nepotism or personal or party connections. The commission endorsed a division of labor along Platonic lines between a small intellectual elite, recruited in youth on the basis of general intelligence, and a mass of clerical and mechanical officials. The result is a civil service that applies uniform procedures across the whole range of home ministries,[3] but within each ministry it is highly stratified.

Today, the very continuity of the higher civil service from its Victorian origins is often a cause of criticism. The higher civil service is seen as a major cause or reflection of "What's Wrong with Britain." The Fulton Committee, the biggest postwar review of the civil service, charged:

> The Home Civil Service today is still fundamentally the product of the nineteenth century philosophy of the Northcote-Trevelyan Report. The tasks it faces are those of the second half of the twentieth century. This is what we have found; it is what we seek to remedy.[4]

Defenders of the higher civil service emphasize that continuity is a necessary and difficult task of governance; in the traditional phrase, the Queen's government must be carried on. But this argument assumes that the problems of governing will remain the same in order to accommodate the preference of higher civil servants for stability. However, in Britain in the 1980s, this is less and less the case.

THE POLITICAL STATUS OF HIGHER CIVIL SERVANTS

The conventional English way of characterizing the civil service is to say that it is nonpolitical.[5] But to say that is to beg the question: What is politics? One way in which the civil service can be said to have nothing to do with politics is to define politics as the business of *elected* politicians, since civil servants are not elected, as are members of Parliament and cabinet ministers. A second sense in which this label can be justified is to describe politics as about *formal* actions of government. Parliament then defines politics, for acts of Parliament authorize what government does, and the cabinet acts as the agent for the majority party there. In this context civil servants are said to be nonpolitical, since they only (sic) advise ministers and administer acts of Parliament. Yet another definition is that politics is *public* controversy about government, whether in Parliament, the media, or an election campaign. Since civil servants are debarred from engaging in public controversies and their discussions in Whitehall are closed, they do not engage publicly in politics.

The Civil Service Department declares; "Administrative trainees and those in equivalent grades are precluded from engaging in political activities."[6] What this means is that administrative civil servants cannot engage in *party* politics or *public* controversy about issues, wherever this might be deemed to impair their usefulness as confidential policy advisors to ministers or to undermine public confidence in their impartiality. Exceptions to this rule typically concern local affairs or interests of an avocational kind remote from a serving official's own work. The European practice of civil servants taking leave to stand for Parliament is unknown in Britain, and it is also unusual for a civil servant to resign to seek election to Parliament and a chance to become a minister.[7] The political socialization required of a would-be minister is sufficiently lengthy and intensive to require the choice of a different career at about the time of leaving university.[8]

In reality, we must start with a prior idea of what politics is about in order to determine whether higher civil servants in Britain have a political status. If politics is defined as the maintenance of public order by the more or less legitimate monopoly of force, then civil servants, as chief administrators of the regime, could be considered more important than party politicians, for the first priority of any state (a concept in England approximately represented by the Crown) is to survive. From this conflict-oriented perspective, the military and the police, who claim most strongly to be "above" politics, are far more political than higher civil servants. Whatever significance such a definition may have in a potentially revolutionary situation or a newly established regime, it has little significance in Great Britain.[9]

In the British setting, politics is appropriately defined as the articulation of conflicting views about government policies, and the authoritative resolution of these conflicts. In the first place, this emphasizes the substantive importance of policies; politics concerns specific programmatic actions of government. Second, it emphasizes generic properties of the policy process, and the inevitability of conflict about what government should do. Third, it stresses the importance of *resolving* conflicts authoritatively by policies that reconcile and dissipate conflict.

Because politics is about policy making and higher civil servants are concerned with policy making (not mere administration), they inevitably have a political status. The status is different from that of MPs, but it is political, nonetheless. The nominal distinction between policy and politics in English (a distinction that does not exist, for example, in the French reference to *les sciences politiques*) may confuse, but should not obscure reality. Nor is the Civil Service Commission backward in attributing a policy (that is, political) role to the higher civil service, promising would-be recruits a career of "policy and planning work or the drafting of legislation or the detailed management of an executive programme."[10] A survey by Richard Chapman found that "policy formulation" was the most frequently cited task of administrative class civil servants. A four-nation study of Britain, Germany, Italy, and Sweden by Robert Putnam found that British higher civil servants showed a greater tolerance for politics than their counterparts in other nations.[11]

Higher civil servants are policy makers by default; their perspective is upward-looking (advising the minister) and outward-looking (negotiating with other departments and major pressure groups). Little time is available for the mere administration of departmental programs on a day-to-day executive basis. This is a task for juniors, or for civil servants who are judged unlikely ever to make the higher civil service. The higher one rises in the civil service, the more remote an individual becomes from the everyday administration of British government, and the more attention is given to advising and discussing policy in the more general sense.

Because higher civil servants in Britain normally spend a lifetime working for government, and the swing of the electoral pendulum has resulted in a fairly regular alternation between Conservative and Labour governments since 1945, they must eschew identification with partisan policies. A higher civil servant cannot rely upon spending nearly all his working life under a single dominant party, as in Italy or Japan. Higher civil servants are not directors but directionless, lacking the authority to announce policies, the prerogative of elected MPs appointed as cabinet ministers. The distinctive contribution of British higher civil servants is to resolve conflicts articulated by parties and pressure groups by engaging in consensus mongering.

The predisposition of higher civil servants in Britain is to deemphasize conflict between parties, treating it as campaign oratory or knockabout parliamentary battle, and divorcing it from policy making. At any point in time, "ongoing reality" is assumed to dictate the particular course of action that government should follow or determine the narrow scope for choice, given external and internal constraints upon the matrix of government policy. Sir William Armstrong, the former head of the civil service, described his perception of the effective scope for policy differences shortly after the 1970 general election, intended by the Conservative victors to produce a new style of government.

> I have now had a good deal of experience of changes of government and been concerned, in the period immediately before each election with the preparation of briefs explaining the situation in the area of government activity for which I was responsible and outlining the problems, and alternative solutions, as I saw them. This work has necessarily been done in ignorance of the result of each election, and experience since 1945 has taught me that the results of elections can often be surprising. It has therefore been necessary to prepare for both parties: and the fact is that the differences between the two sets of briefs have been remarkably small and only what one would expect: a fuller explanation for those who would, if they won, be coming fresh to the scene, a discussion in greater depth of topics which, from the manifestos, campaign speeches, and other indications, one party or the other was known to be interested in and a proper reticence, in the material prepared for one side, about the private affairs of the other. This experience seems to show that there is indeed a great deal of common ground—what I have called ongoing reality—which is properly, necessarily, and desirably the concern of a permanent Civil Service.[12]

The evidence of consensus mongering in policy is to be found in the statute books. In each session of Parliament the government of the day introduces some fifty bills; each measure is virtually certain of enactment because of the government's command of a disciplined majority. Although government legislation must be agreed within cabinet, British parliamentary norms encourage the Opposition party to oppose government bills on principle, and the Opposition need not recommend a viable alternative course of action. Yet in practice, so broad is the policy consensus built by ministerial and civil service deliberations that the Opposition does *not* oppose (that is, vote against) 78 percent of government legislation in the main Second Reading debate of principle.[13]

Higher civil servants are best characterized as *impartially partisan* (in Hazlitt's words, "Be ever stronger on the stronger side"). At the point of execution of policy, civil servants are expected to be impartial in their treatment of ordinary citizens. But, within government, as Jack Straw, a former Labour political advisor now an MP, notes:

> The service is in fact expected to be highly *partial* to the government of the day. A great deal of time of officials at all levels is devoted to promot-

ing the interests of Government, against those of the Opposition (and, sometimes its own backbenchers). . . .

Nor is politically impartial advice—whatever that may be—in my experience ever sought or given. What is sought is technical or expert advice that is intellectually rigorous: advice which does not duck inconvenient questions which may well have been ignored when the policy idea was prepared by party, trade union or pressure group.[14]

The central issue, Straw emphasizes, is simply "whether officials are willing loyally to serve a government even where its views are very different from their own." This norm is common enough in many professions, for example, the law.

The concept of impartial partiality differs from nonpartisanship in the way that bisexuality differs from asexuality. It also differs from the "neutral competence" that Hugh Heclo attributes to senior officials formally advising the American president.[15] In both instances, competence is taken for granted. But the label neutral misstates an important point, namely, that advice on policy cannot be neutral when real decisions have to be made. Explicitly or by indirection, it must favor a course of action. The label differs from Sir William Armstrong's description of policy making by the *force majeure* of "ongoing reality," for it does not try to depoliticize policy making, that is, suggest that circumstances permit only one policy for a government at a given time. It accepts that personnel can serve different masters, but emphasizes that this service is intrinsically partisan, that is, placed at the disposal of ministers engaged in conflicts about policy.

As citizens, civil servants have the right to vote and unusual knowledge for making a choice between the parties. A 1966 survey of younger administrative class officials found that 57 percent had voted Labour, and only 20 percent Conservative, with 13 percent Liberal and 3 percent Nationalist; only 7 percent did not vote.[16] The results reflected a temporary swell of optimism in Labour being able to "modernize" Britain. (A similar survey in 1970 or 1979 could well have found a majority inclined to the Conservatives.) Two-thirds described themselves as floating voters. Notwithstanding their high level of political sophistication, administrative class civil servants are not ideological voters, but appear to vote with the nature of the times.[17]

The higher British civil service might well be described as protean political rather than party political, for the ability to be impartially partisan requires a wide interest in policy and politics—but a limited commitment to specific positions, and a willingness to change views if the political climate or cabinet direction changes. The personality type is not unfamiliar: it might also describe wheeler-dealer, consensus mongering politicians such as Lyndon B. Johnson. But the outlook of British higher civil servants is not positive and prescriptive, as is normally the case with an elected politician. The tolerance of party politicians is often rooted in cynicism, as expressed in such comments as

> I have no time for politicians.
>
> The efficiency of a Government in office tends to influence one's views. . . . In many cases it is difficult to differentiate between parties—they all consist of politicians.
>
> If you are emotionally concerned about party politics, you don't become a civil servant.
>
> I suppose I am really an anarchist.[18]

Civil servants can maintain the public appearance of impartial partisanship only as long as their actions are conducted privately. This is the case in Britain, to an extent perhaps unique in the Western world. The Official Secrets Act of 1911 is the statutory basis protecting civil servants; it requires every civil servant to pledge: "not to divulge any information gained by one as a result of any appointment to any unauthorized person, either orally or in writing, without previous official sanction in writing." The effect is that written memoranda are relatively rarely leaked. Even a directive on open government from the prime minister's private secretary can be classified confidential.[19]

HIGHER CIVIL SERVANTS: SOCIALIZED BUT NOT TRAINED

Higher civil servants in Britain are socialized, not trained. They are formed by the careful selection and cultivation through the years of those who aspire to such a role. The very absence of a formal legal definition of the higher civil service enhances the importance of role socialization in the formation of higher civil servants. The higher civil service is an institution in the sociological, not the legal, sense.

The higher civil service consists of the posts of highest importance, that is, "the relatively few officials, usually at or near the head of their departments, who are in a position to exercise a real and direct influence upon government." In a study of policy making and policy makers, F. M. G. Willson estimated their number at about 300, defined as civil servants in regular personal contact with ministers.[20] By implication, the remaining 700,000 civil servants are in what might be called the "outer" civil service, for they approach ministers in charge of government departments through the inner circle of higher civil servants.

In structural terms, the higher civil service is differentiated both vertically and horizontally. The great bulk of 700,000 British civil servants—

TABLE 1. **The Higher Civil Service and Other Public Employees in Britain**

	N	% OF TOTAL PUBLIC EMPLOYMENT	% OF CIVIL SERVICE
1. Higher Civil Servants	599	0.01	0.1
2. Cadets for Higher Civil Service	2,332	0.03	0.3
3. Diplomatic Service	8,640	0.1	1.2
4. Other Graduate and Qualified Civil Servants	160,158	2.0	22.6
5. Clerical and Industrial Civil Servants	536,071	6.8	75.7
	707,800	8.9	99.9
6. Non-civil service public employment (1976)			
a. Local Government	3,022,000	38.2	
b. Nationalized industries and other public corporations	2,107,000	26.6	
c. National Health Service	1,193,000	15.1	
d. Armed Forces	336,000	4.2	
e. Miscellaneous	544,000	6.9	
	7,910,000	100	

Sources: Derived from *Civil Service Statistics 1980* (London: HMSO, 1980), tables 1, 4 and 6. Richard Parry, *United Kingdom Public Employment: Patterns of Change, 1951–1976* (Glasgow: University of Strathclyde Studies in Public Policy No. 62, 1980), appendix tables 1 and 2.

Notes:

line 1: All Permanent Secretaries and Deputy Secretaries; and Under Secretaries in proportion to those whose jobs corresponded to the pre-1971 administrative class, that is, 65 per cent of the total. Cf. Peta Sheriff, *Career Patterns in the Higher Civil Service* (London: HMSO, Civil Service Studies No. 2, 1976), table 1.

line 2: Assistant Secretaries under age fifty (513), Principals under forty (1,029), Higher Executive Officers—Administration (387), Administration Trainees (403).

line 4: Under Secretaries (214), Assistant Secretaries (627) and Principals (3,445) not in line 2. Also, all Administration Group at Executive Officer or above, comparable grades in Scientific, Professional and Technological and Information Officer Categories, and other comparable qualified staff (including economists, research officers, statisticians, librarians, lawyers, accountants, actuaries, medical officers, psychologists, prison governors, tax officers, inspectors and valuers, school inspectors).

line 5: Industrial civil servants, clerical officers and assistants, secretaries, messengers, draftsmen, etc.

line 6: As enumerated in R. Parry, appendix tables 1 and 2.

what one proponent describes as "the real civil service"—spend a lifetime "doing a solid and unspectacular job . . . of little interest to journalists or even to academics."[21] Three-quarters are in routine clerical and industrial jobs (table 1). The other quarter hold posts requiring a variety of qualifications, whether specialist or a university degree (lawyer, architect, or surveyor). The Civil Service Commission, however, delegates the recruitment of more than 90 percent of civil servants to employing departments, because the work involved is low status. It concentrates upon recruiting the 8.5 percent of entrants requiring a graduate education or its equivalent.[22]

Among graduate civil servants, there is a fundamental *horizontal* division between qualified specialists, and what was formerly called the administrative class civil service, still recognizable as the senior posts within the administration group. About 47 percent of qualified civil servants are employed in specialist posts, e.g., economist, information officer, librarian, statistician, lawyer, engineers, tax inspectors, scientific officers, auditors, and so forth. Among graduates recruited by the Civil Service Commission in 1979, only 5 percent were offered posts within the administrative class.[23] Whereas the vertical division between qualified and unqualified civil servants is normal in every nation, in Britain there are great barriers between the administrative class and other graduate and professional classes. The barrier is of great practical importance, because the higher civil service is recruited almost exclusively from the administrative class.

The recruitment of higher civil servants is from *within* the civil service. These posts are sufficiently important, sensitive, and senior so that they will not be offered to junior staff, to outsiders, or to persons who are in any way "unknown quantities." The opportunity to join the higher civil service is not distributed randomly among public employees. Instead, it is almost exclusively confined to members of what was formerly called the administrative class, and now consists of leading positions in the administrative group, henceforth called by the traditional, very selective term *the administrative class.* To become a higher civil servant, an individual must have joined the administrative ranks upward of twenty years previously, and proven his suitability for such a role to senior civil servants who are the effective "gatekeepers" for entry to the higher civil service.

The administrative civil service in Britain is socially no more representative of the population than in any other country. The recruitment of university graduates ensures that the great bulk of the population is ineligible, since only 4 percent of the labor force in Britain are graduates.[24] Among graduates, a disproportionate number of higher civil servants come from Oxbridge (that is, Oxford or Cambridge), and the same is true of cadets. As of 1980, 74 percent of permanent secretaries and deputy secretaries were Oxford or Cambridge graduates, whereas the proportion of British students attending Oxford or Cambridge thirty years earlier was 18 percent. Among applicants for entry to the post of administrative trainees in 1979, 60 percent of successful candidates were Oxbridge, 24 percent of all candidates sitting the entrance examination were Oxbridge, and 8 percent of all students were at Oxford or Cambridge.[25]

The median higher civil servant is aptly described as coming "from families of great diligence and a little prosperity, rather than great prosperity and a little diligence."[26] They are pure meritocrats rather than the offspring of aristocrats or plutocrats with aptitudes and inclinations for the civil service. The typical higher civil servant is likely to have gone to a fee-paying day school without national prestige, and to have won a place at Oxbridge by academic ability. He or she (for about one-twelfth are women) is reckoned to have improved on a father's career by entering the administrative civil service in a post that offers security, status, and a good salary. The same proportion (21 percent) have come from manual workers' families as from the higher professions and managerial class.[27] Among permanent secretaries, more today come from state secondary schools than from prestigious public boarding schools.

An often overlooked point is that administrative class civil servants are very *atypical* of the hundreds of thousands of middle-class families with a good secondary and university education. The proportion of Oxbridge graduates becoming administrative trainees is no more than 2 percent (that is, 111 of about 6,000 Oxbridge graduates in 1979). Even though surveys find that the civil service has a generally favorable image among university students, only a limited minority have a predisposition to apply for a post, and most who do seek graduate posts outside the administrative class civil service.[28] In other words, while an administrative trainee's job is conventionally viewed as a good job for graduates, the vast majority of British graduates do not seek such a job.

In measured academic ability, the median administrative class civil servant has a good degree (that is, second-class honors), not an excellent degree (first-class honors).[29] More significantly, recruits are not required to relate their studies to the work of government. The great majority are graduates in classics or history, that is, trained to become teachers of the school subjects in which they have been successful. Among successful 1979 candidates, 62 percent studied arts subjects, 30 percent a variety of social science courses, and 7 percent science and technology.[30] The absence of law graduates is particularly notable by comparison with some continental countries.

The justification for recruiting graduates without regard to the subject of their education was laid down at the time of the Northcote-Trevelyan Report. In the words of a classicist, Benjamin Jowett, the influential master of Balliol College, Oxford, "The knowledge of Latin and Greek is perhaps upon the whole, the best test of regular, previous education."[31] Lord Macaulay, one of the promoters of reform (and, in his own right, a distinguished historian), argued;

> If, instead of learning Greek, we learned the Cherokee, the man who understood the Cherokee best, who made the most correct and melodious Cherokee verses, who comprehended most accurately the effect of the Cherokee particles, would generally be a superior man to him who was destitute of those accomplishments.[32]

The rejection of formal training has contemporary advocates among civil servants, such as C. H. Sisson:

> The British administrator travelling abroad is shocked to discover that many countries are administered by men who read books about public administration. This, in the British view, is not only a surprising but a very unfortunate state of affairs, and goes some way to explain the disabilities under which foreigners, in the matter of government, notoriously suffer . . . Such people are committing the crime of learning from books something that one just does.[33]

The Fulton Report recommended that administrative class recruits should have a "relevant" education identified as in "the social studies, the mathematical and physical sciences, the biological sciences or in the applied and engineering sciences." It did not, however, explain why such subjects should *ipso facto* be more relevant to Whitehall administrators than, say, a study of the rise and fall of Roman civilization. In the event, the committee failed to agree about how to test for "relevant" knowledge, and the idea has not been adopted by the Civil Service Commission.[34] But post-Fulton entry examinations have now been redesigned to test for such skills as resolving problems by fitting specific facts to general regulations; drawing inferences from simple tables of social statistics; and following logical diagrams, as well as participating effectively in group problem-solving.

The motives that lead young graduates to apply for the administrative class appear to be more social-psychological than political.

Status: Attraction of an elite group; being at the center of things.

Collegiality: Working with congenial colleagues.

Task related: Interesting, important work; working for the common good; intellectual quality of the work.

Materialistic: Pay; security; lack of interest in other careers.[35]

Civil servants enter Whitehall because they like the idea of succeeding in a prestigious competition offering an interesting job with congenial colleagues, high status, and satisfactory pay. They are not particularly attracted by the substance of policy, or by any particular political motivation. If these recruits had not become administrative civil servants, university teaching would have been their preferred career.[36]

Administrative civil servants see their work, initially at least, as a diffuse status and not as a specific challenge to do things. They expect to *be* somewhere (at the center of things), *not* to *do* something (e.g., change society or put the British economy to rights). Individuals with a commitment to promote policies are likely to go into party politics to groom themselves for a parliamentary and eventually a ministerial career. The difference between ministers and their civil service advisors at the formative stage of their career is not so much in where they were educated, for MPs and cabinet ministers are also disproportionately middle-class Oxbridge graduates, but rather whether they see promoting policy *or* ensuring administrative continuity as more important in government.

Young recruits are ready to be shaped by on the job socialization because they are so untrained for their work. The median recruit enters with a good education in subjects relatively remote from the day-to-day work of government; with a diffuse idea that the job will be interesting; without any particular sense of political purpose; and with a socially acceptable background that would make resignation difficult because of a lack of family wealth and independent status. Moreover, the great bulk of young recruits have never held any other full-time job.[37]

Within the administrative class, socialization is intense. The first task of a young administrative trainee is to learn what he is expected to do, and to demonstrate that he is good at doing that which is expected. Since the number of administrative trainees is more numerous than the number of promoted posts, recruits must promptly demonstrate their abilities to move quickly up the promotion ladder. In their first three years, administrative trainees normally spend two ten-week periods at the Civil Service College, established in obeisance to the Fulton Report. The curriculum includes elementary statistics, economics, public administration, and cognate subjects. But performance on courses does not affect evaluation for promotion, and the courses are often criticized by civil servants for their "lack of relevance" to Whitehall.[38]

Because the higher civil service consists of persons of senior status (only 28 percent are below the age of fifty at the rank of under secretary, the normal qualifying rank for higher civil servants)[39] a young administrative trainee seeks to gain cadet status. The term *cadet* is not normally used in Whitehall, but it is very appropriate to describe youthful civil servants in the fast stream for promotion, heading for a position in the higher civil service in the fullness of time. The usual Whitehall term is *high flier*. The younger a person is in a given rank, the more likely he or she is to be a cadet headed for a higher civil servant's post.

The breakthrough for an ambitious young cadet comes at about age thirty if he or she is assigned one of about one hundred posts as private secretary to a minister (or a permanent under secretary in a major department). The job of a private secretary is to monitor all the activities of "his" minister, acting as the general purpose personal assistant to the minister *and* as the link between the minister and the ministry, including contacts with civil servants higher in rank than the rising cadet. The post gives a young civil servant a unique firsthand view of British government at the top. It also gives those at the top firsthand knowledge of the strengths (and possible weaknesses) of the young cadet.

If the cadet displays the qualities expected, then he or she can reasonably expect to reach the ranks of the higher civil service—but only after about fifteen years of further socialization into the mores of Whitehall. This occurs as a principal, working directly on policy issues but under strict supervision, and then as an assistant secretary in charge of a block of policy issues. Usually the assistant secretary is the last person with some specific familiarity with an issue to see a departmental file before it is passed to higher civil servants for coordination within and between departments and discussion with ministers.

Conventionally, promotion from assistant secretary to under secretary is said to mark persons as higher civil servants. But official ranks must be used cautiously, for the political status of higher civil servants is informal and operational, and not a simple function of rank. Of two civil servants in the under-secretary grade, one can be a higher civil servant at headquarters coordinating the work of several divisions for review by a minister, whereas another will not have the same status if he is in charge, of the regional office of a ministry. Equally, of two civil servants in different grades, the lower ranking will be more important if in a post as private secretary, or a high-flying cadet. Making appropriate allowances, table 1 shows that higher civil servants and cadets constitute only 0.4 percent of civil servants and a minuscule proportion of total public employment in Britain.

An administrative class civil servant can conventionally reckon to have a "ticket for life," that is, an assured job, interesting work, high social status, and a good pension on retirement. Cadets whose careers move more slowly (and may never reach the higher civil service) can count on seniority carrying them a long way. The turnover in the higher civil service is great, because of mandatory retirement at sixty. More than one-quarter of 42 permanent secretaries must be replaced each year, one-fifth of 158 deputy secretaries, and almost one-sixth of 613 under se-

TABLE 2:   The Achievement of Cadet Higher Civil Servants—25 Years On

	N	%
1. Entered as Cadets (Assistant Principals, Open Competition 1945–48)	421	100
2. In post, civil service, 1975		
a) Higher civil servants (Per Sec, Dep. Sec, Under Sec)	182	43
b) Assistant Secretaries (Promotion to Higher Civil Service still possible)	88	21
c) "Failures" (Senior Principals, Principals)	17	4
Total	287	68
3. Died, retired, resigned, for ill health, or women left for domestic reasons	66*	16*
4. Left for other employment	43	10
5. Left at cadet stage because of inefficiency	3	0.7
6. Resigned, reasons unknown	22	5

Source: Derived from Edgar Anstey, *Civil Service Administrators: a Long-Term Follow-Up* (London: Behavioral Sciences Research Division, Report No. 31, Civil Service Department, 1976) pp. 3–4.

*Includes half a dozen or more in higher civil service grades.

cretaries. Analysis of recruits to the administrative class civil service 1945–1948 as assistant principals found that by 1975 nearly two-thirds had either become higher civil servants or still had the possibility of promotion to this grade. Only 5 percent had failed to secure promotion or had been dismissed (table 2). Voluntary resignations are minimal: in 1979, a total of 52 among 5,611 assistant secretaries and principals, and 27 resignations among 875 administrative trainees and higher executive officer (A) grades.[40]

Departure from the administrative class at mid-career is against the mores of the Whitehall community. By definition, those who leave the civil service are unlikely to have any further impact upon those left behind. Nor is there any expectation of promotion by *pantouflage* in the French style. There is virtually no mid-career movement from the civil service to nationalized industries, public corporations, or local authorities or the health service, and mid-career movement into the private sector is also slight. Unlike Washington, where senior civil servants may start (or feel forced) to look outside government once they have accumulated a maximum of twenty years service for a pension, Whitehall's higher civil service does not normally begin contemplating another job until compulsory retirement occurs at age sixty. A significant portion of retired higher civil servants take part-time or full-time posts in Crown appointments (normally outside party politics) as against nonexecutive directorships in profit-making firms.[41] Generous index-linked pensions remove the financial inducement for civil servants to take a job after retirement.

The higher civil service is selected from within a closed community. Entries to the administrative class at mid-career from outside government are relatively few, and at a competitive disadvantage for entering the higher civil service. This is equally true of recruits to the ranks of principal or assistant secretary from executive class or specialist grades within the civil service. A survey of under secretaries and above by Peta Sheriff found that 78 percent had reached their post by conventional socialization procedures; 13 percent by transfer across horizontal barriers from specialist grades and 9 percent by upward mobility from the executive and clerical classes.[42] But late entrants are less likely to have politically central jobs, even when equal in rank to higher civil servants.

The role socialization of administrative civil servants emphasizes commitment to the service (or, more particularly, to the ethos of the administrative class), and not to particular programs, specialisms, or departments. A Fulton Committee study found that the average administrative class civil servant was in a given post for 2.8 years.[43] The presumed advantage of frequent posting is that a high-flying cadet sees different types of work within government, as well as avoiding commitment to any one perspective. A "generalist" outlook is assumed to be a particularly good background for higher civil servants, most of whose work is coordinating or reviewing a very wide variety of programs, or considering their interrelationships. Another consequence of frequent postings is that a civil servant does not develop any specialist knowledge relevant to programs of a ministry or to particular tasks, such as budgeting. For that reason, part of the training at the Civil Service College is consciously designed to instruct young cadets in how "to write briefs on something you know nothing about."[44]

Partially offsetting frequent changes of job is the tendency for administrative civil servants to concentrate their experience in a handful of ministries. Movement from a finance to a program post may occur within the same ministry, or a succession of postings may give an individual a view of two ministries, one program-oriented and the other process (e.g., the cabinet office). Among higher civil servants, 48 percent have served in one or two departments, 27 percent in three, and 26 percent in four or more in the course of a dozen or so postings.[45] Concentration of experience gives administrative civil servants a good grasp of a departmental culture. It also means that their immediate reference group is not several thousand people throughout Whitehall, but a small group within a department; memoranda can be exchanged between people who know each other's strengths, weaknesses, and idiosyncrasies. The ethos of the administrative class, however, discourages departmental identification superseding identification with the civil service as a whole.

> About the worst thing that can happen to an ambitious Assistant Secretary, short of being caught accepting bribes, is to go native—to stay in the same division so long that he is thought to be lost to a particular specialism.[46]

The solidarity of the higher civil service is maintained because promotion is centralized and has been almost entirely in the hands of civil servants. Formally, the civil service division of the Treasury is in charge of personnel. But high fliers quickly become known to seniors by virtue of their private office work. A Senior Appointment Selection Committee of civil servants, chaired by the head of the civil service, keeps available manpower under regular review. The head gives a very high priority to filling a few dozen of the highest jobs each year.[47] This system of promotion strengthens the influence of civil service elders over aspiring cadets.

Politicians, individually and as a class, have very little influence upon the promotion of civil servants. In exceptional circumstances, a minister may voice strong views about a particular permanent secretary or private secretary, both posts where personal relationships with the minister are important. The prime minister is nominally head of the Civil Service Department.[48] There are strong sanctions to prevent a civil servant from using a minister as a patron to secure rapid promotion. A minister has no power of promotion, and any attempt by a minister to influence very senior civil servants on behalf of an individual could backfire. Moreover, ministers are transient members of a department and any civil servant closely identified with a politician would find himself in a lurch when the minister was reshuffled to another ministry, or removed from office by election defeat or retirement. Civil servants have a long-term stake in their career, and any attempt to use party political contacts for short-term advantages would jeopardize their long-term promotion prospects.

The moral solidarity of the higher civil service is sustained by co-optation as the method for entering it. Aspirants work to catch the attention of those above them, so that they will have a sponsor when the highest-ranking civil servants decide promotion. Individual civil servants are not assessed so much by impersonal performance criteria, as by the collective subjective judgments of their superiors. Whilst the term *esprit de corps* is inappropriate because of its overtones of enthusiasm, there is undoubtedly a self-regulating *corps* of higher civil servants in Whitehall whose effective force is all the more impressive because it is not legally denominated but maintained by a continuing process of socialization and co-optation. To rise into the higher civil service, an individual must be a loyal member of the community, and be deemed good at what that community values most. The values of the community are preserved, as Lord Balniel has noted, "not so much by the conscious efforts of the well established, but by the zeal of those who have just won entry and by the hopes of those who still aspire."[49]

GOVERNMENT AS A CONJOINT PRODUCT: THE INTERACTION OF HIGHER CIVIL SERVANTS AND MINISTERS

In formal terms, higher civil servants have a dependent relationship with ministers. The actions of a government department are taken in the name of one individual, a cabinet minister.[50] His name is invoked as the legitimate authority for any major action. A popular metaphor to describe the relationship of a minister with his civil servants is to say that the minister "is the masculine principle and the department the feminine principle in policy making."[51] But this metaphor leaves open whether so-called masculine assertiveness is effective dominance. The very fact that higher civil servants must study their minister carefully and adapt to his behavior may enable them to manipulate the object of their study by responding in ways that turn formally dominant leaders into unwitting followers of their nominal subordinates.

Any new policy must be the joint product of work by ministers *and* higher civil servants. Only ministers (and Parliament) can legitimate the actions of government by choosing and formally endorsing particular courses of action. Within a department, the buck stops on the desk of the minister, and within a government, it stops on the cabinet table. But only higher civil servants are numerous and well informed enough about the established activities of a department to work out in detail the content of a new policy, to carry it out *de novo,* and subsequently carry it on as a routine program. As a token of the status of higher civil servants, 41 officials are paid a higher salary than the prime minister, and another 157 are paid higher salaries than leading cabinet ministers.

Both ministers and higher civil servants are organization people. Government departments are the institutions that simultaneously give force to their actions, and constrain what they do. Ministers and civil servants are jointly engaged in producing a product of an organization, namely government policies. These consist, not only of the intentions of the governing party and the responsible minister, as expressed in party manifestos and speeches, but also in acts of Parliament drafted by civil servants and approved by politicians, and actions taken by civil servants to implement the intentions of politicians that Parliament has approved.

Together, cabinet ministers and the higher civil service provide whatever directive force exists in the massive complex of bureaucratic (and largely self-sustaining) organizations known as government.

Both ministers and civil servants have a common commitment. Together, their reputation immediately stands or falls by what their department does, and how it is regarded in Whitehall and in Parliament. A department that is successful in conflicts with other departments in Parliament and in the media will confer kudos upon both minister and civil servants. A department that is regarded as unsuccessful will harm the reputation of all associated with it.

Many discussions of the relationships between ministers and higher civil servants pose the wrong question: they try to determine which is more powerful, assuming that either one or the other group must govern Britain. In fact, *both are necessary* to the work of British government and, in many instances, each can veto what the other may prefer. Where concurrent acceptance is needed from two groups, it is more relevant to consider the terms of their relationship. The constitutional norm is that ministers and civil servants should be complementary. Ministers normally emphasize mobilizing support for "their" policies, and higher civil servants reconciling differences within government created by the very initiatives of a minister. The relationships between the two groups can involve friction and suspicion. Given that ministers cannot choose their civil servants (or vice versa), complaints will be heard, e.g., from ministers about the political recalcitrance of civil servants who put up "too many" obstacles, and from higher civil servants about ministers who can hardly read, let alone understand, careful discussions of the difficulties of their policy nostrums.

In personal terms, the relationship between ministers and higher civil servants is very intimate. As Headey notes, "In an average week a Cabinet Minister is likely to see at least two civil servants—his Permanent Secretary and his Private Secretary—far more frequently than he sees the Prime Minister or any of his party colleagues."[52] A minister's private office, which arranges nearly all his appointments, monitors his telephone calls, and looks after all other matters but those classified as "party political," is run by a high-flying cadet. He is normally the first person a minister sees at work in the morning and the last at night. The permanent secretary is the minister's chief link with all other higher civil servants in the department, and represents the institutional knowledge of the programs for which the minister is responsible.

As individuals, ministers and higher civil servants have chosen very different careers in government. A minister has the formal authority to make decisions; the public task of representing a department in Parliament and to pressure groups; the private task of negotiating with cabinet colleagues when interdepartmental disagreements arise; and, not least, a host of extragovernmental concerns, including his standing in the party, in the media, and in 10 Downing Street, whence come promotions and dismissals. For a minister, a department may be but a means to an end of furthering his individual political career, involving only a limited or incidental concern with policy making. Headey found that only half the ministers he interviewed were primarily concerned with initiating policies; the other half saw their role in the policy process as confined to selecting between policy alternatives put before them by higher civil servants, or endorsing a specific recommendation from them.[53] A minister is well advised to cultivate a certain detachment from his department, for he is likely to be in a given department for only two to three years. Moreover, unlike civil servants, who spend all their working life within Whitehall departments, the normal minister will spend most of his parliamentary career out of government office.

As individuals with personal careers to consider, higher civil servants or cadet civil servants are secure, inasmuch as the whole of their working life is certain to be spent in or around the policy process. However, a civil servant's reputation does not depend so much upon what he does, but rather, upon the opinion in which he is held by significant others. This is most obviously the case of a cadet, who must cultivate the good opinion of higher civil servants who determine promotion. Within the higher civil service, an individual must be able to adapt his own behavior in order to get along well with ministers with a variety of personal styles as well as opposing parties. A higher civil servant is rarely the overt cause of friction with a minister.

Both ministers and higher civil servants are usually generalists rather than specialists. Both groups have had an arts education at university, and limited outside experience relevant to specific departmental programs. A description applied by the head of the civil service to the experience of the group would also apply to ministers:

> The way to the top has so often been via a series of what one might call in short-hand policy-mongering jobs, without much experience of managing and organizing work and people.[54]

But both groups are remote from the coal face, that is, the levels of government where the actual day-to-day execution of programs is carried out. This is true when the central government is the executive agency, and even more when responsibility for managing and carrying out policies is hived off to extra-Whitehall agencies or carried out by local government or public corporations. Neither higher civil servants nor ministers are meant to be executive officials or managers.

Notwithstanding common concerns and close interpersonal relationships between ministers and higher civil servants, there nonetheless remain major *functional* differences between them, embodied in constitutional conventions and statutes and in informal norms.

One unique function of British ministers is to engage in *public* controversy about policy. A minister's engagement in overt controversy is of pervasive importance in the department. It means that a minister may initiate controversial policies against the wishes of pressure groups, the media, the Opposition party, or even, against advice from his civil servants—if he can gain cabinet endorsement. When controversy is thrust upon a department (e.g., by the disclosure of a scandal or major failure), it is the responsibility of the minister to defend his department, even if he thinks it is in the wrong and had no previous knowledge of the actions complained of.

As the legitimate authority for departmental policy, a minister also enunciates what the department ought to do; resolves intradepartmental differences by selecting between alternative policies put before him; and, provides the necessary formal endorsement of what the department may wish to do. These functions can be important negatively as well as positively. Without a minister's endorsement, civil servants carrying out actions that lead to controversy will find themselves exposed for having acted beyond their own authority. A minister may veto or delay action recommended by his civil servants if he thinks it will result in an unacceptable controversy within or outside government.

The limits of political action by higher civil servants were unintentionally revealed in early 1974 by the leading civil servant of his generation, Sir William Armstrong. Because of his direct access to the prime minister as the head of the civil service and his great experience of Whitehall, Sir William became drawn into advising the prime minister of the day, Edward Heath, about central issues of economic policy.[55] In this, there was nothing new. As Sir William once said, "Many Ministers don't want to be given alternatives; they want to be told what to do." Where Sir William erred, however, was in becoming publicly identified with the prime minister's policies, appearing in public at his side as an advisor at meetings with leaders of unions and industry, and having the prime minister turn to him publicly to request his advice. This set up a reaction by the subsequent Labour government.

A unique function of the higher civil servants in Britain is to provide the "institutional" memory about the work of the department, and how to defend or advance its interests in Whitehall. Even though an individual civil servant may be new to a post, he will have at his command all the previous files relating to a problem (including files connected with the government of the previous party, which are closed to ministers). In addition, every higher civil servant can fall back upon the pool of knowledge of his colleagues, including knowledge of the foibles and concerns of the minister, which is circulated throughout the department by the private secretary.

Higher civil servants are expected to provide ministers with information and advice that reflect a collective, not a personal opinion, the accumulated experience of the department about a problem at hand, what Lord Bridges called "the departmental point of view."[56] The minister may choose to act contrary to that view. But the whole point of having experienced officials at hand is to compare their outlook with the often uninformed judgments of party political debate, in order to create a government policy that will satisfy *both* the intentions of ministers *and* the practical concerns of civil servants with how policies are to be carried out. If conflicts between the two cannot be adjusted, then the constitutional norm is that civil servants should then be prepared to engage in the dutiful execution of ministerially ordained error. A minister who has views and can articulate them clearly and consistently to his higher civil servants is much more likely to have the actions taken in his name accurately reflect the mind of the minister than a minister whose mind is unclear, inconsistent, irrelevant to departmental views, or simply blank.

Given the numerical weight of administrative class civil servants by comparison with ministers, they can (and must) handle the great burden of labor. As a precondition of formulating or carrying out new policies, a minister must see to it that routine departmental responsibilities are satisfactorily discharged. This work is delegated almost entirely to civil servants. Insofar as it has a potential element of political controversy or interest, higher civil servants may supervise what is done, and the minister may be personally asked to approve, or at least to sign relevant documents. The minister is responsible for such tasks as answering questions in the House of Commons, meeting delegations, and delivering speeches at meetings of pressure groups concerned with the department. Higher civil servants will brief the minister on answers to awkward parliamentary questions; on potential demands by pressure groups; and prepare speeches for him to deliver on departmental business.

The making of major policies is dialectical, involving an exchange of influence between minister and higher civil servants. On a major issue, a department's policy cannot be dictated solely by the fiat of a minister. While the initiative may come from the minister and he may make the final and most difficult decisions, too, the investigation of the means by which action can be taken and the review and negotiation of procedures to carry out a policy will be overwhelmingly in the hands of civil servants. The minister lacks the time to carry out what he initiates—and there is no alternative pool of personnel at hand in the ministry. A departmental policy is usually a synthesis of views put forward by the minister and by departmental civil servants.

Within a department, the initial stimulus for ministerial action can come from any of several directions. It may come from within the department, as difficulties accumulate in dealing with a problem, or as civil servants (often assisted by advisory committees and pressure groups) believe they have devised a better way of discharging a department's responsibilities. Or it can come laterally from within government, as the by-product of a cabinet decision (e.g., about public expenditure) or from another department's initiative having interdepartmental implications. The stimulus can also come from national events or events abroad, or publicity in the media.

Wherever the initiative comes from, the file for dealing with the problem will normally start at the bottom of a ministry, that is, with a principal, an administrative grade civil servant immediately concerned with the problem within the department. Often, he will not have any executive responsibility for the problem, but simply be overseeing the relevant work of extra-Whitehall public agencies. The principal may be relatively new to his post, or without special knowledge of the subject because of frequent postings.[57] The file created by the principal is but the first stage in an accumulation of information and opinions, and second thoughts about both. It is then passed to an assistant secretary for review and revision as he thinks appropriate.

When a file goes to the under secretary, it is looked at primarily in terms of broad implications for other policies within the department, being viewed by a higher civil servant likely to have some regular contact with the minister. The Association of First Division Civil Servants describes the work of under secretaries as necessary for "refining" judgments, assuring "an almost judicial consistency of approach, in which each decision is taken and can be defended in the light of government attitudes and activities as a whole, an essential cornerstone of our constitutional practice," and acting as a trouble-shooter and a peacemaker in intradepartmental and interdepartmental disputes.[58] The file on a proposed policy will then pass through two more layers of higher civil servants—deputy secretaries and the permanent secretary. The permanent secretary's job is not so much to impose his view on subordinates (who are themselves better informed on details) but to write a final minute that makes the minister appreciate essential points that he should note in his political interest.

A characteristic bias of the higher civil servant in this review process is negative, searching for objections to almost any course of action that may be proposed, whether by a minister or by an underling, an attitude also cultivated by an Oxbridge arts education. The view was more suc-

cinctly stated by J. H. Thomas, a cockney minister of Ramsay Mac-
Donald, who complained to a civil servant: "I asked you for a paper about
'ow to do this, and you give me a paper about 'ow not." In the opinion of
Sir William Armstrong:

> The chief danger to which politicians and Ministers are exposed is not, as
> is often supposed, that obstructive bureaucrats will drag their feet in
> implementing their schemes, but that their own (i.e. the Minister's) opti-
> mism will carry them into schemes and policies which will subsequently
> be seen to fail—failure which attention to the experience and information
> available from the service might have avoided.[59]

Given conflicts between ministers and higher civil servants about
what is practicable, recurring charges arise that higher civil servants try to
"obstruct" ministers. In the strictest sense, this charge is often true.
There are a multiplicity of reasons why higher civil servants try to dis-
suade ministers from announcing or acting upon general intentions. The
first is to protect the minister from an action he will subsequently regret.
Does the minister understand how to deal with objections that he will
meet if he announces a given intention? The second reason is departmental: to protect the department from an action that it will regret, perhaps
after the minister has been moved elsewhere. A third reason reflects the
collective responsibility of British government: a minister may be propos-
ing a policy that is not approved, or unlikely to be approved by cabinet
collectively, and civil servants with access to the "jungle tom-tom" of
Whitehall will be more aware than the minister of opposition in other
departments, including 10 Downing Street. Finally, objections may be
grounded on a recognition of extragovernmental forces, for example, opposition from foreign countries or industrial, banking, or trade union
groups.[60]
    The ambiguity of deciding what is or is not practicable and desirable
is illustrated by the response to the Fulton Committee's recommendations
for major changes in the civil service. According to one committee member, Lord Crowther-Hunt, a staunch proponent of change, the issue of
principle fought out between the prime minister, Harold Wilson, and the
head of the civil service, Sir William Armstrong, was whether the then
Labour government should pledge itself to take specific actions, or to
investigate a stated course of action, and then do what was deemed practicable. Insofar as the recommendations were practicable, there would be
no difference in the eventual outcome. (That they were practicable is an
assumption of Lord Crowther-Hunt.) Insofar as the recommendations
were impractical, then investigation would prevent the government from

a failure disrupting the civil service. (This was the *assumption* of Sir William Armstrong.) In the event, the second course of action was followed, and many recommendations were aborted in a smothering embrace. The interpretation of Lord Crowther-Hunt is that recommendations were not carried out because they were against the interests of entrenched civil servants, who used the need to investigate practicality as a means of delaying action until Labour left office, and the commitment to change was itself forgotten. But an alternative interpretation could equally be placed upon events by Sir William Armstrong, namely, that the time spent investigating proposals uncovered a host of obstacles ignored by the Fulton Committee, pointing toward difficulties and likely failure.[61]

The difficulty of deciding what is practicable is also particularly sharp when issues arising involving conflicts between different ministries of government, say, between a spending department such as Education or Health, and the Treasury, or between the Department of Energy and Environment, each with different views about building and siting atomic energy reactors. A spending minister may think it obviously desirable not to cut spending by his department, whereas the Treasury may think cutting spending is a good way to achieve desirable economies. But an individual minister's wish is government policy only if it has obtained (or, in minor matters, may be presumed to be consistent with) cabinet policy. In interdepartmental disputes a minister is an interested party: he wishes *his* side to win.

The British system of government is particularly good at resolving disagreements between departments in the name of a collective cabinet.[62] Higher civil servants have a particularly strong role to play in consensus-mongering between departments, for they have a dual loyalty—to their present departmental minister, and to the government as a permanent collectivity. In making policies on an interdepartmental basis, the higher civil service works through official committees that prepare the ground for committees of busy ministers by deciding points of fact and substance that, in the collective judgment of officials, need not be referred to ministers. In the conduct of interdepartmental business, civil servants differ from ministers, for whereas a minister's personal reputation depends upon his effectiveness in winning interdepartmental battles, a civil servant's depends upon his willingness to compromise in order to produce a consensus document for endorsement by a cabinet committee. Whereas a minister wins respect by fighting interdepartmental battles and winning them, higher civil servants usually win respect by avoiding interdepartmental battles. Such is the contrast between the "conflict-oriented" ministers and "consensus-seeking" civil servants that ministers will sometimes complain that their civil servants have made concessions for the sake of consensus that the minister would prefer to have fought against ministerial adversaries.

For ministers to assume that there are no obstacles to their intentions is to assume that whatever a secretary of state or a party committee decides is *ipso facto* "do-able." It is also to assume that ministers relatively uninformed and inexperienced in the work of their department invariably understand the consequences of government action better than do experienced, informed, and politically shrewd Whitehall civil servants.

A more reasonable conclusion to draw about the political direction of higher civil servants' advice is that it is inclined to favor the status quo. By definition, the status quo is "do-able," because it is already being done. Civil servants make a further assumption: that status quo policies will remain doable in future. A new government, upon first coming into office, is likely to identify the civil service with its predecessor's policies, whether Labour or Conservative. This explains why both left-wing Labour politicians *and* right-wing Conservatives can see higher civil servants as "secretly" in sympathy with their opponents, since higher civil servants must accept, as part of the status quo, policies previously adopted by cabinets of each party.[63]

The existing system of minister-civil servant relationships persists, notwithstanding criticism, because both ministers and higher civil servants benefit. There is an exchange of advantages, and not just a unilateral advantage for civil servants. From the day of his appointment, a minister gains a staff of well-informed and politically alert advisors. The frequent alternation of Labour and Conservative governments for two decades means that higher civil servants have continuing practice in being Labour as well as Conservative advisors. Equally important, changing evaluations or fashions in major policy areas, such as management of the economy, makes civil servants adept at making U turns on major matters of economic policy. In return for taking all the blame for mistakes of higher civil servants, a minister also gains the right to take all the credit for what they do well. Since ministers have only a short stay in a department, there is a premium upon acquiring instant expertise, instant loyalty, and instant credit (even if it be for actions prepared by a predecessor of another party). A minister does not have the time to "take over" a department personally. But higher civil servants have the collective experience, knowledge, and political bipartisanship to hand over a department to the minister of the moment. For a minister to undertake a sustained attack upon civil servants might conceivably benefit government in the long run, but in the short run it would render very difficult a politician's chances of securing the normal benefits of being a minister in the British system of government.

Higher civil servants gain a permanent position of influence in the policy process, and a position that is risk free. Formally, civil servants are not responsible for the actions that they take; these are formally taken in the name of a minister. Their careers do not depend upon the success or failure of individual policies, as is the case of a minister. Their careers are risk free because whatever failure may result is not their fault, but can be laid to the door of a minister. The point is strikingly demonstrated by the continuing hegemony of Treasury officials within the higher civil service. A Treasury base for a career remains the most common route to the highest appointments in the civil service. This remains true even though the central and persisting weakness of British policy for the past generation has been the management of the economy.

PRESSURES UPON CONVENTIONS

Higher civil servants in Britain can purchase continuity at the price of adaptability. Their capacity to assimilate change is recurringly demonstrated. For example, in the Second World War outsiders were recruited to carry out additional and novel tasks of wartime government. A significant number remained, and notwithstanding (or because of) their novel socialization, rose to very high ranks before retirement in the 1960s. In the 1960s, the expansion of government created more senior administrative posts than had been allowed for in recruitment decades before. The problem was met by recruiting outsiders at mid-career and by recruiting from other grades within the civil service. These recruits, however, did not significantly alter the ethos of the higher civil service.

In any complex process of change, it is a nice matter of judgment whether preexisting institutions or reforms are altered more in the process of assimilation.[64] The point is well illustrated by the response of higher civil servants to the introduction of noncareer political or policy advisors to ministers, chosen on extra- (or anti-) Whitehall criteria of party loyalty, specialist knowledge, or personal acceptability. Political advisors (typically young persons aspiring to become MPs themselves) have usually been accepted because they have concentrated upon doing work that civil servants would not in any event do, such as maintaining liaison with party headquarters and the parliamentary party. Policy advisors have also been able to gain access to official files and membership of official committees, where their points of view can be effectively inserted in an established policy process. By working with the grain of higher civil servants, policy advisors may upon occasion exercise influence, but the procedures of policy making (about which higher civil servants often care more than the substance) are maintained.[65] The insertion of one youthful political advisor and an academic on leave as policy advisor does not, however, transform the routines of departments with tens of thousands of employees.

The process of assimilating changes in the civil service has its parallel in the assimilation of ministers. Since 1964, all four prime ministers have been meritocrats and two of them former cadet civil servants. On the Conservative as well as Labour side, cabinet ministers no longer come from the old upper-class strata, with an ethos consistent with that of the Northcote-Trevelyan civil service. Yet there are no discernible differences in policy outputs, and it can even be argued that the déclassé status of ministers today (by comparison with an earlier aristocratic era) is an emollient in relations with the higher civil service, who are also now recruited from very similar backgrounds.[66]

Paradoxically, the unchanging nature of institutions is likely to be an unintended source of change, insofar as conventions and practices adopted in one era are difficult to sustain in different circumstances. The most important illustration of unintended change is the doctrine of ministerial responsibility, which has a pervasive influence upon the direction of British government and the role of higher civil servants. There was a time when ministerial responsibility was a fact:

> The most striking feature of British administration in the first quarter of the nineteenth century was the extent to which the work of government departments was performed by the ministers themselves.[67]

In the present era, the doctrine is fiction. Given the volume of work carried on in a Whitehall department today, a minister cannot know about the great bulk of decisions taken by higher civil servants and announced in his name.

While one person remains nominally responsible for a department, the scale and volume of activities within nearly every department have increased substantially through the years, out of all proportion to assumptions of the nineteenth century. There has been no significant expansion in the number of cabinet ministers to meet this increasing volume of work. There were fifteen ministers in 1866, nineteen in 1900, and twenty-two in 1979.[68] Individual Whitehall departments have grown not only in terms of customary activities, but also through mergers with other departments. In the early 1970s five Whitehall superdepartments—the Foreign and Commonwealth Office; the Department of Trade & Industry; the Department of Health & Social Security; the Department of the Environment; and the Ministry of Defense—were in existence, and four still persist. Together, these five superdepartments merged nineteen different ministries in existence in 1952![69] The span of responsibility of an individual minister has been widening, as well as the volume of work increasing.

The increase in the volume of work at the top of Whitehall departments has been met by a very considerable increase in the size of the administrative class civil service. From 1953 to 1967, the numbers at all grades from permanent secretary to assistant principal declined by 10 percent from 2,594 to 2,344. Reorganization of the civil service after 1968 inflated those numbers by assimilating executive and specialist hierarchies to administrative class grades, but there has also been substantial real growth. By 1980, the total in these grades was 7,228, an increase of 64 percent over the comparable total for 1967 and in the ranks of under secretary and above, 788, an increase of nearly 50 percent from the level of 1967. In consequence, the ratio of cabinet ministers to higher civil servants rose from about 1 to 15 to 1 to 35 before Margaret Thatcher commenced a cutback in the size of the civil service.

The increase in numbers is itself a sign of weakness at the top, for a permanent secretary has more activities to coordinate and appear knowledgeable about—even though permanent secretaries were already working flat out to keep up with major departments a generation ago. The result is an increasing *dissociation* between the top people—both ministers *and* civil servants—and the principal or assistant secretary who is close to the file that contains (on paper, at any rate) the problem at hand. In the words of one temporary official, Labour political advisor Jack Straw:

> If a Permanent Secretary does not really know what's going on, it is not going to be very easy for the Minister either. . . . The difficulties that Secretaries of State have in exercising positive supervision over their departments may equally be faced by senior officials—indeed it is part of the same problem.[70]

The higher civil service can contain the effects of change only within the Whitehall community. Growth in British government in postwar years has preeminently been growth in government *outside* the Whitehall community. In 1951, the home civil service and the armed forces, the groups directly under the authority of Whitehall ministries, constituted 25 percent of all public employees; in 1976, they had declined to 13 percent of a larger total of public employees. The home civil service, with 9 percent of total public employment, is one of the smallest of the principal categories of public employees.[71] What is true of numbers of public employees tends to be equally true of amounts of money spent.

Growth in government outside Whitehall makes the higher civil service both remote and competitive. It is *remote* in that so much of its work is now concerned with interorganizational bargaining, in which one partner is outside the immediate bond of cabinet collective responsibility. It is *competitive* because, when only one party to a negotiation is a Whitehall department, there is not the same pressure to seek agreement, as is the case when negotiations are confined within the Whitehall community. A dispute between a Ministry of the Environment and local government authorities will be public from the first, inasmuch as elected local councillors are free to protest, and have an immediate political incentive to do so. Equally, when the Minister of Industry is disputing with the head of a nationalized firm about how much public money it should be given, civil servants know that the head of the nationalized industry can, if he deems it beneficial to his cause, publicize their differences. Local authorities can be suspended, and heads of nationalized industries can be fired—but such measures of overriding authority cannot be interpreted as examples of consensus!

The expansion of government responsibilities for managing the economy today makes higher civil servants in the Treasury particularly subject to buffetings by organized groups and pressures outside the control of their laws or norms. The success of many Treasury measures, such as prices and incomes and investment policies, is crucially affected by decisions taken by industry and trade unions. Time and again, these groups have demonstrated their unwillingness to agree publicly with government, let alone do what would be suggested in polite mandarin tones is the proper thing to do. As Rudolf Klein notes, there is now a form of "disjointed corporatism" dominated by interest groups with "the power to disrupt but lacking the authority to deliver the goods."[72] Even further outside the reach of the moral community of Whitehall are forces in the international economy. In dealings with institutions in which much is accomplished by discussions between officials, e.g., the European Community or the International Monetary Fund, there is no predisposition to produce a consensus on Whitehall terms or in Britain's interest. Nor are businessmen, trade unionists, or international civil servants today likely to be influenced by the social status of higher civil servants, which formerly, according to Peter Nettl, could be used in negotiations with lower status groups to bend them to Whitehall's ends.[73]

The higher civil service has an almost Durkheimian sense of moral solidarity; it is bad form or it is just not done for higher civil servants to compete against each other. In cricket terms, what counts is not whether one wins or loses, but how one plays the game. But local government officials are footballers: they want their team to score the most goals. Over and above organizational differences, social class differences reinforce their sense that Whitehall norms are alien. The fact that local government officials work closely with elected officials who may oppose the government of the day is a further complication. Within nationalized industries, staff tend to be specialists identifying with their industry; they are not indifferent to policy outcomes as are civil servants. Most senior local government officials are specialists, too. Central-local finance controversies or the resolution of financial problems of nationalized industries are far removed from the world described by Heclo and Wildavsky's *The Private Government of Public Money.*[74]

While higher civil servants are the custodians of the chief formal institutions of British government, they are no longer the sole voice of government. They are but spokesmen for one community—and a community viewed with reservations by extra-Whitehall groups. In such circumstances civil servants can no longer speak confidently about what will happen or speak earnestly about what must be done. Imperative language is inappropriate when others do not follow commands. Instead, language becomes conditional: civil servants increasingly speak of what the government *would* like to happen, or *hopes* will happen—if leaders of other organizations with which they must bargain will only act consistent with Whitehall's definition of their interests.

Because of the importance of the moral solidarity of the Whitehall community, any change that threatens this sense of community has potentially great implications. Neither Conservative nor Labour cabinet ministers, individually or collectively, have the readiness or determination to force a major confrontation, let alone change in the higher civil service. The very terms of reference for the Fulton Committee (established by a Labour government) ruled out, in the words of the prime minister of the day, Harold Wilson, "any intention on their part to alter the basic relationship between ministers and civil servants." The consequence was politely described thus: "We found at many points of our inquiry that this imposed limits on our work."[75]

Potentially a greater threat to solidarity can come from trade unions or, trade unionists would say, from government as an employer. Traditionally, to be a public official was to enjoy a status, even though this was less the case in Britain than in Prussia. It was normally an economic advantage as well. Today, public employment is an impersonal office in a large bureaucratic organization, and the vagaries of public sector pay policy have stimulated unionization. In consequence, a higher proportion of public employees in Britain are unionized (72 percent) than in the private sector (34 percent).[76] The cash nexus is replacing the service ethic for employees everywhere, and it appears to be more important in the public sector than in the private sector.

The higher civil service (members of the anachronistically named Association of First Division Civil Servants, now affiliated to the Trades Union Congress) cannot be indifferent to the deteriorating morale and industrial relations in the civil service. The deputy head of the Council of Civil Service Unions, representing lower grade and specialist workers, warns of "a major confrontation posing a major constitutional crisis."[77]

The proclivity of Mrs. Thatcher to attack civil servants and to encourage other ministers to do so has led William Kendall, the secretary-general of the Council of Civil Service Unions, to declare:

> Clearly she is for clobbering something she defines as the bureaucracy. It is part of what H. L. Mencken called "the Rotarian Mind." The danger is that in the end she will produce a politicized civil service because she is attacking the institution itself. The other danger is that the unions will assist the politicization and will become more overt.[78]

Under pressure from militant members at a time of generally factious industrial relations in Britain, the logic of attack is to hurt the politicians, not the public. Already, strikes have occurred in courts, prisons, and staff in Parliament.

The greatest challenge to the community of the higher civil service comes from within: *demoralization*. Many civil servants now in the highest posts were recruited in the years shortly after the Second World War, when there was widespread optimism about the beneficent and positive capability of government. Even in the early 1960s, when What's Wrong with Britain studies became noteworthy, there was also a compensating belief in making the system better. As late as 1969, Sir William Armstrong could express the supreme self-confidence and solidarity of higher civil servants by telling a television interviewer, when asked how he felt about his important responsibilities, "I am accountable to my own ideal of a civil servant."[79]

The generalized British loss of confidence in government has inevitably affected morale among the higher civil servants. Moreover, it has made higher civil servants more vulnerable to external criticisms. High pay, high status, and job security have led to accusations of self-favoritism in policy making. They have also encouraged the present Conservative government to look for ways of reducing the size of the civil service by 10 percent, including significant reductions in the higher civil service itself. Mrs. Thatcher's aggressive manner and readiness to voice criticisms—which higher civil servants feel that they cannot answer—has hurt civil servants who normally make great efforts to be liked by the persons they serve. The consequence is, in the words of specialist reporter Peter Hennessy, "Morale in the civil service is at an all-time low."[80]

The present concern of the higher civil service in Britain with maintaining official secrecy is important for relations with ministers, but it may be self-defeating in a broader context. It obscures whether civil servants or ministers are more responsible for policies that go awry—and there has been no shortage of the latter in Britain in the past decade. Moreover, it excludes interested persons and organizations from full participation in the formulation of policies whose subsequent effects cannot be hidden from them. When a principal political problem of governing is how to handle bad news, then sharing the responsibility of policy making more widely may be an advantage, insofar as it shares the burden of blame.[81]

At present, higher civil servants suffer from a dissociation of influence and responsibility. Whilst collectively (and sometimes, individually) higher civil servants exert considerable influence upon government policies, they are not responsible for the public advocacy or defense of these policies. The insulation of civil servants from public debate and criticism may be considered both a long-term fault in the formation of higher civil servants, as well as a source of "incomplete" policy advice. Equally, civil servants may be too subject to influence by ministers, carrying out policies that they consider nonsense because ministers have so requested them and no personal blame attaches to the civil servants doing so. Various Continental countries have found ways to move selected (and, usually, volunteer) civil servants into positions where they are publicly and personally committed to the success of policies. Instead of trying to place inexpert party politicians in more layers of Whitehall, thus reducing administrative effectiveness, it might be more reasonable to introduce expert governors (that is, select higher civil servants) into the public debate about policies that can no longer be contained within the community of Whitehall.

Any individual who spends the whole of his or her working life in the administrative civil service will have a limited awareness of how other organizations work, or how the government of Britain looks from their perspective. The marginal utility of spending two additional years in the status of principal (a purgatory between private office and assistant secretary) is very low or nil for a high flier by comparison with what could be learned by spending two years *outside* the civil service. The number of high fliers is sufficiently small, their general ability high enough, and their specific knowledge of Whitehall useful enough so that there should be no difficulty in arranging temporary assignments from Whitehall to posts in a host of organizations, profit-making and nonprofit-making (e.g., local government, nationalized industries, trade unions, universities, etc.). To be on the receiving end of dealings with government—or having to act outside the safe community of Whitehall—would be stimulating and educational in the extreme. Such an innovation need not even be required; it could simply be made clear that those who opted for such a move would be favored henceforth for promotion.

AN INTERNATIONAL PERSPECTIVE

Because the functional demands of government are similar across national boundaries, many of the activities of higher civil servants in Britain are similar to those of counterparts in other Western governments. Inevitably, distinctive features are highlighted by international comparisons.

In recruitment, the British administrative civil service is outstanding for the emphasis placed upon general ability rather than upon specific skills deemed relevant to government. The dominance of classicists and arts graduates generally is in marked contrast to the favor shown lawyers on the Continent, and a bias in favor of graduates in public administration (or recently, public policy) in the United States.

On the job, British higher civil servants are distinctive in the identification of a servicewide community. Higher civil servants are not recruited by department and thus divided from each other by departmental loyalties. Nor are they divided into specialist groups, like the French *grands corps*. The Whitehall community, not particular departments, is the primary focus of loyalty for higher civil servants. Promotion by elders of the community (that is, the head of the civil service and a few other permanent secretaries) reinforces this identification. Moreover, the community is an enduring one: turnover rates prior to retirement are very low in Whitehall, by comparison with the United States. Nor is an individual expected to use a Whitehall career as a stepping stone to another career—whether in party politics or as managing director of a state-owned enterprise. A higher civil servant is a lifer, typically having no other work experience prior to entering government and expecting to remain in the civil service until retirement at age sixty.

The higher civil service is a secure, stable community, and its political ministers have tested the service's claims to impartial partisanship, by rotating back and forth between Labour and Conservative governments with considerable frequency. From 1945 to 1979, each party had held office for seventeen years. Hence, while higher civil servants are extremely concerned with politics, they are also anxious to maintain their bipartisan status. By contrast with Continental countries where party membership (or even party activity) can be a means of promotion, in Britain a party label would be a handicap for a high flier. The ability to serve different parties, as well as different personalities, is a sine qua non for a successful higher civil servant in Britain.

The strengths as well as the weaknesses of British higher civil servants are little publicized. The convention of ministerial responsibility, reinforced by the Official Secrets Act, makes higher civil servants cloistered politicians. Within the offices of Whitehall, individual civil servants are not anonymous, nor could cadets afford to be unknown, for promotion reflects individual attributes and achievements. Visibility *intra muros* is both necessary and sufficient for the higher civil servant in Britain. By contrast with elected politicians in Britain, who give great and increasing attention to publicity, the political status of higher civil servants in

Whitehall is a private status. It is nonetheless real and important in government.

NOTES

1. See Henry Parris, *Constitutional Bureaucracy* (London: Allen & Unwin, 1969).

2. See, e.g., G. Kitson Clark, "Statesmen in Disguise," *The Historical Journal* II.L (1959), 35ff. and Richard Rose, "England: A Traditionally Modern Political Culture," in L. W. Pye and Sidney Verba, *Political Culture and Political Development* (Princeton: Princeton University Press, 1965) 83–129.

3. The discussion omits the diplomatic service, because of a very different pattern of work. Nor is attention given to the political status of senior armed forces officials whose judgments can be more than "merely technical."

4. Report of the Fulton Committee, Vol. 1 (London: HMSO, 3638, 1968), p. 9. See p. 101 for a dissenting note by the committee's one sociologist, Lord Simey.

5. For an unconventional opposite view, see the study by the very un-English thinking English writer, Brian Chapman, *The Profession of Government* (London: Allen & Unwin, 1959).

6. Civil Service Commission, *Appointments in Administration, 1981* (London: HMSO, 1980), p. 23. More generally, see the report of the Armitage Committee, *Political Activities of Civil Servants* (London: HMSO, 1978, Cmnd. 7057), and James B. Christoph, "Political Rights and Administrative Impartiality in the British Civil Service," *American Political Science Review* LI:1 (1957).

7. In 1959, 22 MPs were classified by the Nuffield election study as having had a previous career in the civil service or local government, and in 1979, 30. Few MPs have been in administrative class careers, and only in wartime have higher civil servants become cabinet ministers.

8. See Richard Rose, *The Problem of Party Government* (London: Macmillan, 1974), 359ff.

9. Interestingly, in Northern Ireland normal civil administration has been carried on, while real politics creates dissensus about the regime.

10. *Appointments in Administration, 1981*, p. 3.

11. See Richard A. Chapman, "Profile of a Profession," p. 13, in *Fulton Committee Report* III:2 (1968), and Robert D. Putnam, "The Political Attitudes of Senior Civil Servants in Britain, Germany and Italy," 100ff. in Mattei Dogan, ed., *The Mandarins of Western Europe* (New York: Halsted Press/Sage, 1975).

12. Sir William Armstrong, *The Role and Character of the Civil Service* (London: Oxford University Press, 1970), 14–15, Italics supplied.

13. Richard Rose, *Do Parties Make a Difference?* (London: Macmillan, expanded 2nd ed., 1984), 80.

14. Jack Straw, "Power in Government—A Chinese Puzzle" (Convocation lecture, Leeds University, 1978), p. 175.

15. Hugh Heclo, "OMB and the Presidency—The Problem of 'Neutral Competence,'" *Public Interest,* No. 38 (1975). Cf. Richard E. Neustadt, "White House and Whitehall," *The Public Interest,* No. 2 (1966): 55–69.

16. See Chapman, *The Higher Civil Service,* 115–116.

17. Cf. Angus Campbell et al., *The American Voter* (New York: John Wiley, 1960), chap. 10.

18. Richard A. Chapman, *The Higher Civil Service in Britain* (London: Constable, 1970), 115f.

19. See Peter Hennessy, "Secrecy shrouds No. 10 directive on open government," *The Times,* 27 November 1979, and "Civil servants given guide on what not to say and to whom," *The Times,* 22 May 1980.

20. F. M. G. Willson, "Policy-Making and the Policy-Makers," in Richard Rose, ed., *Policy-Making in Britain* (London: Macmillan, 1969), p. 358.

21. R. G. Wendt, in a review of Kellner and Crowther-Hunt (see note 26), in *Public Administration* LVIII (Autumn 1980): 498.

22. Civil Service Commission, *Annual Report 1979* (Basingstoke: 1980), p. 7.

23. *Civil Service Statistics 1980* (London: HMSO, 1980), table 19, reckoned to include diplomatic service as well as administrative trainees.

24. Calculated from *General Household Survey,* 1978 (London: HMSO, 1980), table 6.4.

25. Calculated from Permanent Secretaries biographies in *Who's Who,* 1980; *Returns from Universities and University Colleges 1950–51* (London: HMSO, 1952, Cmd. 8638), p. 5; *Statistics of Education,* Vol. 6 (London: HMSO, 1976), table 5; and Civil Service Commission, *Annual Report, 1979,* p. 40.

26. See Peter Kellner and Lord Crowther-Hunt, *The Civil Servants* (London: Macdonald, 1980), p. 193, which contains a useful description, inter alia, of the examinations for entrants to the administrative class.

27. See Fulton Committee, *Report,* Vol. III, 1, "Social Survey of the Civil Service," p. 19. Note that managerial class I is *not* the upper class.

28. See Fulton Committee, *Report,* Vol. III, p. 323, Psychological Research Centre, "The Recruitment of Graduates to the Civil Service: Survey of Student Attitudes."

29. Fulton Committee, *Report,* Vol. III, 1, p. 98. For updating, see Civil Service Commission, *Annual Report, 1979,* p. 41.

30. See Civil Service Commission, *Annual Report, 1979,* p. 41.

31. Quoted in Richard Rose, "England: A Traditionally Modern Political Culture," p. 117.

32. See *The Life and Letters of Lord Macaulay,* Vol. II (London: Longmans, 1923), pp. 585–586.

33. C. H. Sisson (a non-Oxbridge graduate who spent a long career in the nonprestige Ministry of Labour), *The Spirit of British Administration* (London: Faber & Faber, 1966). He echoes Michael Oakeshott, *Political Education* (Cambridge: Bowes & Bowes, 1951).

34. See Fulton Committee, *Report,* Vol. I, pp. 27ff. and Appendix E, especially p. 162.

35. Richard A. Chapman, "Profile of a Profession," p. 12.

36. See Chapman, *The Higher Civil Service in Britain,* 52, 54.

37. Peta Sheriff, *Career Patterns in the Higher Civil Service* (London: HMSO, Civil Service Studies No. 2, 1976), table 17.

38. See, e.g., *Memorandum,* by Stanley Henig in Minutes of Evidence, Vol. I for *The Civil Service* (London: HMSO, HC535–II, Session 1976–77, Eleventh Report from the Expenditure Committee), p. 191.

39. Civil Service Statistics, 1980, table 5.

40. Ibid., tables 4, 6, and 11, regarding under secretaries and above as equivalent to the higher civil service.

41. See Civil Service Department, "Rules on the Acceptance of Outside Business Appointments by Civil Servants," in *Civil Service Manpower Reductions* (London: HMSO, HC 712–II, Session 1979/80, 4th Report from Treasury and Civil Service Committee), especially Annex 6 and evidence at pp. 166–167. Cf. Grant Jordan and Jeremy Richardson, "Pantouflage: a Civil Service Perk," *New Society* (22 February 1979): 415–416.

42. Peta Sheriff, p. 19.

43. Fulton Committee, *Report,* Vol. II, p. 20.

44. Comment by a teacher at the Civil Service College, quoted in Kellner and Crowther-Hunt, p. 145.

45. Peta Sheriff, table 12.

46. Kellner and Crowther-Hunt, p. 162.

47. See the extensive comments by Sir William Armstrong, quoted in Kellner and Crowther-Hunt, pp. 174–175.

48. Mrs. Thatcher has shown more interest in appointments in the very highest levels, but this has not evidenced charges or cases of political bias. Cf. Peter Hennessy, "Mrs. Thatcher keeps close eye on top civil service postings," *The Times,* 14 February 1980.

49. Lord Balniel, "The Upper Classes," *The Twentieth Century,* No. 999 (1960), p. 432.

50. Terminology varies from department to department. Here, the term *minister* normally refers to the formal head of the department, usually a cabinet member, and often described as a secretary of state. Junior ministers are excluded from this essay. The chief civil servant in a department is known as the permanent secretary or permanent under secretary, and will here be called the permanent secretary.

51. Bruce W. Headey, *British Cabinet Ministers* (London: Allen & Unwin, 1974), p. 151.

52. Ibid., 153.

53. Ibid., 60.

54. Quoted from *Eleventh Report from the Expenditure Committee,* Vol. II–1, p. 659.

55. See Stephen Fay and Hugo Young, "The Fall of Heath," *Sunday Times,*

(3 parts), 22 and 29 February, 7 March 1976.

56. Sir Edward Bridges, *Portrait of a Profession* (Cambridge: University Press, 1950). Departments differ in the way in which they make up their collective view. See, e.g., Headey, chap. 7, and sources cited therein.

57. For a principal's point of view, see, e.g., W. J. L. Plowden, N. D. Deakin and J. B. L. Mayall, Memorandum No. 139, Fulton Committee, *Report*, Vol. V (2), pp. 998–1004.

58. For full details see Peter Hennessy, "Little saving seen in Civil Service Grade Cut," *The Times*, 17 June 1980.

59. Sir William Armstrong, *The Role and Character of the Civil Service*, p. 14.

60. See Richard Rose, *Do Parties Make a Difference?*, chap. 8.

61. For a lengthy and one-sided account, see Kellner and Crowther-Hunt, chap. 4.

62. See Richard Rose, "British Government: The Job at the Top," in R. Rose and E. Suleiman, eds., *Presidents and Prime Ministers* (Washington, D.C.: American Enterprise Institute, 1980), 1–49.

63. See, e.g., Kellner and Crowther-Hunt, 287ff., and recurring reports by Peter Hennessy in *The Times*.

64. Robert D. Putnam, "The Political Attitudes of Senior Civil Servants in Britain, Germany and Italy," presents data indicating that there are some differences in attitudes between cadet and higher civil servants. Time will tell whether the differences are generational or life-cycle.

65. See, e.g., Rudolf Klein and Janet Lewis, "Advice and Dissent in British Government: The Case of the Special Advisers," *Policy and Politics* XI:1 (1977); Tessa Blackstone, "Helping Ministers Do a Better Job," *New Society,* 19 July 1979; Brian Abel-Smith, "Don't have a go at romantic fiction if you know nothing about sex," *Times Higher Education Supplement,* 27 June 1980; and Maurice Peston, "A professional on a political tightrope," ibid., 11 July 1980.

66. See Dennis Kavanagh, "From Gentlemen to Players" in William B. Gwyn and Richard Rose, eds., *Britain: Progress and Decline* (London: Macmillan, 1980), 73–93.

67. D. M. Young, *The Colonial Office in the Early Nineteenth Century,* quoted approvingly by Henry Parris, *Constitutional Bureaucracy,* p. 24.

68. Junior ministers have increased to a greater extent—but their influence in the policy process is still very limited.

69. Cf. L. J. Sharpe, "Whitehall—Structures and People," in Dennis Kavanagh and Richard Rose, eds., *New Trends in British Government* (London: Sage Publications, 1976), especially p. 55.

70. Jack Straw, "Power in Government—A Chinese Puzzle," pp. 181–182. The pressure is not new. See, e.g., Lord Strang, Permanent Under Secretary in the Foreign Office thirty years ago, *Home and Abroad* (London: Deutsch, 1956), chap. 10.

71. For details, see Richard Parry, *United Kingdom Public Employment: Patterns of Change, 1951–1976* (Glasgow: Strathclyde Studies in Public Policy No. 62, 1980).

72. In a review of Barbara Castle's *Diaries, New Society,* 25 September 1980.

73. Cf. J. P. Nettl, "Consensus or Elite Domination: the Case of Business," *Political Studies* XIII:1 (1965).

74. Hugh Heclo and Aaron Wildavsky, *The Private Government of Public Money* (London: Macmillan, 1974).

75. See Fulton Committee, *Report,* Vol. 1, Appendix A, p. 107.

76. See Richard Rose, *Changes in Public Employment: A Multi-Dimensional Comparative Analysis* (Glasgow: Strathclyde Studies in Public Policy No. 61, 1980), p. 41.

77. Peter Jones, quoted by Peter Hennessy, "Militant civil service unions 'heading for constitutional crisis,'" *The Times,* 9 May 1980.

78. See Peter Hennessy, "Mrs. Thatcher gets warning of a politicized civil service," *The Times,* 12 August 1980. Note also, Paul Routledge, "Civil service vows to hurt the politicians," *The Times,* 29 October 1980.

79. Quoted in R. A. Chapman, *The Higher Civil Service in Britain,* p. 141.

80. "Where an initiative could stop the slide into defeatism," *The Times,* 16 September 1980. See also Sir Ian Bancroft's statement, "Whitehall concerned over public hostility," *The Times,* 10 December, 1980.

81. See Dennis Kavanagh, "Political Leadership: the Labor of Sisyphus," in Richard Rose, *Challenge to Governance: Studies in Overloaded Polities* (London: Sage Publications, 1980), 216ff.

GERMAN FEDERAL BUREAUCRATS

A Functional Elite between Politics and Administration

Renate Mayntz

THE SETTING OF THE PROBLEM

In studies of top civil servants, the issues at stake are usually the elite character of this group and the effective power it wields. In this connection, questions after the social origin and political attitudes of top civil servants are of a derived nature because these features reflect the group's elite character or permit one to predict for whose benefit the group is likely to use the influence it has. In Germany, the political implications of the role played by top civil servants have traditionally commanded predominant interest. The core problem has received its best-known formulation in Max Weber's treatment of bureaucracy as the administrative staff typical of legal-rational political orders (Weber 1964, chap. 3). To maximize rationality, political authority must not only be based on law, but the execution of political decisions must also be rational in a technical or instrumental sense. Weber constructed his ideal-typical conception of bureaucracy so as to maximize this instrumental rationality in the execution of political decisions. In his historical analyses, however, he never tired of pointing to existing tendencies for the bureaucratic staff to escape its instrumental role and assume a position of power in its own right—a political variant of the Marxist concern with the expropriation of the expropriators. Nor was this a new concern when Weber formulated the problem of bureaucratic power; the invention of the term *bureaucracy* itself in early eighteenth-century France was meant to criticize the tyrannical and self-serving rule of high civil servants (Dunsire 1973, chap. 4). The ideal of legislative control that assigns a merely instrumental role to the bureaucracy expresses the basic legitimatory belief of modern parliamentary democracies: the publicly elected parliamentary representatives are to formulate the popular will, and the bureaucracy, directed by the political executive, is to implement it. Reality has probably never fitted this ideal, but it is evident that with increasing state interventionism, growing public sectors, and a general orientation toward public planning, the policy-making functions of the ministerial bureaucracy have become ever more pronounced. As Alfred Grosser (quoted by Dogan 1975, p. 7) puts it: "Everywhere the legislative initiative has passed into the hands of the administrations. The legislatures sometimes amend, rarely reject, usually ratify. The members continue, indeed, to call themselves collectively 'the legislative power' on the law books, but in most cases they merely participate in a procedure of registration." While this may be overstating an undeniably general tendency, there is obviously scope for variation in the role played by top civil servants.

In Germany, the instrumental character of the bureaucracy has for specific historical reasons remained a particularly live issue up to the present. The German civil service has traditionally been seen to represent public interest in general against the partisan claims of the emerging political parties (Frowein 1967, p. 9), but it has, in fact, never been a politically neutral instrument. When the modern civil service developed in the course of political centralization and the growth of an extensive state administration, higher officials quickly came to play a prominent role. The period when high civil servants, especially in Prussia, effectively assumed government functions and thus became for all practical purposes a ruling elite lasted from the latter part of the eighteenth century until 1848 (Gillis 1971). In Prussia, an absolutist monarchy that was late to industrialize, there were at the time no elites that could effectively compete for governing power. The bourgeoisie was as yet but weakly developed and largely lacked political awareness and ambition, there was no autonomous group of political decision-makers, and the landed aristocracy had found a mode of accommodation with the bureaucracy (Armstrong 1973) by increasingly entering the higher civil service and taking public office especially at the provincial level. Since entry into the higher civil service had early become tied to requirements of training and demonstrated ability (examinations), it is not surprising that the bureaucracy, by virtue of its superior education, administrative experience, and political skill, became the driving force of national welfare and progress (Rejewski 1973, p. 29). Though not partisan in a party political sense, the bureaucracy before 1848 played anything but an instrumental role.

With the constitutional reforms introduced after the 1848 uprisings, in which a part of the reform-oriented civil servants had actively participated, this general situation changed. Though tolerated rather than welcomed by the king and all convinced monarchists, the new political institutions provided the basis for the growth of a separate group of political decision-makers, and the bureaucracy had to define its own position in relation to it. At the same time, especially after 1870, new competing elites developed in the economic and in the scientific and cultural fields. During the second half of the nineteenth century the bureaucracy gradually lost its position as an effective ruling elite. Repeatedly subjected to disciplinary action designed to assure the identification of the civil service with the conservative monarchists and the established political order, the bureaucracy increasingly withdrew from active political life, but at the same time and for largely the same reasons it became partisan (that is, overwhelmingly conservative and monarchist) in its attitude (Morsey 1972).[1]

It is indicative of this political orientation of the higher civil service that with the advent of the Weimar Republic, about 10 percent of the Prussian officials working in general administration made use of an option given them by an ordinance of February 1919 and retired prematurely on the grounds that they felt they could not loyally serve a republican government (Runge 1965, p. 102 f.). But the majority of the conservative civil servants remained in office, and for them the appeal to a norm of nonpartisan, expert service to the public welfare undoubtedly assumed an important protective function and made it possible for them to continue working without feeling obliged to give active support to a government and constitution to which they felt no personal loyalty. The level of political activity of the higher civil service was correspondingly low. The efforts of succeeding governments in the period of the Weimar Republic to instill democratic values into the bureaucracy through measures of personnel policy (Fenske 1972) did not basically change its orientation, so that the government in turn had reason to insist on the norms of neutrality and obedience in order to get a recalcitrant conservative bureaucracy to implement social democratic policies.

When Hitler came to power, he seems to have been more successful in bending the bureaucracy to his will. The personnel measures that he took to cleanse the civil service of such democratic and socialist elements as had been introduced came quickly and were radical (Runge 1965, pp. 237–241). Hitler made political partisanship explicitly a condition for obtaining and retaining office, defining the readiness to support the National-Socialist (NS) state unconditionally and at all times as criterion of admission to the civil service (Brandt 1976, p. 111, p. 129). At the same time, however, the state bureaucracy was subjected to the direct control of the national Socialist party. It is probably no exaggeration to say that the German civil service has never before been so much instrumentalized or played so subservient a role.

In retrospect, the Nazi experience has had a dual effect. It served first, to reinforce the ideal of a nonpartisan civil service whose relative independence permits it to hold its own against arbitrary political claims for compliance. At the same time, however, the civil service was not to be apolitical, but to support actively the new democratic constitution. These expectations are reflected in the civil service policy and administrative personnel measures in the young Federal Republic (Morsey 1977).

THE STRUCTURAL BACKGROUND OF BUREAUCRATIC POWER

The chance that a given bureaucracy escapes political control and becomes a power center in its own right rests in the general fact that in order to fulfill its tasks, it must dispose, not only of expert knowledge and the requisite resources, but must also have a certain scope for discretionary action. This functionally necessary and practically inevitable degree of autonomy implies, of course, the danger that knowledge, resources, and the scope for independent decisions will be used for purposes of bureaucratic self-aggrandizement or of imposing the bureaucracy's own preferences in the development and implementation of political decisions. The extent to which this danger becomes real and the exact shape it takes depend, not only on the characteristics of higher civil servants themselves, such as their origin, professional orientation, and social status as a professional group, but also on a number of structural properties of the bureaucracy and of its sociopolitical environment.

Probably the most important structural characteristic is the degree of political centralization, which directly affects the tasks assigned to top civil servants at the national level. Aside from the degree of political centralization it is also of importance whether a given national administration predates the development of constitutional political institutions (as in Germany), or has grown alongside or even after them (as, for instance, in the United States and Great Britain). With respect to the sociopolitical environment, the existence of a plurality of relatively powerful social groups with divergent, but not antagonistic, interests enhances the potential influence of the bureaucracy by offering it the opportunity to form coalitions and gain outside support for its favorite policies (Eisenstadt 1958). It is further obvious that a powerful and stable political leadership curtails the chances of the bureaucracy to escape political control. Dogan points out that the pluralism or fragmentation of the party system enhances bureaucratic power. He illustrates this by reference to socialist one-party systems, where the ruling party is the true center of policy decisions so that even the top bureaucracy is more or less restricted to the tasks of implementation (Dogan 1975, p. 11). Italy, in contrast, might serve to illustrate the opposite extreme of a highly fragmented political system where the internal differentiation of the parties and parliamentary party groups into wings and currents and their linkage with diverging interest groups weaken the power of political integration and enable the central bureaucracy to form changing coalitions, offsetting the pressures of one with that of some other groups, thus gaining a measure of political influence (Ferraresi 1968).

Starting with the last of these factors, the party system of the German Federal Republic is characterized by a restricted pluralism. Governmental stability is remarkably high. Though all major parties are occasionally beset by internal tensions, there exist nothing like the fragmentation and factionalism characteristic of the earlier Weimar Republic or of present-day Italy. The system of organized interests is similarly pluralistic. The big sectoral interests are represented in a limited number of large, well-integrated, nationwide organizations. German labor unions, for instance, based on the industrial instead of the (more fragmented) craft principle to begin with, jointly form the powerful labor association (Deutsche Gewerkschaftsbund (DGB). These contextual features are important for the way top bureaucrats go about fulfilling their tasks, but they do not visibly sway the balance either in favor or disfavor of bureaucratic power.

Of the various contextual factors that impinge upon the role played by higher civil servants in central government, the German federal constitution and certain structural details of governmental organization are of more directly visible influence. Germany has never reached the same degree of national political centralization as France. Nevertheless, the constitutional distribution of powers assigns today most legislative functions to the federal level. Policy implementation, on the other hand, is largely the task of the German *Länder* (states). The federal goverment has full responsibility for policy implementation only in the areas of defense, rail transport, and postal services. Tax administration is under the joint supervision of the competent federal and Länder authorities. There are, of course, a number of programs administered by federal departments directly, mainly financial incentive and subvention programs. But program management and implementation have never been a predominant task of federal departments. In several policy areas large-sized programs not delegated to the Länder for implementation are managed by federal agencies that operate largely free of departmental control. An example is the Federal Labor Agency, which administers federal labor market policy including unemployment insurance. This distribution of functions has important consequences for the role played by higher civil servants in federal government: Their predominant concern—even in terms of working time—is policy making and program development rather than program management (Mayntz & Scharpf 1975, p. 63).

Several features of governmental and departmental organization also shape the role of the higher ministerial bureaucracy. The first significant fact is that the chancellor and his cabinet receive aid, information, and assistance, not from any special staff outside the regular organization of government, but from the civil servants in the chancellor's office, a federal agency organized and staffed according to the same principles as the federal departments. The second important feature is that staff help at the top of the federal departments is also very limited. The departmental executive typically consists of the minister and his state secretaries. There are two types of state secretaries, the traditionally existing tenured state secretary and the parliamentary secretary. While the former has normally been a career civil servant and is generally responsible for the continuity of departmental administration (Echtler 1973), the parliamentary secretary must be a member of Parliament, and his term of office ends with the legislative period. The minister commands the aid of a personal assistant, usually a younger civil servant, a press and/or public relations assistant, and a small office (or an officer) for cabinet and parliamentary matters. In addition, there is a small ministerial bureau taking care of more routine clerical and administrative tasks. The state secretaries have usually only one personal assistant and a secretary, but no further staff. There exists nothing like the French ministerial cabinet, nor like the large and ill-defined circle of personal advisors to be found in American federal departments. Nor is there any other reservoir of advisors, planners, and policy analysts within the German governmental structure who could compete with top bureaucrats for these tasks. This means in effect that most of the corresponding functions must be fulfilled by the normal departmental personnel. By virtue of the tasks that naturally devolve upon higher civil servants in a government organized in this way, top bureaucrats will obviously play a role of great influence in the development of policy.

TOP CIVIL SERVANTS: POSITION, ORIGIN, TRAINING AND RECRUITMENT

Given the organizational background and the clear-cut and relatively uniform structure of the German civil service, it is easy to circumscribe the group here under consideration both in terms of function and rank. With a very few exceptions this group consists of tenured civil servants. The vast majority belongs to the topmost ranks of the nontechnical, general administrative service. The personal ranks involved are mainly four: state secretary, *Ministerialdirektor, Ministerialdirigent,* and *Ministerialrat*.[2] Though there is no one-to-one correspondence between personal rank and position, the last three ranks by and large correspond to the positions of division, subdivision, and section chief. Section chiefs are here included among top bureaucrats because the sections *(Referate)* are the basic organizational unit where the bulk of departmental work, including policy development, is actually performed. The federal budget for 1980 lists roughly 1,700 positions of the ranks just mentioned for the 16 federal departments, the chancellor's office, and the press office.[3] Estimating on the basis of the salary information given for these positions, the group of 1,700 top bureaucrats should be composed of 2 percent state secretaries, 19 percent division and subdivision chiefs *(Ministerialdirektoren* and *Ministerialdirigenten),* and 79 percent section chiefs *(Referenten).* This group of top federal bureaucrats accounts for less than 2 percent of the civil servants employed by the federal administration.[4]

German higher civil servants of today do not possess a special elite status on the basis of social origin, recruitment, or occupational prestige. This used to be very different in the past, when especially in Prussia the high civil service was not only an effective power elite, but also an uncontested social elite, recruited from the landed aristocracy and the leading families of the educated bourgeoisie, well paid and often disposing of a substantial private income in addition. In 1820, 42 percent of the higher administrative officials were noble (Gillis 1971, p. 30), coming either from families of the old landed aristocracy or from the new nobility; as Armstrong reports, in the eighteenth century higher officials of bourgeois origin were often ennobled, and public service frequently became a tradition in these families, contributing to the high degree of bureaucratic self-recruitment that characterized the Prussian administration (Armstrong 1973, pp. 79–81). This pattern of elite recruitment continued even into the twentieth century; in 1911, for instance, 31.7 percent of the higher civil servants employed in the general administration of the provinces belonged to the old aristocracy, with an additional 5.5 percent belonging to the new nobility; nearly half of them were sons of officials or of officers (Fenske 1973, p. 352). But at that time the socioeconomic position of the higher civil service had already suffered a serious decline. As previously mentioned, competing elites developed during the second half of the nineteenth century and vied with the higher officialdom in education, influence, and income. After 1870 it was especially the quickly developing industrial sector that offered much more attractive economic opportunities. Civil service salaries did not only lag behind in relative terms, they did not even permit officials to maintain their former standard of life any more, so that having a private source of income now became a necessity and sometimes even an explicit condition if one aspired to higher civil-service positions (Most 1915, Reinke 1979, pp. 116–124).

In the Federal Republic today, top civil service salaries, though easily surpassed by the income of a successful physician, dentist, or manager in industry, are still considered to be good and permit, if managed well, a middle/upper-middle-class style of life. Though no longer in economic straits, however, today's top bureaucrats have not regained a special elite position.

The social background of most higher civil servants is middle and upper-middle class; this characteristic is shared by university graduates in general and is due to the social selectivity inherent in the German second-ary school system. The social origin of higher civil servants is, therefore, in no way superior to that of other functional elite groups, such as man-agers in industry, university professors, or free-practicing professionals including lawyers. Their only special feature is still a remarkably high degree of recruitment from families of former civil servants (Luhmann & Mayntz 1973, p. 140). Higher civil servants do not receive their academic training in schools of particularly high prestige, as is largely the case in France and Great Britain. Most higher civil servants in general adminis-tration have studied law at one of the many German universities, with no recognizable concentration on one or a few schools. Finally, the prestige of higher civil servants is in general not superior to that of other academi-cally trained groups.

German civil servants are generally recruited for a career, that is, for entry into a category and not for specific positions. Their training is sup-posed to enable them to fill a variety of positions. This is particularly true of the general administrative service, a functional category that plays a generalist kind of role. Roughly two-thirds of the top civil servants have studied law (H. G. Steinkemper 1980, p. 105). The discipline of law came to supplant the evolving sciences of national economics and public admin-istration in the training of higher civil servants already in the course of the nineteenth century. Epsecially in the general administrative service it became thereupon possible to speak of a "monopoly of jurists." While today such a monopoly no longer exists if the higher civil service as a whole is considered, top bureaucrats in the federal bureaucracy are still largely jurists. This predominance of jurists is reinforced by the fact that higher civil servants with a training in law have a considerably better chance to reach top positions (Luhmann & Mayntz, 1973, p. 142). The requirement of a legal background for higher civil servants may make sense where ministerial work consists largely in drafting laws, decrees, and ordinances, even though legal training in Germany focuses on the application and not the development of legal norms. But with an increasing emphasis on long-range public planning, this character of ministerial work has shifted. Planning puts more emphasis on substantive expertise, and the ability to put a program in the proper legal form becomes an adjunct rather than a focal aspect of the task. For this reason the continuing predominance of legally trained higher civil servants has become a subject of heated controversy.

Having received their first academic degree, prospective higher civil servants must enlist in the so-called preparatory service, a combination of theoretical learning and on-the-job training. The institution of the preparatory service has historical roots going back to the eighteenth century, when a period of work as unpaid assistant became a normal precondition of obtaining a position in the higher civil service (Breuckmann 1965). Today law students enter this service after their first legal examinations. The preparatory service is not specifically directed to an administrative career; it provides recruits with practical experience, not only in public administration, but also in the work of a lawyer and of the courts. Accordingly law students can choose among these different careers upon concluding the preparatory service with their second legal examinations. Recruits to the higher civil service who have some other diploma than law enter a preparatory service, too, but in this case the training is specifically aimed at familiarizing them with the administrative context in which they will have to work later on.

According to the principles of the German civil service, the group of top positions previously circumscribed in terms of rank and function should be filled through the promotion of career civil servants. The promotion of career civil servants is largely based on seniority, with performance a secondary criterion if a choice must be made among several candidates with the same formal qualifications. To aid promotional decisions, higher civil servants in the federal departments are subject to a periodic evaluation in the form of reports written by their immediate superior. Promotional decisions, as well as recruitment decisions, are departmental prerogatives. The Federal Personnel Committee has a number of consultative functions and is involved in recruitment decisions only in those exceptional cases where candidates do not possess the normal career prerequisites. Within the federal departments, personnel management is generally the function of a specialized section in the general service division, but where top positions are concerned, the departmental executive (state secretary or even the minister himself) is directly involved and makes the final decision, which—for all the positions here under consideration—also needs formal cabinet approval.

Together with the lack of homogeneity in social (and/or regional) background and the absence of a common educational experience at one or a few elite schools, the departmental recruitment practice militates against the development of a corporate identity among the members of the higher civil service. This is a feature that seems to distinguish German top bureaucrats noticeably, for example, from their British counterparts (Headey 1972, pp. 43–48). The personal loyalty of German higher civil servants is to their particular department rather than to the service (or their service class) as a whole. Nor is the pattern of subjective identification significantly weakened by the relatively high mobility of higher civil servants both in federal and in Länder ministries (Luhmann & Mayntz 1973, pp. 182–192); especially since most of this mobility takes place within a given department (between hierarchical levels, but also between sections and divisions).

CIVIL SERVANTS AS MINISTERIAL AIDS: A DILEMMA AND ITS SOLUTION

Given the lack of a sufficiently large and freely disposable personal staff, the German political executive group is obviously faced with a serious problem: it needs collaborators who share the executive's general political outlook and policy orientation, but must rely mainly upon civil servants recruited according to a different set of criteria. The clash between the functional needs of the political executive on the one hand and the career principles of the civil service on the other hand is mitigated, however, by the existence of a special category of civil servants, the so-called political civil servants *(politische Beamte)*. Though not a legal term in the strict sense, the term is used to designate a special group of civil servants who can be temporarily retired at any time because they hold positions where full agreement with the goals of a given government is essential (Kugele 1976, p. 10 f.). This group is clearly defined by law, mainly the Federal Civil Service Law of 1953 with a few later additions. Leaving aside certain top ranks in the Foreign Service and a number of special positions like that of the Chief of the Press Office, political civil servants are those who at the federal level hold the ranks of state secretary and Ministerialdirektor (that is, most division chiefs). Political civil servants are not appointed as such; career civil servants rather move into this special category by being promoted to the corresponding ranks. In principle, therefore, normal civil service criteria apply to the selection and appointment of political civil servants, while the ease with which they can be disposed of stands in sharp contrast to the job protection enjoyed by other civil servants, who can be dismissed only under very exceptional circumstances, such as conviction for a criminal offense, and who cannot even be freely shifted to other positions against their will. If a political civil servant is sent into temporary retirement, the minister need not even give any reasons at all for his decision. The temporarily retired civil servant is paid the pension he is entitled to according to his rank and age.

Though sometimes (for instance, Kugele 1976) interpreted as an attempt to solve the contradiction between the norm of civil service neutrality and the individual freedom of political action, the purpose of this institution is, in fact, to enable the political executive to get rid of persons in functionally important top positions who do not enjoy his or her full trust. The legal chance to dispose of leading civil servants so as to maximize political congeniality and personal trust in the relation between the political executive and top civil servants is not a new invention of the Federal Republic. The tenured civil servant who is protected against arbitrary personnel decisions of the sovereign was only achieved with the Prussian General Code of 1794. Immediately, however, the need for a more flexible handling of the incumbents of top positions made itself felt. At first a number of decrees were issued that made it possible under certain conditions to dismiss a civil servant against his will, but no clear distinction was made between cases of "normal" misbehavior and cases where other (political) considerations played the main role. In a new ordinance regulating disciplinary action enacted in 1849, which in a modified form received legal status in 1852, it was stipulated that certain categories of higher civil servants down to the level of *Landrat,* the provincial magistrate, could be "put to disposition," that is, sent into temporary retirement against their will and on general political grounds. Though this legal possibility was used sparingly at most times, it never fell into disuse and served repeatedly as the instrument of imposing political discipline upon officials, especially in the second half of the nineteenth century (Rejewski 1972). Today the institution of the political civil servant is not meant as an instrument of political regimentation, but as a means to fill top positions with incumbents of the political executive's special trust. The institution of the political civil servant recognizes, as it were, that the incumbents of *top* departmental positions must be able and willing to act in the interest of the government of their own accord and without the need of specific orders, while officials at lower levels are expected to be controlled more closely by their immediate superiors (H. G. Steinkemper 1980, p. 56).

The institution of the political civil servant does not contradict, but rather underlines or reflects the fact that, in general, civil servants in Germany enjoy the uncontested right to engage actively in politics. That this could be an issue became visible only with the legalization of political parties after 1848. The Prussian General Code of 1794 had defined a special norm of loyalty for all officials, but made no special reference to political activities. In fact, until 1848 high officials enjoyed a considerable political freedom in their opinions and activities, partly because they were the effective governing elite, and partly because, by virtue of their origin, education, and position, their basic loyalty was not in doubt. The participation of at least a part of the higher civil service in the 1848 uprisings ushered in a period of greater political restrictiveness through a narrower interpretation of the legal norm of special loyalty. Thus participation in organizations considered hostile to the existing political order—which included, not only some parties, but also unions—was considered an infringement of the loyalty norm. Repeatedly attempts were made to get higher officials to give active support to the candidates of the conservative government party, but in general engagement for all political parties not considered to be anticonstitutional was permitted. There was a parallel debate about the implications of the norm of special loyalty for officials elected to Parliament. Though here, too, the government's attitude oscillated between more and less permissiveness, the dominant position was that such MP's could oppose individual government proposals, but should refrain from basically questioning the constitution (Rejewski 1972; Wunder 1977). In the Weimar Republic full freedom of political opinion for all civil servants was even written into the constitution; it became somewhat restricted only toward the very end of that period when membership in right or left parties such as the German Communist Party (KPD) or the Nazi Party (NSDAP) was defined as incompatible with civil service status (Runge 1965). Under Hitler, of course, it was not only the civil servants who lost their political liberties.

The civil service law of today only expects the civil servant to fulfill his official tasks in a nonpartisan way; he is otherwise free to engage in all kinds of political activity, though in doing so he is legally held to observe such moderation and self-restraint as necessary in view of his position in society and the duties of his office. It is manifestly difficult to make this legal norm operational, and the courts were repeatedly called upon to clarify its meaning on the basis of concrete cases. As Frowein (1976) shows, the usual interpretation is very wide, indeed. Judging from a variety of court sentences, it seems that only such things as joining a declared anticonstitutional party, campaign activities during office hours that seriously disturb the work process, or public criticism of the government of such vehemence that it must undermine the public's trust in the critic's impartiality in making official decisions, are sanctionable violations of the norm of political moderation.

THE POLITICIZATION OF CAREER PATTERNS

The institution of political civil servants affords important opportunities for recruitment to top positions according to explicit political criteria. If these chances are fully utilized, the end effect might be a highly politicized top civil service, politicized in the sense of party allegiance and affiliation. In fact, the political parties might well be able to colonize, through the personnel decisions of the ministers who are their own members, growing segments of the federal bureaucracy. To what extent this has really happened is a controversial question. There are those who, like Seemann (1980), argue vehemently that the German ministerial bureaucracy has become politically colonized—mainly by the Social Democratic party—and who agree with Dyson (1980) that in Germany a "party-book administration" has developed, with the boundary between party organization and administration becoming increasingly blurred and career lines linking the two sectors closely. But data about the career patterns of top federal bureaucrats can also be interpreted in a different way. In fact, Dyson's own argument seems to apply more to the Länder and local government levels than to the federal bureaucracy, and he himself adduces evidence of counterforces to the general pressure toward politicization.

In evaluating data about the characteristics and careers of top civil servants the problem is often to judge whether a given percentage is "much" or "little"—whether the glass should be called half full or half empty. But even taking this difficulty into consideration, it seems safe to state that the politicization of the federal bureaucracy is limited both in quantitative and in qualitative terms. The quantitative aspect is reflected in figures about the recruitment and party membership of top civil servants, as well as in the use made of the opportunity to send political civil servants into temporary retirement.[5]

To begin with the last aspect, it seems significant that of the 100 federal state secretaries who have held (and left) office between 1949 and 1977, only 38 were temporarily retired (H. G. Steinkemper 1980, p. 97). Since this top rank is likely to be most easily subject to a decision of temporary retirement, the percentage should be significantly lower at the level of division chiefs. Decisions of temporary retirement are mostly taken when there is a change in the governing majority, but it is not unusual that a minister sends a state secretary or division chief into temporary retirement in the normal course of the legislative period. The most spectacular changes occurred when the SPD/FDP coalition government was formed in 1969, but even then, as Dyson recounts, the new ministers used their formal power to fill top positions with persons of their own choosing to very different degrees (1980, p. 135 f.). In fact, attempts to use this formal power extensively and blatantly have caused so much ill-will among federal civil servants at large that ministers have sometimes tried to use substitute strategies such as creating new additional positions or working with task forces of trusted persons drawn from the existing departmental units.

It would appear quite natural that the institution of the political civil servant is not only used to recruit top officials according to political criteria, but that this also increases the chance of competent and trustworthy outsiders to achieve high positions in the federal bureaucracy. Civil service principles, however, do not only fix educational entry requirements that are extremely difficult to circumvent, but also favor quite definitely recruitment from within the service, as higher positions are generally expected to be filled by promotion from lower ranks. The result of these countervailing tendencies is reflected in the figures H. G. Steinkemper (1980) has compiled on the basis of data collected in a larger study carried out in 1972; they show that one out of every four political civil servants in the federal government (25.3 percent) can be called an outsider by virtue of his atypical career (p. 108). That the institution of political civil servant is an important avenue for the entry of outsiders can be seen in the fact that among top officeholders below that level, the percentage drops considerably (12 percent among Ministerialdirigenten and only 7 percent among Ministerialräte; p. 109).

"Outsiders" are such top officeholders who entered, not only the given department, but the bureaucracy from the outside when they assumed their present or the immediately preceding position. To include the latter category of persons among the outsiders is meaningful because of the widespread practice for external recruits to enter the bureaucracy one level below that of the office for which they are informally designated. Since most outside recruits (with the significant exceptions of judges and university professors) do not have civil service status when they enter the federal bureaucracy, their status is at first that of a salaried employee. After a certain time, procedures are initiated with the Civil Service Commission to confer civil service status on them. This can be obtained more easily and more quickly if the candidate has already demonstrated his competence on the job. This practice means, too, that at any given time there will be a few top officeholders who have the status of employees. Of the top federal bureaucrats analyzed by H. G. Steinkemper, 4.6 percent had that status (1980, p. 95).

If outsiders account for less than one-fifth of all top civil servants, those with a purely administrative career are today likewise a minority. This holds for both regional and federal government officials (B. Steinkemper 1974). At the federal level H. G. Steinkemper found only 28 percent of top officials to be of this type (1980, p. 108). The majority, in fact, display mixed career patterns, having started their administrative careers elsewhere (that is, in law, science, business) or having at some time interrupted them, but without being, therefore, outside entrants in the sense previously defined. No longitudinal study of recruitment patterns exists, but a comparison of the age structure of outsiders and classical career civil servants, together with consideration of the entry dates of outsiders into the federal bureaucracy, permits the conclusion that outsiders have been recruited increasingly since the end of the 1960s, while before that time their number was rather insignificant (B. Steinkemper 1974, p. 74 ff.). Incidentally, in a historical perspective this is not the first time that a significant number of outsiders has entered the top civil service; in the Weimar Republic the new government parties, and especially the Social Democratic party, sought in this way to "democratize" the civil service and to place some loyal partisans among the top bureaucrats. Especially the SPD had to resort to genuine outsiders, including even union officials or trusted party members without academic background because, as a consequence of previous political restrictions, it could not draw on a reservoir of partisans among civil servants (Runge 1965). These outsiders were later dismissed by Hitler on the grounds of lacking the proper educational requirements and/or lack of political (NS) reliability (Wunder 1977, p. 373).

Among outsiders, politics is the most important recruitment area (33 percent), followed by science and education (20 percent) and the economy (18 percent) (H. G. Steinkemper 1980, p. 110). In fact, the more the career pattern deviates from the normal civil service model, the more likely has party allegiance played a decisive role in recruitment to top positions. It is, therefore, significant that over two-thirds of the outsiders are members of a political party while the same is only true of 25 percent of the career civil servants in top positions (H. G. Steinkemper 1980, p. 124). With the increasing recruitment of outsiders the top civil service has thus become increasingly politicized. In this connection, rank plays a decisive role. While most state secretaries are members of a political party, this is only true of every second Ministerialdirektor (division chief). One level farther down, already 70 percent deny being members of a party. The difference is biggest, however, between the two topmost ranks, both of which belong to the category of political civil servants. Quite in line with this the vast majority of division chiefs deny that active participation in a political party was an important factor in their career, while state secretaries agree significantly more often that this has been the case (H. G. Steinkemper 1980, p. 116).

THE DISTINCTNESS OF ADMINISTRATIVE AND POLITICAL CAREERS

The recruitment pattern that emerges from these data so far shows that there is a tendency to select top officials according to criteria that increase their value and utility as ministerial aids. The institution of political civil servants makes this easier to achieve, but it does not have the effect of blocking top positions for regular civil servants by reserving them for outside entrants selected according to specifically political criteria. It is clear that the pressure to fill civil service positions on the basis of political considerations is strongest for the very top office of state secretary, but in general political considerations need not be narrowly party-political in nature or considerations aimed at the aggrandizement of the party. Political considerations may, in fact, make it seem wise to retain a patently nonparty member as official or even someone whose sympathies may lie with the opposition party. Not all top offices, especially at the divisional level, are politically sensitive to the same extent, and often expert experience or the good links to a particular clientele group will appear more important than party membership or partisan attitude. In fact, if only one-third of the outsiders, themselves a minority among top federal bureaucrats, have come from the political sector and if one-third of this group do not even avow political party membership, this indicates quite clearly that party allegiance is only one among several qualifying criteria that the political executive takes into consideration in selecting the closest collaborators.

If high-level cross-overs from politics into the federal bureaucracy are relatively rare, a career moving in the opposite direction—from administration into politics—is likewise exceptional. H. G. Steinkemper (1980, p. 79) reports that even of the state secretaries who held and left that office between 1949 and 1977 only 10 percent became ministers or members of Parliament; that quota should be significantly lower at the next levels, where fewer of the incumbents have strong party links to begin with. This weak career linkage between political leadership and top civil service is, however, often overlooked, clouded as it is by the statistical fact that about 40 percent of the federal MP's and nearly half of all members of regional parliaments are public servants (Hess 1976). The federal parliament in the period 1976–1980 counted for instance (Deutscher Bundestag, 1979)

- 10.3 percent members of the present and previous political executive (including parliamentary state secretaries),
- 30.5 percent civil servants, and
- 5.0 percent public service employees.

Historically, this strong parliamentary representation of the civil service is not new. When parliamentary institutions evolved in nineteenth-century Germany, the elite character of the higher civil service and its familiarity with the functions of governing provided rather strong motivations to candidates and voters alike, so that between 1848 and 1880 civil service representation in German parliaments was about as strong as it is today. This proportion decreased toward the end of the nineteenth century and continued to be relatively weak during the Weimar Republic, but rarely dropped below 20 percent (Hess 1976; Molt 1963; Ritter 1976). Throughout the history of German parliamentarism it has never been considered incompatible for a civil servant to engage in politics and to run for office. Of course civil servants elected to the federal Parliament today do not continue in their jobs. In 1953 it was stipulated by law that they had to go into temporary retirement for the time of their parliamentary office, continuing to draw pension pay, while since 1977 with the change of the former parliamentary allowance to what is effectively a substantial salary, duties *and* (pecuniary) rights of civil servants entering the federal Parliament become dormant. Only university professors still are a partial exception to this, since they may continue with at least part of their academic work and be remunerated accordingly (Evers 1980).

A closer look at the statistical data reveals, however, that at least today the civil servants in the federal Parliament are anything but a homogeneous block and that top bureaucrats in particular play only an insignificant role. Thus only one-third of the 30.5 percent civil servants in the federal Parliament are higher civil servants who have held positions in administration; only 0.6 percent belonged to the category of political civil servants (Deutscher Bundestag, 1979). Among the remaining 20 percent the largest contingent are university professors, schoolteachers, and other university personnel (10.6 percent all together). The proportion of higher civil servants and particularly of political civil servants in the federal Parliament has lately even been decreasing, while the group of teachers is growing steadily.

The significance of these figures comes out even more distinctly if it is recalled that a successful political career in the Federal Republic is typically started after having learned a first profession (Herzog 1975). The young lawyer, teacher, and so forth then become active in their local party organization and often stand at the local level for their first elective office. By the time they reach the federal Parliament, a good part of this group have turned into professional politicians and their ties to their first vocation have grown thin. Classifying the members of the 1957–1961 legislature into four big types (professional politicians, interest representatives, public servants, and part-time employees), Loewenberg (1969, p. 298) designates 24 percent of them as professional politicians and only 10 percent as public servants; since then, the first category, if anything, has further grown in proportion. Politics, that is to say, has become a career all of its own in the Federal Republic, and among the late and lateral entrants to this particular career top civil servants play only a rather unimportant role.

What is true of the federal Parliament also holds for the political executive: federal ministers are politicians, not bureaucrats. The career ladder of the higher civil service normally does not lead to a high political office. To aspire to the office of minister a civil servant would do better to renounce his civil service career and become a professional politician. Lange mentions that until 1972, the end of the period he surveys in his study, there has been only one case where a minister came to his office directly from a position in the bureaucracy (1973, p. 165). Looking, however, at the occupations of federal ministers between 1949 and 1969 *before* they became politicians, we find fully 26 percent of them had been civil servants in public administration (Lange 1973, p. 143). This pattern still holds today. Analyzing the ministers of the first socialist-liberal coalition, v. Beyme (1971, p. 269) characterizes two of them as politicians with an earlier career in administration, but the predominant trend is toward the complete predominance of professional politicians, with a supplementary tendency toward the selection of candidates with management experience in business and with a background in science (university professors).

Even if top civil servants rarely cross over into politics, this does not mean that they are immobile and normally wait to be retired either permanently or temporarily. In fact, of the one hundred state secretaries who held and left this office between 1949 and 1977, only twenty-eight were retired after having reached the age limit; another two had died. H. G. Steinkemper was also able to show that two-thirds of the political civil servants in federal government, and an equal portion of the whole group of top officeholders, mention specific job alternatives they see for themselves should they lose their present office (1980, pp. 97, 100). This is not at all illusionary. A civil servant leaving the service does not retain his pension rights, but the state buys him into the general old-age insurance scheme of the German welfare state. While this is usually not fully equivalent to the civil service pension he would have drawn, this arrangement assures at least that the loss of accumulated pension rights is no big barrier to outward mobility. The world of business (industry, commerce, finance) and free professional practice seem to offer the best job alternatives, given the fact that most top civil servants are trained in law and have often acquired useful contacts with the business world in their official capacity. In fact, H. G. Steinkemper reports that only a minority of 2.3 percent of top civil servants with perceived job alternatives see these in the field of politics, while business or industry and the liberal professions account for fully 45 percent (1980, p. 100). This again strongly supports the thesis that, for all the apparent politicization of higher civil servants, their career lines remain quite distinct from the political sector.

THE ATTITUDES OF FEDERAL CIVIL SERVANTS: TRADITIONAL OR POLITICAL BUREAUCRATS?

It is not surprising that the previously described recruitment tendency has a correlate at the level of attitudes and orientations, but care should be taken not to construct too close and simple a linkage between the growing importance of party membership and party allegiance for recruitment to top positions in the federal bureaucracy on the one hand and the attitudinal patterns to be described on the other hand. The important fact is that, irrespective of an increasing percentage of party members among federal bureaucrats, there is a general process of attitudinal change that holds for the civil service as a whole, including the lower service classes, and that is quite obviously to a large extent a generational phenomenon. This change process, described in more detail in Luhmann and Mayntz (1973, pp. 335–352), has two aspects. As far as the functional self-image of public personnel in their relations to the target groups of their work is concerned, the change might be described as a shift from the concept of "servant of the state" to "advocate of the public." Obviously this has a somewhat different meaning depending on the rank and functional position of the civil servants concerned. The attitude of lower-level civil servants is, for instance, characterized by a growing client orientation, which includes the willingness to have public control over administrative actions strengthened. Another aspect of this change is an increasing rejection of the traditional norm of neutrality and nonidentification with respect to the claims of special interest groups. At the higher levels of the civil service the changing functional self-image is well reflected in the fact that today only a minority of roughly 25 percent see the essence of their job in the enforcement or implementation of laws and only a similar minority still subscribe to the traditional norm of the civil servants' political neutrality. Thus in the study by Luhmann and Mayntz (1973, p. 348) 67 percent of the top group of civil servants rejected the statement that those who work in the public service must be willing not to act on their own political convictions and to identify with the intentions of the legal government. Nor did this statement find much more agreement at lower levels of the civil service, but age correlated strongly and consistently with this attitudinal factor. Higher civil servants at the level of the federal as well as the Länder governments seem to identify less with any specific government or minister than with something they define as general public interest. Perceiving themselves as advocates of public interest, they also feel fully legitimated to defend their own opinions and program proposals against the intentions of their minister or the government in power. The increasing political awareness and the increasing recognition of the political aspects of top bureaucratic roles support and reinforce the change in recruitment patterns, but are not directly and solely caused by it.

The second dimension of change in the orientation of public servants concerns their relation to the state as employer. Here the general trend of change can be described as an increasing employee-consciousness, that is, the consciousness of a special civil service status with its characteristic privileges and duties finds increasingly less support; and public servants, whether they are tenured civil servants or mere public employees, begin to conceive of themselves as just another category of the gainfully employed.

This general change in orientation, which is much more a generational effect than linked to specific positions or changes in recruitment pattern, can be described in more detail for the group of top civil servants in the federal bureaucracy on the basis of a number of attitude studies. The most important of these by virtue of its comparative character is Putnam's research (Putnam 1975). Using data from intensive interviews and questionnaire responses of top civil servants in several European countries, Putnam distinguished two polar types, the "classical bureaucrat" and the "political bureaucrat." While the classical bureaucrat corresponds roughly to the idealized stereotype of the Weberian (or the nineteenth-century Prussian) higher civil servant, the "political bureaucrat" is "both more aware of 'political realities' and more willing to treat political influences on policy-making as legitimate. He recognizes the need to bargain and compromise, yet at the same time he does not necessarily shrink from advocating and even fighting for his own preferred policies. Whereas the classical bureaucrat is 'procedure-oriented' or 'rule-oriented,' the political bureaucrat is 'problem-oriented' or 'program-oriented.' Whereas the classical bureaucrat views the politician as a troublesome or even dangerous antagonist, interfering with the efficiency and objectivity of government, the political bureaucrat sees the politician instead as a participant in a common game, one whose skills and immediate concerns may differ from his own, but whose ultimate values and objectives are similar" (Putnam 1975, p. 90). This ideal-typical characterization of a new self-image must strike anyone who has frequent contacts with top-level federal bureaucrats in Germany as a remarkably adequate description of the predominant type of orientation in this group. In fact, Putnam finds to his own considerable surprise that by and large his German respondents tend more toward the pole of the political than of the classical bureaucrat. He concludes that "top level civil servants in Germany in 1970 displayed great sensitivity to and support for the imperatives of politics in a democracy. By all the measures now available, they are hardly less egalitarian, hardly less liberal, hardly less politically responsive or programmatic in outlook than their British or Swedish counterparts" (1975, p. 113). Putnam's German respondents are, however, unique in another respect: His German sample is characterized by an unusual degree of attitudinal inhomogeneity. This is in turn related to a relatively inhomogeneous age composition, reflecting the discontinuities and disruptions caused in the German civil service by the Nazi regime and World War II. Putnam, too, has recognized that the political orientation of his German respondents is more related to age, and hence a generational effect, than to political party allegiance (1975, p. 115).

Corroborating evidence for the political orientation of top federal bureaucrats has been supplied by Peter Grottian (1972), who questioned seventy-two federal bureaucrats engaged in tasks of planning. Trying to summarize the attitudes of his sample, Grottian concludes that 22 percent of them are actively oriented toward structural change, with another 38 percent oriented toward structural modification, where these innovations involve, not only social reforms, but also administrative reforms. Only a small minority of 16 percent emerged as passively conservative in Grottian's study. In this research, too, it turns out that the more innovatively oriented planners are, not only more often members in a political party, but that they are characterized even more significantly by lower average age.

WORKING RELATIONS BETWEEN CIVIL SERVANTS AND POLITICIANS

From the discussion of career patterns it has emerged that the civil service sector and the political sector in the German federal government are clearly distinct. There is no blurring of recruitment patterns and career lines, no easy crossing-over between the two sectors. It is true that some professionally qualified party members have entered the federal bureaucracy as outsiders, as it is true that civil servants who have not yet reached top rank may enter upon a political career. But with the partial exception of the small group of state secretaries who have become most strongly politicized, top civil servants do not change sides and become members of the political executive. Nevertheless, it should not be denied that the distinctness of the two sectors that is highlighted here is, not only a matter of degree, but also of perspective. The distinctly bounded character of German top civil servants becomes most clearly visible in comparison to the American case described in this volume, while the distinctness of career lines emerges particularly in contrast to the French example.

It might still be asked whether the (relative) distinctness of the political and administrative sectors in the German federal government does not pose some problems. In terms of systems theory, the distinctiveness of functional subsystems is, of course, a necessary correlate of superior performance and hence functional rather than dysfunctional. Nevertheless, it creates the need for coordinative mechanisms as well as for internal structural adaptation at the subsystem level. Both phenomena can, in fact, be discovered in the German case.

The felt need for a special coordinative mechanism has probably found its clearest expression in the creation of the role of parliamentary state secretary in 1967. If most top civil servants can be characterized as political bureaucrats, this does not mean that they represent and bring to bear party-political views in the process of policy development and executive decision. The minister himself, on the other hand, is unable to do so single-handedly. The creation of the parliamentary state secretary is, therefore, a deliberate attempt to strengthen the political element in the executive and to intensify its relations to Parliament and the political parties (Laufer 1969). The parliamentary secretary serves as deputy to his minister in cabinet meetings and especially in Parliament, where he has, for instance, taken over the function of answering queries addressed to the department during question time, responded to formal parliamentary requests for information and even taken part in plenary debates (Wahl 1969, p. 334). The parliamentary secretary also helps to maintain closer contact with various party groups than the minister himself can (Fromme 1970). Finally he shares in the process of departmental management, where his specific function is to guide the work of the divisions and sections according to political criteria of importance and rationality.

As far as structural adaptation is concerned, the previous analysis has shown that there is no sharp break, no pronounced discontinuity in the characteristics and orientations of the various levels of top civil servants. Taken as a whole, the career patterns of political civil servants do not, for instance, differ significantly from that of other top federal bureaucrats, as H. G. Steinkemper's analysis was able to show (1980, p. 131 f.). Nevertheless, there are significant gradual differences between the succeeding ranks, and these reflect the different functional roles played by state secretaries, division heads, and section chiefs. As we move up these ranks, both the recruitment criteria and the orientation of the civil servants become more explicitly political. This corresponds to a parallel difference in the pattern of task distribution between these topmost levels of the bureaucracy. The nearer one gets to the top, the more do the generally political functions of conflict resolution, consensus building, the management of outside (extradepartmental) relations, and promotional work for the departments' programs dominate. At the lower levels, on the other hand, the normal tasks of program development, information gathering, drafting of proposals, and so forth assume increasing importance.

Just as there are gradual differences rather than a sharp break in the characteristics of the various ranks of higher civil servants, there is also no dichotomous split in the task structure. While generally political functions dominate at the very top and program development functions at the level of the sections, the divisional leadership plays an important mediating role between these levels. The divisional leadership is in direct day-to-day contact with the work going on in the sections. The mediating function of the divisional leadership has two aspects. On the one hand, it must transmit the general directives and political intentions of the departmental executive to the sections and see to it that their work is oriented accordingly. On the other hand, the divisional leadership must represent the views and proposals of the sections to the departmental executive and promote its projects in the interactive relations with other parts of the political-administrative system. Division chiefs may differ in the emphasis they put on the downward or the upward direction of this mediating function, but extreme cases of identification either with the sections versus the top executive or vice versa are rare. The function of mediating between the levels is an accepted characteristic of divisional leadership.

Among the various ranks of top civil servants, the state secretaries may today find it particularly difficult to arrive at a consistent role definition. State secretaries, though tenured civil servants, are the most highly politicized category in the federal bureaucracy. Their role is truly boundary-spanning. There is an obvious danger that this leads to a blurring of the distinction between the role of the tenured state secretary and that of the parliamentary secretary. Originally, the introduction of parliamentary secretaries was intended to relieve the state secretary of functions that do not correspond to the traditional role of a nonpartisan civil servant. However, the tenured state secretary, formally defined as a political civil servant, is increasingly being recruited from the outside and according to political criteria. As a consequence, and on the level of actual behavior, there is much variety in actual role performance and in the evolving patterns of task differentiation between the two types of state secretary (Mayntz & Scharpf 1975, pp. 87–89). Among the several roles that state secretaries can be found to play, one can be called the "administrator." The administrator acts as departmental manager with a heavy emphasis on personnel, organization, budgeting, and accounting functions. This role is played with preference by the few remaining nonpartisan, career civil servants who have advanced to this rank. The second role played by state secretaries is that of "professional expert" who engages actively in program development and has intensive, though somewhat selective, working contacts with those units in the department dealing with the subject matter the secretary is mainly interested in. This role is often preferred by professionals recruited from outside the career civil service; it is rarely played either by career bureaucrats or by parliamentary secretaries. The third possible role, that of "promoter," can be played by regular as well as parliamentary state secretaries. This role requires, not only political skills, but also some political power and is, therefore, no likely choice for a strictly nonpartisan civil servant. The promoter role shades easily into the fourth possibility, the role of "politician." This role "is played mostly by parliamentary secretaries, though by no means all of them could be thus classified. In the pure case, the 'politician' has little substantive interest in any particular policy field and little professional expertise. He is a generalized promoter, sponsoring projects which he expects to become political assets for his party or his minister, always intent to enhance the power position and slate of 'successes' of his party, his minister, and himself" (Mayntz & Scharpf 1975, p. 89). There usually develops some pattern of task differentiation between the regular and parliamentary state secretaries in a department. A typical and often fruitful combination is that between regular state secretaries playing the role of professional experts and a parliamentary secretary who combines the roles of promoter and politician.

Except for the true boundary-line role played by most state secretaries, the working relations of top federal bureaucrats with the political sector are selective in functional terms and—while of great importance for them—not very intensive in terms of the frequency of direct contact. To make this clear, let us first look at the interaction between civil servants and the political leadership within federal departments.

While each minister is formally responsible for all the activities of his department and can be called to account for them by the Parliament, he normally does not attempt to monitor all departmental activities himself. In fact, the sections, as the basic departmental operating units, are officially granted a certain degree of autonomy. The *Referent* as section chief is formally responsible for the substantive policy area assigned to his section. In German federal departments this assignment of tasks is explicit and detailed and pretends to be a comprehensive distribution of all functions that formally belong to the department's jurisdiction. While higher level departmental leaders have the authority to give specific orders to a section chief, this authority is generally expected to be used only as a type of management by exception. The section chief is expected to develop himself initiatives and proposals within his area of competence. This basically decentralized process of planning and policy development within the department is controlled by the departmental executive in three related ways: by giving—more ad hoc than systematic—general directives that can serve as guidelines within certain policy areas or call for specific proposals to be developed; by intervening ad hoc in ongoing program-development processes as these come to the executive's attention; and by making a final selection among proposals submitted for final endorsement. If the political executive decides to give a specific directive or to intervene ad hoc in the department's ongoing work, this means in every case a selective allocation of attention. The political executive is manifestly unable to control departmental activities comprehensively. The criteria according to which the executive allocates attention selectively have elsewhere been formulated as follows: "(1) Executive attention is allocated to politically controversial problems and to policy initiatives which are likely to trigger intense political conflict. (2) Executive attention is given to projects and proposals which serve the management of an acute crisis. (3) Selective attention is paid to the development of programs which are likely to receive wide publicity and to gain public acclaim. (4) Executive attention is given to issues which have provoked public criticism of the department and to cases where the department has bungled something visibly. (5) Attention must be given to matters brought forth by another cabinet member, a member of the executive's party group, or some other politically important person. (6) Finally, executives normally develop personal interest in specific matters or in some specified policy field; these interests are often biographically determined and channel executive attention selectively" (Mayntz & Scharpf 1975, p. 91). The operation of this pattern of selective attention grants a certain measure of autonomy to the department's working units, an area where top civil servants can work more or less undisturbed—even though the wall of this secluded area may unexpectedly break down. In general, this pattern of selective executive attention grants civil servants more scope for discretionary action where the political topicality of an issue is low.

Since leading federal bureaucrats enjoy using the effective power and influence that their position affords them, they try to avoid or at least minimize the occasions for executive intervention. From this results a tendency to develop preferably such initiatives and plans that, on account of their rather incremental and noncontroversial nature, are less likely to call the executive's attention and trigger intervention. To steer around the cliffs of executive attention is, in fact, a conscious strategy. However, this does not mean that top civil servants want to evade political control and push their own policy ideas even against expressed wishes of the political executive. Federal bureaucrats do not need the executive's attention and cooperation in program development, but they depend fully on them for subsequent endorsement and support. This never-forgotten dependence motivates federal bureaucrats to take, not only the executive's expressed wishes, but also the likely preferences and the constraints to which the executive's decisions are subject very seriously as guidelines for their every-day work. This complex relationship is quite well expressed in a passage from an interview quoted by Putnam (1975, p. 102):

> We are not here to receive orders, mentally to click our heels, and to say "Jawohl!"—that's not why we are here. On the contrary, if they (senior civil servants) have a different conception (of the problem)—and they should always have a political conception—they must, under certain circumstances, use their conception in conjunction with their expertise and simply say, "But I would propose thus and such for this reason." And if the Minister says, "No, politically we can't do that on account of

these reasons," then all right, it will be done as proposed [by the minister, R.M.]. It must be this way, because the Minister is the responsible official, who must have the last word. That can't be avoided.

The minister and Parliamentary state secretary are the most important contacts that federal bureaucrats have with the political sector. Even those federal civil servants who are members of one of the governing parties are usually not expected to function as go-between between party leaders and the bureaucracy. Their party contacts help them to assess the climate of opinion in party and Parliament and thus the likely reactions to given departmental proposals. But since their personal contacts with politicians will be normally of the lower level type (that is, not with the parliamentary party group's leadership, not with the party's executive board), expressed wishes and explicit proposals from the political sector to the bureaucracy will rather be transmitted through the departmental executive, state secretaries often included.

The most salient contacts of top civil servants with the federal Parliament take place in the framework of parliamentary committees and are connected with the need to get parliamentary approval for departmental proposals or projects, with defending budgetary claims, or with responding to parliamentary questions. The higher level civil servants are more concerned with direct parliamentary contacts than are section chiefs. Even though not all departmental projects must take the hurdle of parliamentary approval, and even though in these cases other and possibly more difficult hurdles (like that of cabinet approval) must be taken first, federal bureaucrats seem to work in full consciousness of the existence, if not always of the precise nature, of political restrictions impinging upon the eventual success of their projects. Since they actively try to discern the relevant restrictions that circumscribe their own scope for action, the relatively low frequency of direct parliamentary contacts does not imply that this is an unimportant relationship.

If one were to analyze the federal bureaucrat's pattern of personal contacts in detail, one would probably find that political contacts are less important than either extradepartmental contacts with other civil servants (mainly from the federal, but also from the regional level), and nonpolitical external contacts with client groups, interest representatives, scientific advisors, and government-supported institutions of a nonadministrative kind (including research institutes). The same large elite survey on which H. G. Steinkemper and B. Steinkemper based their analyses also supplied some information about the nonpolitical outside contacts of top federal bureaucrats. The scope of these contacts is less impressive than their intensity. The respondents reported an average of 2.5 different outside sectors with which they had direct personal contact.[6] The pattern of sectoral contacts proved to be rather similar to that of the political elite, where labor unions, the churches, and economic organizations (including large corporations and banks) dominate, while contacts with the agricultural, social welfare, and scientific-educational sectors are weaker in comparison (Neumann 1979, p. 71 f.) The network of nonpolitical outside contacts supplies an important part of work-related information to the federal bureaucrats. In addition it should be mentioned that a vast majority of the many existing governmental advisory committees are structurally located at the divisional or even section level of the departments and that in this context less formal, often bilateral, contacts with interest representatives and advisors also take place.

This system of external working relationships is reinforced by a number of more formal links that top bureaucrats have with other sectors in society. To begin with, about two-thirds of the top federal bureaucrats report at least one membership in some nonpolitical organization (Neumann 1979, p. 124 ff.). Moreover, 47 percent of the federal top officeholders analyzed by H. G. Steinkemper (1980, p. 102) mentioned holding one or more offices—sometimes honorary, but often remunerated—outside of the civil service. It is significant, but, after what has been said so far, no longer surprising, that only 6.5 percent of these additional offices are in politics (typically some office in the party organization), while functions in science and in industry or business clearly predominate. As far as positional links with the economic sector are concerned, governing board positions in public corporations or state-controlled enterprises seem to account for a good part of them; in fact, as Neumann (1979, p. 111) points out, civil servants must accept such assignments as part of their official duties. This interpretation is supported by the fact that outsiders do not differ significantly from traditional career bureaucrats in holding such positions (B. Steinkemper 1974, p. 87). Often, however, it will be difficult to tell whether holding a given office is the civil servant's private affair and important because it affects his income and career alternatives, or whether the information, knowledge, and chances to exert influence afforded by it are of importance for his work in the bureaucracy; in fact, one does not really exclude the other. In any case, the intensive involvement of higher civil servants with other sectors of the society both in their work roles and beyond them is an important structural feature of the German civil service elite.

This fact is also reflected in the way the administrative elite is perceived by other social groups. About 80 percent of the respondents in the elite survey previously mentioned who did not themselves belong to the political-administrative system reported having personal contacts with the federal bureaucracy, while 50 percent of all respondents ranked the administration in the two top groups of a scale to assess the importance of different information sources (B. Steinkemper 1974, p. 93 f.). Though closely followed by the Länder bureaucracies, the federal bureaucracy proved to be the dominant political access point for organized interests, more important than the federal and Länder legislatures and political party organizations (Neumann 1979, p. 63 f.). Considering this fact together with the information on personal contacts, memberships, and outside offices of bureaucrats, one has to agree with Neumann, who concludes that federal and Länder bureaucracies occupy clearly the dominant position in the communication network linking the political system to the other subsystems of German society (1979, p. 132). While this does not recover for the top civil service the ruling elite status it enjoyed more than one hundred years ago, it does show that high federal bureaucrats are a functional elite of considerable weight in the political process. Their influence is curbed, however, by the fact that in the context of Germany's federal constitution it is largely limited to policy *development* and does not extend to program management and execution.

In conclusion, the question might be raised in whose interest this elite wields such influence as it has, though, by implication, the answer should already have emerged from the foregoing analysis. It is clear that the top ranks of the civil service cannot be considered the extended arm of political party organizations. Not only are politicians and top bureaucrats clearly distinct groups in terms of formal position and career lines; it is also necessary to understand correctly the very special nature of the increasingly "political" orientation of higher civil servants. There remains a basic divergence of outlook between politicians and bureaucrats that defines "political" in a different way for both. To overstate the case a bit, the top bureaucrat is political in the sense of being policy- or program-oriented: he knows that his job is in policy development, and he is fully aware of the power implications of this process. Conflict resolution, negotiation, and consensus building, therefore, form an integral part of his job. He identifies with program and policy proposals and wants them to be successful and does what he can to assure their success. The politician, on the other hand, is power-oriented rather than policy-oriented, he identifies strongly with a specific social group, such as his party or some wing or faction within it, with his party leaders, a given government or chancellor. If the chips are down, he will give up supporting a given policy proposal if this gets in the way of the short-term or long-term interest of the government or party.

The program orientation of high civil servants and the career orientation linked to it are reinforced by the previously mentioned lack of cohesion and homogeneity among high civil servants as a group. Neither their academic training nor their preparation for public service has established close personal ties and a common outlook among top bureaucrats. The fact that careers do not often cross departmental lines, and the strong generational differences in general outlook work in the same direction. In the absence of a homogeneously socialized group to identify with, departmental policies and one's own career provide the most likely alternatives as personal reference points. This means that the higher civil service, instead of sharing and jointly promoting the collective interest of any particular social class or group, reflects the full range of diverse and often conflicting interests that are organizationally represented in the departments and departmental divisions of the federal bureaucracy. Intensive outside contacts of a relatively limited sectoral scope reinforce this pattern of orientation: departmental identification and sectoral or client orientation complement each other.

The preceding analysis has shown that while high German civil servants in central government play a crucial role in policy development and planning, it cannot be said that in doing so they have escaped political control. Interestingly enough, however, the effectiveness of political control seems to rest less in the political sector's stability and cohesion—though this, too, may play a certain role—but in the willingness of high bureaucrats, oriented at the success of their programs and proposals, to take political constraints seriously, to anticipate them correctly and to avoid conflict and confrontation with those in a strategically superior position. However, the same pattern of orientation and behavior that assures the primacy of politics, tends to generate policy proposals and programs that are incremental in nature, cautious in scope, and coordinated down to the lowest common denominator.

NOTES

1. Armstrong (1973) seems to miss the point of an important change in the influence, position and attitude of Prussian officials in his comparative analysis of the interventionist or noninterventionist attitude of higher civil servants vis-à-vis economic development, partly due to his choice of examples.

2. The higher civil service includes three further ranks below that of Ministerialrat, but by virtue of their rank and normal functional position, these will not be considered as part of the top civil servants.

3. Bundeshaushaltsplan für das Haushaltsjahr 1980, Bonn, S. 52–55. The respective figures of the Federal Department for the Postal Services and Telecommunication, which are not included in the federal budget, were added on the basis of the entries in: *Die Bundesrepublik Deutschland. Staatshandbuch Teilausgabe*

Bund, edited by E. Schiffer (Federal Department of the Interior), Carl Heymann, Köln/Berlin 1980, pp. 390–392.

4. This figure was 111,184 in June 1979; it does not include the armed services, the Federal Railroad, and the Federal Postal Services; see Wirtschaft und Statistik 11/1979, Statistisches Bundesamt Wiesbaden, p. 815.

5. For a review of the practice of temporary retirement which is based on more complete and recent data, see Renate Mayntz, "The Political Role of the Higher Civil Service in the German Federal Government," in Bruce L. R. Smith (ed.), *The Higher Civil Service in Europe: Lessons for the United States* (Washington, D.C.: The Brookings Institution, 1984); Hans-Ulrich Derlien, *The Politicization of the Civil Service in the Federal Republic of Germany: Facts and Fables* (Verwaltungswissenschaftliche Beiträge Nr. 15, Universität Bamberg, 1984).

6. The sectors covered were: industrial corporations and banks, industrial and business associations, agriculture unions, professional associations, churches, education and scientific institutions, voluntary associations with social welfare and common interest goals.

BIBLIOGRAPHY

Armstrong, John A. *The European Administrative Elite.* Princeton: Princeton University Press, 1973.

Beyme, Klaus v. "Regierungswechsel 1969: Zum Wandel der Karrieremuster der politischen Führung," in Gerhard Lehmbruch et al., *Demokratisches System und politische Praxis der Bundesrepublik.* München: Piper Verlag, 1971.

Brandt, E., ed. *Die politische Treuepflicht: Motive, Texte, Materialien.* Karlsruhe/Heidelberg, 1976.

Breuckmann, Elmar. *Die Vorbereitung auf den höheren Verwaltungsdienst; Schriftenreihe der Hochschule Speyer,* vol. 28. Berlin: Duncker & Humblot, 1965.

Deutscher Bundestag, ed. *30 Jahre Deutscher Bundestag: Dokumente, Statistik, Daten.* Bearb. v. Peter Schindler, Bonn, 1979.

Dogan, Mattei, ed. *The Mandarins of Western Europe: The Political Role of Top Civil Servants.* New York: John Wiley, 1975.

Dunsire, Andrew. *Administration: The Word and the Sciences.* London: Martin Robertson, 1973.

Dyson, Kenneth. "Die Westdeutsche 'Parteibuch'—Verwaltung," *Die Verwaltung* 12 (1979) 2, pp. 129–160 (translation of: "The West German 'Party-Book' Administration: An Evaluation," *Public Administration Bulletin* no. 25, December 1977, p. 3ff.).

Echtler, Ulrich. *Einfluß und Macht in der Politik: Der beamtete Staatssekretär.* München: Goldmann Verlag, 1973.

Eisenstadt, S. N. "Bureaucracy and Bureaucratization: A Trend Report." *Current Sociology* 7, no. 2 (1958).

Evers, Hans-Ulrich. *Professorenamt und Abgeordnetenmandat, Mitteilungen des Hochschulverbandes,* vol. 28 (1980), pp. 297–300.

Fenske, Hans. "Monarchisches Beamtentum und demokratischer Staat: Zum Problem der Bürokratie in der Weimarer Republik." *Demokratie und Verwaltung: 25 Jahre Hochschule für Verwaltungswissenschaften Speyer.* Berlin: 1972.

————. "Preussische Beamtenpolitik vor 1918." *Der Staat* 12 (1973), 339–356.

Ferraresi, Franco. "Modalità di intervento politico della burocrazia in Italia." *Studi di Sociologia* VI (1968), 228–273.

Fromme, Friedrich Karl. "Die Parlamentarischen Staatssekretäre." *Zeitschrift für Parlamentsfragen* 1 (1970), 53–83.

Frowein, Jochen. *Die politische Betätigung des Beamten.* Tübingen: J. C. B. Mohr/Paul Siebeck, 1967.

Gillis, John R. *The Prussian Bureaucracy in Crisis (1840–1860).* Stanford, Calif.: Stanford University Press, 1971.

Grottian, Peter. "Zum Planungsbewußtsein der Bonner Ministerialorganisation." *Politische Vierteljahresschrift, Sonderheft* 4 (1972), 127–152.

Headey, Bruce. "The Civil Service as an Elite in Britain and Germany." *International Review of Administrative Sciences* 38 (1972), 41–48.

Herzog, Dietrich. *Politische Karrieren: Selektion und Professionalisierung politischer Führungsgruppen.* Opladen: Westdeutscher Verlag, 1975.

Hess, Adalbert. "Statistische Daten und Trends zur 'Verbeamtung der Parlamente' in Bund und Ländern." *Zeitschrift für Parlamentsfragen* 7 (1976), 34–39.

Kugele, Dieter. *Der politische Beamte: Eine Studie über Genesis, Motiv, Bewährung und Reform einer politisch-administrativen Institution.* München: Tuduv-Verlagsgesellschaft, 1976).

Lange, Rolf-Peter. "Auslesestrukturen bei der Besetzung von Regierungsämtern," in J. Dittberner, R. Ebbighausen, eds., *Parteiensysteme in der Legitimationskrise.* Opladen: Westdeutscher Verlag, 1973.

Laufer, Heinz. *Der Parlamentarische Staatssekretär: Eine Studie über ein neues Amt in der Bundesregierung.* München: Beck Verlag, 1969.

Loewenberg, Gerhard. *Parlamentarismus im politischen System der Bundesrepublik Deutschland.* Tübingen: Rainer Wunderlich Verlag, 1979.

Luhmann, Niklas und Mayntz, Renate. *Personal im öffentlichen Dienst: Eintritt und Karrieren.* Baden-Baden: Nomos Verlagsgesellschaft, 1973.

Mayntz, Renate und Scharpf, Fritz W. *Policy-Making in the German Federal Buraucracy.* Amsterdam/Oxford/New York: Elsevier Verlag, 1975.

Molt, Peter. *Der Reichstag vor der improvisierten Revolution.* Köln/Opladen, 1963, Tab. IV, p. 78.

Morsey, Rudolf. "Zur Beamtenpolitik des Reiches von Bismarck bis Brüning," in *Demokratie und Verwaltung: 25 Jahre Hochschule für Verwaltungswissenschaften Speyer.* Berlin: 1972.

————. "Personal- und Beamtenpolitik im Übergang von der Bizonen- zur Bundesverwaltung (1947–1950)," in R. Morsey, ed., *Verwaltungsgeschichte, Schriften der Hochschule Speyer*, vol. 66. Berlin: 1977.

Most, Otto. "Zur Wirtschafts- und Sozialstatistik der höheren Beamten in Preussen." *Schmollers Jahrbuch für Gesetzgebung, Verwaltung und Volkswirtschaft*, Jg. 39 (1915), pp. 181–218.

Neumann, Helga. *Zur Machtstruktur in der Bundesrepublik Deutschland*. Melle: Ernst Knoth, 1979.

Putnam, Robert D. "The Political Attitudes of Senior Civil Servants in Britain, Germany, and Italy," in M. Dogan, ed., *The Mandarins of Western Europe*. New York: John Wiley, 1975, pp. 87–127.

Reinke, Herbert. "Bürokratie im politischen System Deutschlands," Diss. Köln, 1979.

Rejewski, Harro-Jürgen. *Die Pflicht zur politischen Treue im preussischen Beamtenrecht (1850–1918)*. Berlin: Duncker & Humblot, 1973.

Ritter, Gerhard A. "Entwicklungsprobleme des deutschen Parlamentarismus," in ders., *Arbeiterbewegung, Parteien und Parlamentarismus*. Göttingen, 1976, p. 158.

Runge, Wolfgang. *Politik und Beamtentum im Parteienstaat: Die Demokratisierung der politischen Beamten in Preussen zwischen 1918 und 1933*. Stuttgart: Klett, 1965.

Seemann, Klaus. "Die Politisierung der Ministerialbürokratie in der Parteiendemokratie als Problem der Regierbarkeit." *Die Verwaltung*, vol. 13 (1980), Heft 2, pp. 137–156.

Steinkemper, Bärbel. *Klassische und politische Bürokraten in der Ministerialverwaltung der Bundesrepublik Deutschland*. Köln: Carl Heymanns Verlag, 1974.

Steinkemper, Hans-Günter. *Amtsträger im Grenzbereich zwischen Regierung und Verwaltung: Ein Beitrag zur Problematik der Institution des politischen Beamten in der Bundesexekutive*. Frankfurt/Main: Peter D. Lang, 1980.

Wahl, Rainer. "Die Weiterentwicklung der Institution des parlamentarischen Staatssekretärs." *Der Staat*, vol. 8 (1969), pp. 327–348.

Weber, Max. *Wirtschaft und Gesellschaft*. Köln/Berlin: Kiepenheuer & Witsch, 1964.

Wunder, Bernd. "Die Rekrutierung der Beamtenschaft in Deutschland." *Leviathan* (Jg. 1977), no. 3, 360–377.

TOP CIVIL SERVANTS IN NORWAY

Key Players—on Different Teams

Per Lægreid and
Johan P. Olsen

PRELIMINARY CONCLUSION

In Norway, top civil servants are key participants in public policy-making processes. They are not acquiescing instruments for arbitrary intervention by elected political leaders or social groups. Nor have they usurped all power and created a "dictatorship of the bureaucrats."[1] Rather, top civil servants act within institutionalized networks of organized public and private interests. The ways in which influence is achieved and exercised depend upon these intra- and interorganizational networks and the coalitions built within them. Their views are formed by the tasks they are responsible for, by the institutions and the professions

The authors want to thank the participants in the Madrid Conference on the Role of Higher Civil Servants in Central Governments, and Morten Egeberg, Dick Elmore, Donald Matthews, Reidun Tvedt, and Mariann Vågenes for their help and support.

to which they belong, and by the parts of the environment they interact with. Thus top civil servants seldom act as a unitary group. They share a policy-making style, but they differ in terms of the causes, values, and social groups they defend. They play on different teams, and when conflicts arise they take sides in predictable ways. Yet, policy making is characterized more by compromise than by confrontation. Analysis, anticipated reaction, persuasion, and bargaining are more frequent than force, commands, and rules.

TOP CIVIL SERVANTS AS LEADERS OF ORGANIZATIONS

Max Weber considered bureaucratization the most significant feature of the modern Western state, and he predicted a continuing spread of bureaucratic administration. Fully developed, that would mean an office hierarchy, with the means of administration concentrated in the hands of one master—a social structure very hard to destroy.[2]

For the most part, public administration in Norway is formally bureaucratic. Yet, the world of most top civil servants differs in many ways from a weberian ideal bureaucracy.

There are many interpretations of how a modern administrative apparatus works. Some locate power to the political institutions, assuming that top civil servants are responsible to and totally subordinated to Parliament or the cabinet. Others emphasize social power, viewing civil servants (as well as elected politicians) as the instruments of a ruling class, powerful organized interest groups, the mass media, or of impersonal technological, economic, demographic, or cultural forces. For smaller countries especially, such forces are often located outside national boundaries.

An alternative emphasizes bureaucratic immunity from political and social intervention. If power is located in the administrative apparatus itself, top civil servants may act as a unitary elite, as leaders of petty kingdoms with considerable autonomy, or as rivals in permanent conflicts over administrative territory and jurisdiction. Power may also disseminate to the lower ranks of the hierarchies. Top civil servants, like elected politicians, may be overwhelmed by the expanding public agenda, and depend on their subordinates' willingness to cooperate. The more comprehensive and complex the public agenda, the more expertise, information and real decision-making power accrue to the lower echelons of the central administration, or to local and regional units that implement central decisions.

We believe each of these perspectives captures some aspect of the public policy-making process and of the role of top civil servants. Their

TABLE 1. Central Government Employees by Service Group and Salary Grade. Full-time Employees 1978

SALARY GRADE	MINISTRIES	OTHER CENTRAL ADMINISTRATIVE AGENCIES	OTHER CIVIL SERVICE	UNIVERSITIES AND THE LIKE	GOVERNMENTAL ENTERPRISES	DEFENSE	HEALTH SERVICES	TOTAL
1–14	590	2,817	12,541	3,516	39,327	11,652	4,358	74,801
15–18	431	1,702	9,385	2,490	12,519	4,609	1,524	32,660
19–25	1,102	3,600	8,205	4,241	3,790	6,579	1,308	28,825
26–30	492	844	795	1,118	354	468	396	4,967
31–35	126	79	169	19	22	42	63	520
TOTAL	2,741	9,042	31,095	11,884	56,012	23,350	7,649	141,773

Source: Wage and employment statistics for central government employees. Central Bureau of Statistics, Oslo. NOS B 32.

perceptions, attitudes, behavior, and influence emerge from rather complex intra- and interorganizational processes that cannot be adequately captured by concepts of total autonomy or subordination.

Under what conditions will the criteria laid down at the top of an organization, or by outsiders, actually govern the thinking or behavior of the employees who make the day-to-day decisions or provide services?[3] Under what conditions will public decisions be accepted by the groups involved, or by society at large?

Top civil servants are leaders of organizations operating in an environment primarily populated by other organizations. We are interested in how their thinking and behavior are influenced by the organizations they head, by the environment they face, and by their social background. Furthermore, we consider how these factors affect their ability to form and give direction to their organizations and to society. We need to understand which resources top civil servants have of their own, as well as the extent to which they are backed by a nesting of reserve sources of authority and power.[4]

By *top civil servants* we mean the top administrative positions in the ministries: secretary general, director general, and assistant director general. In 1978 these amounted to 126 persons (table 1). Together with deputy directors general and heads of division (492 persons) they constitute the "administrators." The term *civil servants* also includes executive officers in the ministries (grades 19–25). Civil servants outside the ministries are only included under certain circumstances. The same applies to the political leadership of the ministries.

While we observe some tendencies that are inconsistent with Weber's prediction of a universal bureaucratization, he provided a framework for studying actual administrative development. Particularily useful is his treatment of how the thinking, behavior, and influence of civil servants is affected by *the organization of careers, expertise, and authority.*

First, we consider the degree to which careers of civil servants—recruitment, promotion, and departures—are controlled from within the administrative apparatus or by groups or forces in the political or social system. Second, we analyze the extent to which top civil servants monopolize expertise and information, whether secrecy is an available resource, and which factors affect their beliefs and attitudes. Finally, we analyze the role of authority. To what extent is everyday life of top civil servants governed by an impersonal and legitimate order of authority—shared understandings of the rights to command and the duty to obey? Or, does the concept of interest coalitions better portray how top civil servants relate to each other, to their subordinates, to politicians, clients, and to other social groups?

To provide a perspective for this discussion, we will provide a brief account of the roots of the present system.

THE ROOTS: A CIVIL SERVANTS' STATE PAR EXCELLENCE

In 1814 the Danish-Norwegian union was dissolved, a new Norwegian state was founded, and a new Swedish-Norwegian union established, all in a matter of months.

These events remind us how a small nation is subjected to events beyond its control—in this case the defeat of Napoleon. At the same time they illustrate the robustness of an administrative system in the face of external turbulence. The civil service continued to function—bolstered by its deep roots in the Danish-Norwegian absolute monarchy. Norway was a typical civil servants' state for two hundred years—from 1680 to 1880, probably more so than any other state in Europe. The historian Sverre Steen aptly describes this by stating that, prior to 1814, the civil servants governed the country in the name of the king. After 1814 the same men governed in the name of the people.[5]

The position of Norwegian civil servants during the first half of the eighteenth century is typified by their irremovability and protected careers, their professional qualities, their unity, and the absence of competing political and socioeconomic elites.

The king and his court were far away in Stockholm. There was little or no nobility. The bourgeoisie was weakly developed. Norway was primarily a nation of small-holders. In other words, the social elites that dominated most other countries did not challenge the hegemony of civil servants in Norway. Potential rivals also lacked adequate political organization. Organized political activity and campaigning were prohibited by law in 1828. There were few interest organizations, and the prevailing ideology was that special interests were disqualified from participation in public policy making.

The cabinet was generally an integrated part of a civil service career (table 2). Unlike in most other countries, civil servants dominated the *Storting* (Parliament). The Constitution of 1814 was their creation, and they wrote into it extensive protection for the civil service. The risk of losing office was slight indeed. The recruitment process was virtually closed, and civil servants developed a life-style quite different from that of the nation they governed. They were closely knit by a common Danish-European culture; by a common higher education—primarily in law; by the Latin language; by a considerable professional self-confidence; and by extensive intermarriage. Their ideology came close to what Weber later labeled an ideal bureaucracy operating under legal-rational authority. The main task of civil servants was seen as the implementation of enacted rules—to find the proper solution and to guard the public interest, unhampered by arbitrary outside pressure. The role model was the objective and impartial judge, and their primary loyalty was toward an impersonal system of laws.

TABLE 2.   Ministers, 1814–1978, by Occupational Background and Time Periods (Percentages)

OCCUPATIONAL BACKGROUND	1814–1884	1884–1920	1920–1945	1945–1978	TOTAL
(Public) administrators	84	58	31	31	48
Other public employees	1	11	16	18	12
Private employees	0	1	7	18	4
Business/liberal professions	13	21	27	19	20
Farmers	1	9	18	8	9
Manual workers, fishermen, others	0	0	1	6	3
Numbers	(70)	(114)	(77)	(129)	(390)

Source: The Norwegian Social Science Data Services.

The political environment has since changed considerably. There has been a general tendency toward political mobilization and reduced political illiteracy, as well as cycles of dispersion and concentration of political power. In periods of power concentration, political authorities gather initiative and responsibility in their own hands. They emphasize that the role of civil servants is to be reliable instruments for the exercise of political power. In periods of power dispersion, initiative and responsibility are spread. Civil servants are encouraged to be active and independent.[6] Such cycles are related to the level of political conflict in society. In periods of little conflict the administrative apparatus routinely handles problems in a predictable and—for the governing coalition—acceptable way. Imbalances between administrative routines and the demands/interests of leading political and social groups tend to set off demands for political power concentration. Then the criteria for recruiting to the civil service are discussed. The definition of expertise and the relevance of various types of knowledge are debated, and attempts are made to change the formal authority.

The interplay between political mobilization and the growth of the public sector has a long history. From the 1840s new services, new professions, new agencies, and new clientele relations were introduced—often in conflict with the established bureaucratic tradition. Thus, the increased number of civil servants and the growing indispensability of their services did not automatically increase their power. The main tendency was toward a more heterogenous civil service—an administrative apparatus where internal conflicts could occur. And they did. Conflicts between "bureaucrats" or generalists—trained in law and located in the ministries, and specialists trained in various disiplines and often located in new agencies outside the ministries—illustrate the classical conflict between the needs for hierarchical coordination and technical sector expertise.

The traditional rule-orientation was challenged by an increased interest in the consequences of administrative intervention. More often than previously expertise and information were located at the lower levels of the hierarchy. Top civil servants had difficulties comprehending and controlling the activities of their subordinates. Rules of competence and authority became more vague and open. In sum, an expanding public agenda moved real decision making downward in the administrative hierarchy.[7]

This expansion took place alongside demands for participation in public policy making from groups that discovered that the state could be used for material or professional development. As subjects became citizens, the old bureaucratic rule, that any group with a special interest in a decision was disqualified, was challenged. Gradually it was replaced by the idea that democracy would benefit from the participation of those affected by public policies.[8]

The result is that the administrative apparatus consists of layers of agencies established to deal with problems in terms of specific values, goals, and technologies. The original intentions are reflected in the recruitment patterns, in the definitions of expertise, and in the distribution of authority, which are often institutionalized and internalized. A consequence is a reduced ability to learn and adapt. It is difficult to transform an agency even when situations change and the consequences of established routines are quite different from what was intended or expected. It is even harder to dissolve an agency, and it is nearly impossible to discontinue functions and services. In Norway the standard procedure has been to move tasks and offices around.[9] Professions, political and social groups who have occupied a niche are difficult to drive out.

Consequently the analysis of the impact of intra- and interorganizational networks on the thinking and behavior of top civil servants should be supplemented by an archeological perspective. Structures, procedures, and rules are formed by their "time of birth" and specific historical context.[10]

After World War II there was a restoration of the civil service to considerable prestige and influence, and a willingness to spread authority, initiative, and responsibility.[11] This trend rested on a fairly widespread political consensus; the country had to be rebuilt, and it could best be achieved through economic growth and class cooperation. Organized interests, and especially the economic producers' groups, became integrated in governmental policy making.[12] At the same time there were new aspirations for planning and governance.[13] These aspirations originated from the Labor party, out of office for only seven years since 1935, and from the economics profession. Planning agencies were set up in the ministries, and the economists emerged as the new generalists of the civil service. "We could not get enough of them," a former prime minister, minister of finance, and chairman of the Labor party once said.[14]

Political consensus and cooperation contributed to a steady economic growth and to slack resources. Throughout the "confident 60's" responses to new problems often involved establishing new institutions. Lately the growth has leveled off—in spite of oil money from the North Sea. Labor party majority governments have been succeeded by minority or coalition cabinets. The merits of economic growth are increasingly questioned, and the confidence in economic theory and macroplanning as the major instrument of governance is reduced. More organized interests demand participation, and a rising level of education increases the political capabilities of the average citizen. We want to indicate the bearings of these changes on the functioning of higher civil servants by going into more detail about the organization of careers, expertise, and authority.

ORGANIZATION OF CAREERS

Theories of bureaucracy describe promotions as a major mechanism of motivation and control. The disciplining effect will be the most effective if: employees see their lives as organized into a lifelong career—a succession of promotions; superiors have promotions to allocate; subordinates want to be promoted; there is a close connection between promotion and previous performance; and subordinates are aware of such connections.[15] If objective criteria of merit exist, the appointing authorities will be bookkeepers of necessity. If there are no such set standards, we need to know who defines merit and who judges individual merit. These theories are highly relevant because the careers of higher civil servants in Norway deviate little from those in the weberian ideal bureaucracy.

A dominant norm is recruitment based on merit—traditionally university achievement. Except for the diplomatic corps, the civil service does not provide special education or examinations.

Only 6 percent of the administrators in the ministries have no university degree. For top civil servants a degree is required (with a few exceptions) by law. Training in law has dominated: in 1884 95 percent of administrators held a law degree, the figure for 1914 was 67 percent, and 52 percent for 1976. Twenty-one percent of ministry administrators hold a degree in economics. The rest are trained in agriculture, philology, science, social science, medicine, or they have military training. Thus, while the lawyers are still the largest group, the trend is toward professional differentiation. This tendency is even stronger in the central agencies outside the ministries. Here engineers dominate, with 41 percent with a university degree. The role of jurists is proportionally reduced.[16]

A result of the close ties between recruitment and university degrees is a civil service highly unrepresentative of the population as a whole. The pattern is well known—an overrepresentation of males born in the geographical center and in higher social strata.[17] Yet, the emphasis on merit has not produced a civil service like the one Weber expected—detached anonymous bureaucrats isolated from political life. On the average, civil servants engage more in political parties, interest organizations, and other activities than does the population. Can such civil servants be disciplined through career control? If so, by whom?

Potential for discipline. Norwegian ministries have a great *potential* for discipline through promotions. The main pattern is recruitment of young people to the bottom of the hierarchy, of which a majority expect to pursue a career within the ministry. Of the top civil servants (1976), 44 percent had been recruited before the age of thirty. Only 8 percent were forty-six years or older, and the average recruitment age was thirty-two years. Sixty-one percent started at the junior executive level. Among the top civil servants who resigned in the period 1970–1974, 81 percent had been employed in the ministries for more than twenty years.

The organizational form of the ministries, in terms of the number of positions at various hierarchical levels, is also pertinent to the career potential with respect to internal promotions. Interministerial mobility is low. In the period 1970–1974 only 7 percent of the civil servants moved from one ministry to another. However, such moves seem more common among administrators. Of the top civil servants appointed in this period 55 percent were recruited from their own ministry, while 24 percent came from other ministries, among which the Ministry of Finance is an important supplier. The rest came from central government agencies outside the ministries or other civil services. Horizontal (outside) recruitment to top positions is rather rare, and usually occurs from proximate state institutions. Ninety percent of the civil servants in the ministries have lived in the capital for most of their occupational career. In general, the mobility between the public and the private sector is insignificant. The interaction between top civil servants and organized interests in society has not resulted in personnel mobility and cooptation.[18] Civil servants do not want to move, or outside job offers are few (table 3).

The result is that civil servants realistically perceive their career opportunities as better inside than outside the ministries, and better in the public than in the private sector. In the ministries, civil servants are frequently rewarded, and the system of stepwise promotions makes the

TABLE 3.   Indicators of the Potential for Disciplination and Socialization in the Ministries

(a)	Number of executive officers/heads of division	2.2
(b)	Number of heads of division and deputy directors/secretaries general and directors general	3.7
(c)	Top civil servants recruited from outside (1970–74)	11%
(d)	Average service as administrators (for those who left the ministries 1970–74)	8 years
(e)	Average no. of years till retirement for top civil servants	12 "
(f)	Plan/wish to leave the ministries:	
	top civil servants	6%
	other administrators	21%
	executives	30%
(g)	Job offers from outside last year:	
	top civil servants	21%
	other administrators	25%
	executives	25%
(h)	Job offers received *and* plan/wish to leave:	
	top civil servants	2%
	other administrators	8%
	executives	10%
(i)	Average time of service, civil servants	13 years
(j)	Percentage of civil servants with 10 years or more of service	49%
(k)	Average time between promotions (1970–74)	4 years
(l)	Number of veterans/newcomers 1970–74)	6
(m)	Replacement of new personnel (personnel recruited 1970–74) who left within three years in percentage of average intake of personnel during a three-year period)	47%

Source: Based on Lægreid and Olsen, *Byrakerabi*.

road to the top long and time-consuming. Hence people occupy top positions for fairly short periods of time, a fact that further increases the disciplining potential.

The potential for discipline is high and it is used to reward insiders. But do civil servants want to be promoted? The folklore is that promotions are less attractive than before because leaders are subjected to more constraints and stress. So far, however, there are few data supporting this argument, and we assume that promotions still are attractive. Do civil servants then see any connection between performance and promotion? Who or what controls the process of promotions?

Recruitment is based on written applications and interviews. The formal procedure is that administrators are appointed by the cabinet after nomination by the minister, who is advised by the top civil servants. Executives are appointed by the minister after nomination by a board where the employees have two representatives (an arrangement that has been in operation since World War II). Decisions may be appealed to the Storting. This happens very seldom and almost never with any success. The Storting has defined its role as controlling the adherence to formal rules.[19]

This reflects a tradition of decentralized control over recruitment, which the ministries have fought fiercely to retain since 1814.[20] For a long time, only low-level positions were publicly advertised, and public announcement of top positions was written into the rules as late as 1953. Yet the trend has been toward open competition for more positions.

At all levels disagreement is focused on the question of external or internal recruitment. Initial recruitment is based primarily on university exams. At the executive level promotions primarily follow internal seniority. At higher levels, job performance is important, together with the superiors' knowledge of and evaluation of personal style, i.e., ability to cooperate, loyalty, and decisiveness. There is a tendency to take political affiliations into account when choosing between several well-qualified candidates. Party politics does not disqualify for top positions, and some key positions have been occupied by active members of the governing party.[21] Party background cannot, however, compensate for lack of formal education and administrative experience, and the Labor party has not used its long period in power to fill the ministries with party members. Even today the Labor party is stronger in the population than in the ministries.[22] This is partly due to the fact that the employment authorities' choice of applicants for departmental positions is very limited.

The participants in the recruitment process report that the immediate superior has considerable influence. Division heads are the most important when hiring executives, and directors general are central in the appointments of division heads and deputy directors general. The influence of the political leadership is primarily related to top-level appointments. Still, ministers seldom deviate from the nominations by top civil servants, and outsiders rarely have any influence, despite frequent demands for a part in the process.[23]

In sum, the recruitment process takes place within a framework of strong norms based on the merit principle, as traditionally defined by the ministries themselves, and disallowing political promotions and intervention by special interests. These norms make arbitrary intervention by political leaders or organized interests illegitimate, and violations are very likely to result in criticism from the opposition in the Storting and from the mass media.

Attempts to change the system have met with little success. Some top positions outside the ministries have been made nontenured, but almost all incumbents have stayed as long as they wanted.

Likewise, efforts to weaken the constitutional protection of top civil servants, so that discharges would not require legal proceedings, have all failed.[24] The same has been true for challenges to other rights and for efforts to change the recruitment pattern in general.

The 1945 joint program of all political parties explicitly stated as a high priority goal that the civil service should recruit more from the private sector, and also that the mobility between local and central agencies and between various sectors of the state be increased. As with many other attempts to change the recruitment patterns, these statements have had few effects. The changes that have occurred have been related to the establishment of new agencies and new functions. The most important has been the gradual weakening of the hegemony of people trained in law, and the inflow of economists and other professions, especially to the planning units. Changes in the social composition of the civil service have been influenced more by changed recruitment to higher education than by changes in the recruitment policies of the ministries.

During the past few years the political demands for a more representative civil service in terms of social class, sex, geography, education, and vocational experience have grown stronger. So far, the demand for more women in the civil service has received the most attention, but it is still too early to infer a general change in recruitment practices.

If theories of bureaucratic motivation are correct, the disciplining potential of the Norwegian system should be considerable, but difficult to manipulate. The effect would be greatest for newcomers, least so for top civil servants approaching retirement and with pension rights secured. The thinking and behavior of senior civil servants might be better understood as a product of socialization than of the disciplining effects of expected promotions. While the weberian theory focuses on behavioral control, and a separation of personal beliefs, values, and bureaucratic behavior, a theory of socialization must focus on attitude formation and the internalization of the prevailing values in a ministry.

Potential for socialization. Theories of bureaucratic socialization are less developed than theories of discipline, but it seems likely that Norwegian ministries have a strong potential for socialization as well as for disciplination. The average time of service is long. Even in periods of growth, the ratio of veterans to newcomers has been fairly high, and the average tenure considerable. There is an ejection effect. Nearly half of the appointees leave before they have served three years.[25] While there are many reasons for this, those who leave are not representative of those who stay. Both in terms of attitudes and behavior they deviate in various ways. In the long run this process will generate a more homogeneous civil service.[26]

The more important the socialization process, the more important it is to understand how ministerial ethics and conception of events diffuse and are internalized. The more important the disciplination processes, the more important it is to understand how civil servants evaluate costs and benefits of behavioral alternatives. Presently we only conclude that Norwegian top civil servants reach the top after going through several filters of both socialization and disciplination.

We draw three conclusions. *First,* in spite of extensive changes in the environment, civil servants have been able to retain their historical rights, written into the 1814 constitution. This protection against arbitrary intervention from politicians and organized interests provides a basis of autonomy for the civil service.

Second, a result of the present system is that the behavior of top civil servants is fairly predictable. They are unlikely to introduce measures that deviate strongly from established ministerial norms. Consequently, they are likely to be predictable coalition partners, and those who share their values and beliefs may be willing to grant considerable autonomy to the civil servants.

Third, a decentralized recruiting procedure with strong mechanisms of socialization and disciplination should produce a heterogenous civil service in terms of knowledge, attitudes, and "models of the world."

ORGANIZATION OF KNOWLEDGE AND BELIEFS

Bureaucracy essentially means domination through knowledge. Those who want to control a bureaucracy need both authority and knowledge. The autonomy of the bureaucracy increases with a monopolization of technical knowledge gained through formal education and training, and of practical knowledge growing out of experience in the service.[27] The bureaucratic influence also increases with the ability to keep secret their intentions and knowledge.

Monopoly on knowledge? For Weber the only challenge to the bureaucrats' monopoly on expert knowledge came from private economic interests, which are superior to the bureaucracy in matters of business.[28] Today the situation is different. The expanding public agenda—with more interventions in the everyday life of citizens and a variety of services—has broadened the competence base of the bureaucracy. This is reflected in the number of professions attracted to the ministries. At the same time, organized interests have also strengthened their base of competence.

In Norway, the trend is fairly clear. The Storting and political parties have seen their relative position weakened, while organized interests, and especially economic producer groups, have established their own bureaucracies of a size and professional level that match those of the ministries.[29] Institutions of research and higher education also have relevant expertise, and they are increasingly involved in public policy making. The same is true for the mass media, for private firms, and even ad hoc civic action groups frequently mobilize expertise of considerable magnitude.[30] For most professions, less than 1 percent of the graduates are employed in the ministries. Hence there is always a potential for "counter expertise." Furthermore, Norwegian bureaucrats are frequently confronted with expertise from other countries as well as international organizations.

Civil servants in Norway have extensive education, long training, and considerable expertise. But they do not have a monopoly on knowledge. They are comparatively stronger in terms of practical knowledge gained from experience in the service. Long careers, most often within one sector, give specialized knowledge, but seldom a monopoly. Nearly half of the civil servants in the ministries report that they depend on knowledge and expertise from the outside.[31]

The configurations of expertise vary across policy fields. In certain sectors ministerial staffs are well developed, in other sectors not. The same is true for external groups. Also, in some issue areas (e.g., morals, abortion) expertise is less relevant than in others (e.g., economics, health care). The importance of expertise as a power base depends on the unity of various expert groups—the degree to which they fight or cooperate. It also depends on the degree to which civil servants are able to keep their knowledge secret.

Secrecy. In 1848 the cabinet refused to increase the openness of the administrative process because it would make the process slow and more expensive, and because the bureaucracy more often would have to defend and explain its decisions. This argument was based on the view that the role of the bureaucracy was to implement laws and rules given by the Storting without intervention from the outside. "Publicity would reduce the independence which a correct procedure demands."[32]

This view has frequently been challenged, and an important chapter of Norwegian administrative history is the struggle between ministry jurists and the mass media about what constitutes a reasonable level of openness. Still, the media have focused more on the parliamentary arena than on the administrative process. It was not until 1970 that Norway got a law on publicity in administrative affairs, giving the public better access to the administrative process. The Storting stated that while there would have to be exceptions to the general rule on publicity, these should be restricted to a minimum.

Empirical research also indicates that civil servants more often than previously give information on their own initiative; that information is provided earlier in the process; and that civil servants refuse less frequently to give information to the media.[33] Still the media behavior of the civil servants in the ministries differs from that of other elites. It is generally characterized by a willingness to give information when approached by the media, but a reluctance to take the initiative.[34]

The demand for public information is reflected in a recent wave of criticism against "the bureaucracy" for being inhuman, inefficient, overcentralized, high handed, and arrogant,[35] and a demand for less use of the classified stamp—especially in military and foreign affairs.[36] The perceived need to provide such information is reflected in a surge of public relations positions and agencies in the ministries, and in an increasing number of ombudsmen. A much less frequent political strategy has been leakages from the civil service.

In sum, the use of secrecy is still a relevant aspect of the political-administrative process, but its importance seems less than assumed by the weberian theory of bureaucracy. Civil servants in Norway have been better able to protect and control their careers than to keep their monopoly on expertise and information, and to keep their knowledge secret. They have also been less able to maintain *unity*.

Bureaucratic unity—and some sources of differentiation. What are the normative views of top civil servants? How do they perceive the world and their work? What do they agree/disagree about, and which factors form their models of the world?

The ideal weberian bureaucrat is rational, objective, and disciplined, and such norms are still strong in Norwegian ministries. Civil servants emphasize their professional authority and independence. They claim they will forward a proposal they think is professionally right even if they know that their superiors are against it. They say that official channels of authority and information should be followed, and they are strongly opposed to leakages to the public. There are norms of moderation of political participation. Civil servants should participate in political processes, but they should avoid job-related issues. The higher the respondent's position, the more restrictive the view on political participation.[37]

Among civil servants there is a high level of satisfaction with the way the administrative apparatus operates today. Civil servants perceive

TABLE 4.   Perceptions of Problem-Solving Instruments among Civil Servants
(Percentages)

INSTRUMENTS	TOP CIVIL SERVANTS	OTHER ADMINI- STRATORS	EXECU- TIVES	TOTAL
More information and knowledge	93	84	78	82
Strenghthening the public apparatus (more money, people)	66	51	47	51
Reorganization of the administrative apparatus	46	36	30	34
Strengthening international cooperation	45	28	31	31
Extensive changes in political, economic, and social relations in Norway	11	10	13	12
Extensive changes in inter- national political, economic, and social relations	13	11	13	12
Transferring tasks to the private sector	6	4	4	4
Number of respondents	(80)	(285)	(396)	(761)
Number of nonrespondents	(2)	(7)	(14)	(23)

Note: Data are based on the respondents' replies to the following survey question: "When considering the most important problems in your own field, how do you judge the following instruments for confronting these problems?" (Respondents were given the list above.)

themselves as initiators, but their orientation is definitely incremental-istic.[38] Their attitudes are illustrated by their response to how major problems in their own field should be dealt with. Very few want major changes in political, economic, or social relations in Norway or abroad, and they rely heavily on solving problems by means of more information and better knowledge. Few believe that problems can be solved by reducing the level of governmental intervention and transferring decisions to the private sector (table 4). Civil servants are also satisfied with the present structure of participation and representation in administrative decision making. They seldom want to include new groups, and when they do want changes, it is to increase the participation of organized interests already present. Likewise, they are satisfied with the way various interests—especially organized groups—are treated by the administration. The main tendencies are clear, but there are variations in perceptions, attitudes, and values. Typically, these variations can be explained by role-related factors like formal position, type of function, institutional belonging, external networks of contact, and profession. As should be expected from the strong potential of socialization and disciplining in the ministries, the social biography—with the exception of educational background, but including party affiliation—is of little or moderate importance in explaining variations in the civil servants' models of the world.[39]

The defense of traditional bureaucratic values and the level of satisfaction are strongest among those most integrated in the ministries, i.e., with high positions and long tenure, and those who belong to traditional ministerial professions and who have traditional functions. Conversely, those of lower position and short tenure give less support to bureaucratic values. They are less satisfied, and they are more change oriented. The same is true for those who belong to professions that are either new or small in the ministries, and for those who work with comparatively new functions like planning and public relations. This general pattern can be illustrated by an analysis of the civil servants' perceptions of their own roles.

Role perceptions. In the Norwegian bureaucratic culture the role of a civil servant has traditionally been compared to that of judge.[40] This conception is still strong. More than half of the top civil servants and 37 percent of all the civil servants in the ministries see a resemblance between their own job and the role of a judge (table 5). This similarity is linked to the fact that a ministry is the highest bureaucratic authority—the top of a hierarchical chain of command and appeal. Traditionally a ministry has also been the highest professional authority, and this function is reflected by the fact that 40 percent find similarities between their own job and the role of a scientist. Interestingly, this sense of expertise varies little between hierarchical levels.

The role conceptions of the civil servants reflect a shift from organizational forms based on hierarchical command and professional expertise to forms relying on bargaining and persuasion. "Negotiator"/"mediator" is the role mentioned most often, and negotiations and persuasion are an aspect of the job of nearly all top civil servants, and of 40 percent of the executives (table 5). Likewise, more top civil servants find a resemblance with the role of company manager than with the role of judge.

The element of bargaining and persuasion does not make top civil servants see similarities between their own job and the role of party politician or representative of an interest group. The distance to party politicians is emphasized the most. And only "accountant" is ranked below the "representative of an interest organization."

Resemblance between one's own job and the role of a judge is related

TABLE 5.   Role Perceptions of Civil Servants in the Ministries (Percentages)

ROLE	TOP CIVIL SERVANTS	OTHER ADMINI- STRATORS	EXECU- TIVES	TOTAL
Judge	54	44	30	37
Scientist	44	43	36	40
Negotiator/ mediator	89	65	40	54
Company manager	81	51	15	35
Accountant	5	10	15	12
Party politician	9	7	5	6
Representative of interest organization	26	13	13	14
Number of respondents	(80)	(286)	(390)	(756)
Number of nonrespondents	(2)	(6)	(20)	(28)

Note: Data are based on the respondents' replies to the following survey question: "A list of occupations is presented below. We would like to know—for each of them—if they, in your opinion, have anything in common with your present position?"

to training in law and to functions that traditionally have been occupied by jurists—the preparation and implementation of laws and rules. At the same time, this view is related to contacts with persons who only represent themselves or their nearest family, rather than with representatives of organized interests or institutions (table 6). When civil servants confront organized interests that can forcefully back up their views, it is often not enough to find the appropriate rule or the right professional solution. It becomes necessary to balance various views and interests and to find compromises.

The same tendency can be seen in the analysis of the role as negotiator/mediator. This resemblance is mentioned most often by top civil servants, those in contact with economic producer organizations, those whose major function is coordination, and those who work in the two ministries with the most contacts with other countries—the Ministry of Foreign Affairs and the Ministry of Commerce. There is also a weak tendency related to the respondent's sex—females see a resemblance with the negotiator/mediator less often than men, even when we control for all other factors.

Two major reasons exist for finding resemblance between one's own job and the roles most strongly repudiated—party politician and interest group representative. One is having a position that ties the civil servant into a network of contacts with various political institutions at the na-

TABLE 6. Perceived Resemblance between Own Position and the Role of a Judge; by the Civil Servants' Education, Function, and Contact with Individuals[a] (Percentages)

3. Education	Not trained in law				Trained in law			
2. Main function	All others[b]		Making laws/ rules, or single decisions		All others		Making laws/ rules, or single decisions	
1. Contact with individuals	Seldom/ never	Often	Seldom/ never	Often	Seldom/ never	Often	Seldom/ never	Often
Percentage who see resemblance with the role of the judge	13	20	27	53	61	76	79	80
Number of respondents	(209)	(75)	(55)	(30)	(57)	(42)	(66)	(81)

E^1: 12 percent, E^2: 16 percent, E^3: 46 percent.

Note: a) Individuals here refer to people who represent only themselves or their nearest family, and not an organized interest or an institution.
b) The list of "other functions" is found in table 7.
Source: Lægreid and Olsen, *Byråkrati*, p. 140.

224

tional level. The other is related to the civil servants' own political activity. This factor matters most to young people in executive positions with job offers from outside and not committed to a lifelong career in the ministry. Also, people trained in law generally find fewer similarities with these roles than others.[41]

The roles of higher civil servants are complex, but the analysis illustrates a simple point. While social background is important in determining who is recruited to the ministries, it has little effect on values, attitudes, and perceptions. In Norway, unlike some other countries, there does not seem to be a generation gap in the civil servants' view of the world.[42] Age is not an important factor, and has little explanatory power when controlling for other characteristics. On the other hand, tasks, professional background, position, institutional connection, and the task environment are important sources of *differentiation.* Norwegian civil servants are not likely to agree on which values, beliefs, and clients to defend. They have more in common in terms of philosophy of governance—a definite incrementalistic style.

The analysis is also consistent with an "archeological perspective." The defense of bureaucratic values is strongest in the professions, the task groups, and the institutions established during the nineteenth century. People trained in law usually adhere to bureaucratic norms. The same is true for those whose work primarily is rule implementation, i.e., the application of rules to individual cases. Their opposites are those who primarily have planning functions. The institutional stronghold of bureaucratic values is the Ministry of Justice, while the Ministry of the Environment (established in 1972) more frequently deviates from bureaucratic norms. Finally, bureaucratic values and beliefs flourish where there is a clear difference in power between civil servants and their clients. The more densely populated a ministry's environment is by organized interests, the less likely traditional bureaucratic values are to thrive. We will now show that the same is true for bureaucratic authority and processes of coordination.

ORGANIZATION OF AUTHORITY AND INTERESTS

The idea of a legal-rational authority and a shared understanding of a normative order is useful to gain insights into how top civil servants relate to each other, to subordinates, politicians, clients, and others. But we also have to take account of the constellation of material and ideal interests within which they act, bargaining relations, and coalitions formed. Recent empirical studies describe the administrative apparatus as a conglomerate of semifeudal, loosely allied organizations with a substantial life of their

own. Agencies are acting on the basis of different perspectives, information, and resources. They compete for influence, resources, and prestige.
They defend their domains and jurisdictions and enlist allies. Their rivalries are major obstacles to coordination and joint policy-making attempts
at coordination are often seen as unwanted intervention.[43]

What, then, do Norwegian civil servants actually do, how and with
whom do they interact? The largest group is still those performing a
classical bureaucratic function—the application of rules to individual
cases that affect a single person, firm, or institution, or a limited group of
such entities.[44] The second largest group is engaged in planning. While
coordination is an important task for top civil servants, rule application is
central even at the top. Likewise, junior civil servants fairly often engage
in planning. They are not restricted to routine activities (table 7).

There are, however, differences in work style. The proportion spending most of their time at their desks decreases from 46 percent of the
executives to 6 percent of top civil servants. Along the same line, 45

TABLE 7.   **Main Functions of the Civil Servants**
            (Percentages)

MAIN FUNCTION	TOP CIVIL SERVANTS	OTHER ADMINISTRATORS	EXECUTIVES	TOTAL
Personnel administration	15	13	11	12
Budgeting	1	8	6	6
Preparing laws/ rules	10	13	8	10
Planning	18	22	19	20
Rule application (Single decisions)	21	25	31	28
Control	1	3	8	5
Coordination	27	6	6	8
Public relations/ information	0	5	6	5
Other	7	5	6	6
Number of respondents	(73)	(265)	384	722
Number of non- respondents	(9)	(27)	(26)	(62)

Note: Data are based on the respondents' replies to the following questions. First:
"Approximately how much of your working time did you spend last year on each of the
functions listed below?" (The list was presented.) Then: "Into which of the categories
mentioned would most of your work fall?" The table presents responses to the last question.

percent of the top civil servants, compared to 9 percent of the executives, spend most of their time in meetings. The pattern reflects a stepwise decision-making procedure, as assumed by theories of bureaucracy, but the process does not end with a decision by a single top civil servant. Instead, the result of the bureaucratic stepwise procedure is presented in meetings, where a decision is (sometimes) taken. Two-thirds of the civil servants in the ministries report having participated in intra- or inter-ministerial task forces in the last year. Among top civil servants three-fourths have participated. The share is smallest among those with typically "bureaucratic" functions—rule application or control. Top civil servants are even more active on committees and boards where organized interests also participate. Eighty-eight percent of the top civil servants report membership of at least one such committee, compared to 40 percent among executives. Such activity may counteract the tendencies toward specialization. Committee members, however, are often more concerned with promoting the interests of their own institutions than with cross-sectorial evaluation. Committee work may thus result in a "negative" coordination, where members are better at defending their institutions against external influence than at promoting their own ideas and premises.[45]

In general, the bureaucrats have extensive patterns of contacts. The closest connections exist between divisions in a ministry (table 8). There are more extensive contacts with other administrative organs than with the political leadership. As regards organized interests, there are well-developed relationships with economic organizations. Civil servants have three times as much contact with these as with other types of organizations, as much as with municipal authorities. It should be noted that contacts with the Storting are few, and even less so with ad hoc groups.

There need not, however, be a singular relation between contact frequency and importance. Some groups may be taken account of by anticipated reaction. Top civil servants may, for example, keep informed about Storting debates without direct contacts.[46]

Top civil servants take care of a traditional leadership function—transactions with the environment and especially with the decision-making centers (table 8). But with an expanding public agenda, transactions with the environment are spreading down the hierarchy. At the same time, most top civil servants meet with their ministers daily, alone or in small groups. They report that they are quite able to anticipate which issues the ministers will be interested in, and what solutions they prefer. Ministers agree with this evaluation.[47] Relations between top civil servants and ministers are most of the time characterized by trust and cooperation.

Contact patterns are *specialized*, i.e., civil servants usually interact

TABLE 8.   The Contact Patterns of Civil Servants (Percentages of weekly
            contact with various groups or institutions)

WEEKLY CONTACT WITH	TOP CIVIL SERVANTS	OTHER ADMINI- STRATORS	EXECU- TIVES	TOTAL	NUMBER NOT RESPONDING
Storting and its organs	4	2	1	2	5
Individual members of the Storting	13	2	1	2	13
Minister, under secretary in own ministry	80	44	9	30	7
Other departments in own ministry	94	78	68	74	12
Central agencies under the ministry	66	40	38	42	100
Local, regional agencies under the ministry	36	44	39	41	69
Other ministries	57	47	33	41	0
Local, regional agencies, under other ministries	10	8	7	8	54
Local and regional authorities	15	20	16	17	47
International agencies, other countries	22	13	8	11	2
Economic producer organizations	35	22	11	18	24
Other organized interests	9	8	4	6	42
Ad hoc actions	0	—	1	1	17
Individuals acting on behalf of them- selves or nearest family	25	25	18	21	16

Note: The high number of nonrespondents for central agencies and local/regional agencies under own ministry reflects that some ministries have few such agencies. Nonrespondents are otherwise likely not to have contacts, so that the actual percentages with contacts are lower than indicated.
    —: less than .5%.

with *one* committee in the Storting, a small number of administrative agencies, interest groups in their own sector and so forth. Variations in contacts are even greater than variations in attitudes and beliefs related to the top civil servant's formal position, profession, function, and institutional belonging. Such variations are connected weakly, or not at all, to the social background—including party affiliation—of the individual civil servant.

As a result, the role of top civil servants as bureaucrats is more important than their political role. Forceful ministry norms differentiate between administrative work and political activity. The majority of civil servants do not favor political engagement in own field. Those with central ministerial positions are the most willing to restrict political activity. Also, the Constitution states that civil servants in the ministries may not be elected to the Storting. Civil servants are not, however, excluded from political activity. More than one-third of top civil servants hold or have held party office, and 14 percent have been nominated for election, primarily for local elections (table 9).

Civil servants also hold jobs in the political leadership of the ministries. Many of the political staff have public service experience. One-third of the cabinet ministers have been public administrators (table 2), as have more than half of the under secretaries. Many, however, do not come from central government.

In Norway, the political leadership of a ministry consists of the ministers, the under secretaries, and the political secretaries. Each ministry usually has a political staff of three, totaling fifty persons in all the ministries. The political staff of the prime minister's office is weakly developed, and the cabinet has no separate planning capacity. Thus, ministers are

TABLE 9.   **Political Activity among Civil Servants in the Ministries (Percentages)**

ACTIVITY	TOP CIVIL SERVANTS	OTHER ADMINI- STRATORS	EXECUTIVES	TOTAL
Party representative (present)	13	13	9	11
Party representative (former)	23	10	12	13
Nominated for public election (former)	14	18	12	14
Number of respondents	(80)	(288)	(401)	(770)
Number of nonrespondents	(1)	(4)	(9)	(14)

largely dependent on the civil service for assistance and support, and such cooperation is normally smooth. The relations between civil servants and their political leadership are perceived as very peaceful. Generally, civil servants are inclined to see harmony in their own field.[48] Those who report disagreements most often mention conflicts between the ministry and its clients, usually related to disagreements among groups of clients.

To some degree external contacts are a source of conflicts. Civil servants do not perceive Norwegian society as totally homogeneous. Their views of the level of conflict and of major cleavages coincide with those of other elites and the population in general, focusing on economic organization and allocation, regional conflicts, and conflicts related to meritocracy.[49]

The views of the civil servants deviate little from other descriptions of elite interaction in Norway.[50] The major tendency has been cooperation and a mutually satisfactory division of labor, rather than conflicts and jurisdictional strife. Policy making has been characterized by attempts to have one's views accepted as premises for decision making and to achieve as broad acceptance as possible. This is reflected in the coordination process. Internal as well as external transactions differ from those assumed by standard theories of bureaucracy.

Only one-third of the civil servants say their daily activities are determined by rules or established procedure. The proportion varies only moderately across hierarchical levels. While people lower in the hierarchy are less programed than assumed by theories of bureaucracy, top civil servants are constrained by rules, codes, and agreements reached through interaction with representatives of other organized interests. Still, programing through rules is primarily related to classical bureaucratic functions like control, accounting, rule application on single decisions; to a low level of conflict in the work field; and to contact with the ministry's own regional and local agencies.

The use of another classical bureaucratic means of control, direct corrections—for example, superiors making substantive changes in the recommendations by their subordinates—is even less common. Only 10 percent say it happens regularly, and generally these respondents have a low degree of integration in the ministries.[51]

Moderate use of hierarchical control like rules and direct corrections would be expected in organizations with a high potential for socialization and disciplination. Our data also indicate that socialization may be more important than disciplination. Only 7 percent of the civil servants report that they often have to prepare or to implement decisions with which they personally disagree. Such tensions between behavior and preferences are primarily related to conflicts with the minister, and to plans for leaving the ministry.[52]

The response pattern also indicates that civil servants do not see ministerial policies as products of external pressure or constraints. They are able to retain their autonomy, and are also relatively successful in getting their proposals accepted by external groups.[53] They perceive the most success in their dealings with constitutional bodies and the least success with groups directly affected by policies and public opinion.

More than two-thirds of the civil servants feel that their ministry has succeeded well in having its views accepted in the Storting, the cabinet, or the implementing agencies, while 50 percent have the same view of success with public opinion. Top civil servants consider the penetration force of their divisions with all groups greater than do other administrators and executives.

The perceived success does not reflect a bureaucratic power monopoly. Other groups also report satisfaction with the processes. In a study of employees of economic producer organizations, only 10 percent state that their organization has been unsuccessful in having its view accepted by public authorities. Six percent say there is little consistency between what the organization proposed and what public authorities have done, and 15 percent claim that members of their organization have benefited less than the average citizen. A similar study of elected officials in economic producer organizations shows the same pattern (respectively 15, 13, and 22 percent). And in a national survey only 9 percent of the population say that public policies run contrary to their organizations. Fourteen percent say people in their community have received fewer benefits from society than average, and the respondents are generally satisfied with the distribution of influence in Norway.[54]

The level of acceptance may be related to the fact that Norway is a small and fairly homogeneous country, as well as to the policy-making institutions. As more and more discretion has been transferred to the ministries, organized interests have tried to influence that discretion. A "two-tier" system has been institutionalized as the territorial channel of representation has been supplemented by a "corporate" channel. During the last decades the bureaucratic demand for "distance" from affected groups has been replaced by a norm of participation by such groups in policy-making processes. The main participants in this channel are top civil servants, representatives of organized interests, and experts from institutions of research and higher learning. Elected politicians participate only rarely.[55]

As a result the borderline between the private and the public sector has become less clear, and hierarchical command based on formal authority or expertise has become less prevalent as a form of coordination.

Internally in a ministry the relevance of hierarchical authority and command is reduced because of strong socializing mechanisms. Such

coordination is harder because the professional qualifications of subordinates often match those of their superiors; and because stronger interest
organizations among civil servants and increased employee participation
are weakening the hierarchy and changing leadership roles. Employee
consciousness has increased, and participation rights are expanding from
issues related to wages and working conditions to administrative systems.[56]

Hierarchical authority is restricted in transactions between ministries
and sectors because the division of labor has become more complicated
with more decisions affecting several ministries, because ministries have
different types of expertise, and because each may enlist external support. Furthermore, there are obvious constraints on the hierarchical authority of elected leaders in terms of capacity and insights, and because
civil servants have other political references and external sources of support. Finally, ministries cannot always claim hierarchical authority over
well-organized clients with well-trained staffs and with political and economic clout.

If the top civil servants' interaction with subordinates, each other,
elected politicians and organized interests is not prompted by hierarchical
authority, what coalitions are formed? When are civil servants attractive
coalition partners?

Civil servants have useful resources. They have protected careers,
expertise, and practical information, and their numbers as well as their
material resources have increased. Their predictability as coalition partners is high, but their unity has decreased. They have also been better
able to protect their rights than their external political positions. Civil
servants are still overrepresented in the Storting, the cabinet, in local and
regional elected assemblies, and in political parties, but they do not dominate. Their social status is high, but not exceptional. The difference in
salary between top civil servants and new recruits has declined. In 1819
the difference was 6:1. Today it is 2.1:1. Top civil servants make approximately 80 percent of the salaries for comparable positions in the private
sector.

In sum, civil servants should be interesting coalition partners, and the
traditional view of a bureaucracy united against the politicians is not very
accurate. Virtually no battles follow such lines. Less explored is a potential coalition between the two major groups in the corporate channel—
full-time employees in the ministries and in economic producer
organizations. Do groups of experts act as a united bloc, or do they
constitute counterexpertise and adversaries?

We do not believe in a conspiracy view of bureaucratic influence,
where bureaucrats agree on policies and then sell the result to their "mas-

ters" in the ministries and the interest organizations. Neither are politicians and elected leaders in organizations so powerless, nor bureaucrats so united. The two groups of bureaucrats have different careers with little exchange of personnel. Their socialization and their incentives deviate sharply. There are also divergences in attitude toward future cooperation between ministries and organized interests. Two-thirds of the civil servants do not want expanded cooperation, while two-thirds of both bureaucrats and elected leaders in economic producer organizations are in favor.[57] Moreover, each group of bureaucrats is in many ways heterogeneous and represents opposing views.

Consequently we are also skeptical to the concept of a united elite—a grand coalition of politicians, civil servants, and organized interests (at least partly) in opposition to ordinary people.[58] The idea of an intimate collaboration of the elites—a Society for Mutual Benefits based on a tacit treaty, implicit bargaining, and expressed in self-restraints—captures only part of reality.[59] Norwegian policy making takes place within a normative order emphasizing incrementalism and compromise. Attempts to gather political, administrative, and organizational elites in a general corporate policy-making organ at the cabinet level have been unsuccessful. Most initiatives of this nature have come from top political leaders.[60] Organized interests have been unwilling to commit themselves and to become too closely identified with public policies. Top civil servants have also been reluctant.

The Norwegian pattern is not one great Society for Mutual Benefits, but rather several smaller societies. Corporate representation typically takes place at the ministerial or departmental level rather than at the cabinet level. The political system has been segmented into specialized coalitions of politicians, civil servants, organized interests, experts from institutions of research and higher learning. Internal disagreement may occur (and the members may hold different opinions on the value of expanded cooperation), but they share a basic perspective. Conflicts usually evolve between segments, or between a segment and institutions trying to coordinate across segments and sectors.[61]

The actual coalitions depend on the organization and resources of public agencies and affected groups, as well as on the level of engagement among politicians, parties, mass media, and public opinion. The more politicized the decision becomes, the more the influence of civil servants is likely to be reduced. In the few confrontations between politicians and civil servants since 1945, the latter have been defeated.[62] In major conflicts, such as the debate about Norwegian membership in the European Common Market, the influence of civil servants was inversely related to the level of conflict. In this debate, top civil servants were attacked for taking partisan views.[63] Also, when politicized issues, like free abortion, are promoted by the governing party, the influence of civil servants is insignificant.

The power of civil servants thus depends on the issues, the decision-making arenas, and the level of conflict. This would imply that compromise may not be a "bureaucratic mentality"[64] but a rational strategy.

The capacity for focusing on issues is much less for the Storting and the public than for the administrative apparatus and for organized interests. Since the Storting and the public focus on a very small set of issues at a time, issues and conflicts compete for attention. Selection depends on the degree of conflict between the agencies and groups participating in the first phase of the process. Intervention and politicization are least likely when a compromise is reached in this phase.[65] If a task force is split into several factions, a conflict is likely to become socialized in the sense of Schattschneider's term.[66] The issue may become a "garbage can" for new participants, problems, and solutions,[67] resulting in less predictability and reduced influence for the groups that dominated the first phase of the policy process.

Governmental Leadership and the Role of Top Civil Servants

Our interpretation is that the influence of top civil servants is primarily based upon (a) lifelong careers protected against arbitrary intervention by politicians or organized interests, and (b) support from stable coalition partners. Top civil servants are attractive coalition partners because they bring expertise, information, and energy, and because they are predictable. However, since their basic orientation is incrementalistic, they are more attractive for conservatives and moderates than for groups that want radical changes in established programs or procedures. We view the use of secrecy, control over political positions (cabinet, Storting, or in local government), formal bureaucratic authority, and bureaucratic unity as less important.

What is, then, the potential for governmental leadership in a system dominated by stable coalitions rather than by hierarchical legal-rational authority? How will a (likely) change toward less stable coalitions affect governmental leadership and the role of top civil servants?

The ideology of ministerial responsibility originated in a period when the number of decisions, the complexity of issues, the size of the administrative apparatus, and its relative independence from organized interests in society allowed ministers considerable control over everyday life in the ministries. When the parliamentary principle was introduced, the normative base for influence and responsibility was further strengthened.

Today ministers act within a complex network of interdependent and interpenetrated formal organizations, the interaction of which is characterized by persuasion and bargaining. A main feature of the system is segmentation, with stable, nonhierarchical functional coalitions. Ministers are important actors in such a system, but no political superstars. Their influence is related more to their ability to organize policy-making processes than to make policy choices. Their capability to direct is constrained by the political-administrative system but, since ministers often are recruited from within a segment, they seldom have an incentive to make dramatic changes.[68]

Norway may represent an alternative to "consociational democracies"—segmented societies linked by an integrated political system and elite cooperation. Norway is fairly homogenous with a well-developed division of political labor—a segmented state in an unsegmented society.

Since 1945 economic growth has produced considerable slack resources. This, along with sequential attention to goals and local (segmental) policy making, has buffered differences in values, beliefs, and social identification.[69] The smallness of the system has enabled anticipated reaction to become a major form of coordination.[70]

Reduced slack has triggered demands for more coordination, planning, and leadership. In 1979 a new Ministry of Coordination and Planning was established. The need to focus more on the integrated system rather than on its components has been emphasized. However, the resources of the new ministry are very modest, and its leaders are advocating planning as a pedagogical exercise rather than governance.

Changes in the political and social system may simultanously create a need for more planning, and make planning less possible. Specifically, both political and social coalitions have become less stable.

No party can expect a majority in the Storting in the near future. In the major party—the Labor party—discipline is dwindling and individual initiatives discomfort party leaders. Reduced slack and budget cutting may cause organized interests to be less enthusiastic about integrated participation in governmental policy making. This also because organized interests face increasing competition from citizens' initiatives. Participation is related to education, and implies that with a higher level of education the potential for political action will increase. People who do not want continuous participation in parties or interest organizations get involved in citizens' initiatives under certain conditions, and create uncertainty. Furthermore, these initiatives focus on other issues than do participants in the corporate channel. Questions of life-style and morals are more important than economic issues. Consequently, it is more difficult to claim authority based on expertise.[71]

Thus, established segments are challenged by citizens' initiatives, and the reduced slack makes it more likely that segments will challenge each other. A result may be that Norway will enter a cycle of political power concentration—not in terms of concentrating political power in the hands of one group, but that major decisions will be made within a joint political arena, rather than in many segmented arenas. Such politicization is more likely as more major conflicts are related to collective goods or issues.

A possible result is that the Storting and political parties become increasingly influential, and that ministers will emphasize their party affiliation more than their administrative position. The distribution of influence between the participants in each segment may also be modified. Contact with and influence in the general political arena may become more valuable.

The role of civil servants will be weakened if issues become more politicized, and if there is less agreement on who should be considered experts.[72] Still, the future power of civil servants depends more on their ability to defend their most important strongholds—the merit principle and the autonomy of protected careers. The career system may be attacked in three different ways.

First, the stronger the organizations of the employees, the more emphasis on seniority rather than merit. This may reduce the possibility of rewarding talent, but will strengthen the identification with specific institutions and sectors.

Second, politicians may work harder to make the civil service more representative. So far they have not succeeded, and if they do, the results are uncertain. Socialization and disciplination are strong enough to erase or modify socioeconomic identification, with the exception of education. These mechanisms will be diluted if *many* new recruits with similar identifications enter a ministry at the same time. Such extensive hiring, however, is less likely in periods with little growth than when growth is strong.[73] It is unlikely that a "spoils"-system will be introduced in the next five to ten years.

A third possibility is increased turnover. So far, high mobility has been limited to certain sectors, especially the oil sector. If this pattern should spread, the mechanism of socialization and diciplination will be weakened, and probably change the operation of central administrative agencies in fundamental ways.

NOTES

1. Max Weber, "Der Sozialismus," in *Gesammelte Aufsätze zur Soziologie und Sozialpolitik* (Tübingen, 1924), p. 46.

2. H. H. Gerth and C. Wright Mills, *From Max Weber* (London: Routledge & Kegan Paul, 1970), pp. 221, 228, 232.

3. Arthur L. Stinchcombe, *Creating Efficient Industrial Administration* (New York: Academic Press, 1974).

4. Arthur L. Stinchcombe, *Constructing Social Theories* (New York: Harcourt, 1968), pp. 158–160.

5. Sverre Steen, "Ole Gabriel Ueland og bondepolitikken," in Sverre Steen, *Tusen års norsk historie* (Oslo: Cappelen, 1958), p. 168. In this part we also rely on Per Maurseth, *Sentraladministrasjonens historie 1814–1844* (Oslo: Universitetsforlaget, 1979). Edgeir Benum, *Sentraladministrasjonens historie 1845–1884* (Oslo: Universitetsforlaget, 1979). Jens Arup Seip, *Utsikt over Norges historie* (Oslo: Gyldendal, 1974). Francis Sejersted, "Rettsstaten og den selvdestruerende makt," in Rune Slagstad (ed.), *Om staten* (Oslo: Pax, 1979).

6. Knut D. Jacobsen, *Teknisk hjelp og politisk struktur* (Oslo: Universitetsforlaget, 1965). Also, Knut D. Jacobsen, "Public Administration under Pressure: The Role of the Expert in the Modernization of Traditional Agriculture," in *Scandinavian Political Studies*, 1966, vol. 1, pp. 59–93. Jacobsen uses the terms *political contraction* and *detraction* for power concentration and dispersion, respectively.

7. Benum, "Sentraladministrasjonens historie." Jan Debes, *Realiteter og illusjoner i statsadministrasjonen* (Oslo: Universitetsforlaget, 1961).

8. Johan P. Olsen, "Folkestyre, byråkrati og korporativisme," in J. P. Olsen (ed.), *Politisk organisering* (Bergen: Universitetsforlaget, 1978), pp. 13–114.

9. Paul G. Roness, *Reorganisering av departementa* (Bergen: Universitetsforlaget). See also, Herbert Kaufman, *Are Government Organizations Immortal?* (Washington, D.C.: Brookings, 1976). While Kaufman's own answer is affirmative, Nystrom and Starbuck have challenged the analysis. Their argument is that the death rate is as high in the public as in the private sector. Paul Nystrom and William Starbuck, "Designing and Understanding Organizations," in Nystrom and Starbuck (eds.), *Handbook of Organizational Design* (London: Oxford, 1980).

10. Arthur L. Stinchcombe, "Social Structure and Organizations," in James G. March (ed.), *Handbook of Organizations* (Chicago: Rand McNally, 1965), pp. 142–193. Øyvind Østerud, *Det planlagte samfunn* (Oslo: Gyldendal, 1979).

11. John Highley, Karl Erik Brofoss, and Knut Grøholt, "Top Civil Servants and the National Budget in Norway," in Mattei Dogan (ed.), *The Mandarins of Western Europe* (New York: Wiley, 1975), pp. 253–274. Knut D. Jacobsen, "Ekspertenes deltakelse i den offentlige forvaltning." Oslo: Paper presented at the Scandinavian Political Science Association's meeting in Helsinki, 1968.

12. Johan P. Olsen, "Integrated Organizational Participation in Govern-

ment," in Paul Nystrom and William Starbuck (eds.), *Handbook of Organizational Design* (London: Oxford, 1980).

13. Vidar Haugen, "Det Norske Arbeiderparti 1940–1945. Fra forbud til gjenreisning." Bergen: Unpublished dissertation, 1979. Trond Bergh and Helge Pharo (eds.), *Vekst og velstand* (Oslo: Universitetsforlaget, 1977). Edvard Bull, *Norge i den rike verden* (Oslo: Cappelen, 1979).

14. Trygve Bratteli, interview, 1974.

15. Stinchcombe, *Creating Efficient,* chapter 5.

16. The data are based mostly on a survey administered to ministry employees, from executive officers to top civil servants during 1976 (784 respondents), reported in more detail in Per Lægreid and Johan P. Olsen, *Byråkrati og beslutninger* (Bergen: Universitetsforlaget, 1978), on which, for the most part, this essay is based.

17. Only 10 percent of the administrators in the ministries are women; one-third grew up in the capital (Oslo), and 40 percent were born in a family where the main breadwinner was a university graduate or self-employed (Lægreid and Olsen, *Byråkrati*).

18. The oil sector is an exception. Here, the movement of personnel from state agencies to oil companies has become so high that it is perceived as a problem by political authorities (Forhandlinger i Stortinget, 1980, pp. 2836–2837). A result has been special salaries for civil servants employed in the oil sector.

19. Per Lægreid, "Rekrutteringskriterier og karrierekontroll i norske departement" (Bergen: mimeo, 1980).

20. Maurseth, *Sentraladministrasjonens,* pp. 241–243, 397.

21. Lægreid, "Rekrutteringskriterier."

22. Lægreid and Olsen, *Byråkrati.* The survey of the civil servants did not ask directly for party affiliation. The conclusion is based on information about whether they have been active in parties, and which union they belong to.

23. Lægreid, "Rekrutteringskriterier." Kåre D. Tønnesson, "Et departement med det rette hjertelag for næringslivets vel," in *Historisk Tidsskrift,* 44, 1965, pp. 1–16.

24. Lægreid and Olsen, *Byråkrati.* Torstein Eckhoff, "Regjeringens adgang til å avskjedige embetsmenn," in Eckhoff, *Retten og samfunnet* (Oslo: Tanum-Nordli, 1976). The cabinet most often presents such changes as solutions to practical problems, while the opposition frequently argues in terms of power. Recently the parliamentary leader of the Conservatives, Kåre Willoch, explicitly defended the independence of civil servants as a counterweight to the political power of the Labor party (Forhandlinger i Stortinget, 1980, p. 2670).

25. They do leave—they are not fired.

26. In Norway there is a low correlation between various aspects of the social biography of a civil servant (e.g., class, sex, geographic background, education, practical experience, party membership, activity in interest organizations, etc.). If a high correlation produces a more unambiguous prebureaucratic socialization, Norwegian civil servants are not "presocialized" and may, therefore, be more receptive to socialization in the ministry. Lægreid and Olsen, *Byråkrati.*

27. Max Weber, *Economy and Society* (New York: Bedminster Press, 1968), vol. 1, p. 228.

28. H. H. Gerth and C. W. Mills, *From Max Weber* (London: Routledge and Kegan Paul, 1970), p. 235.

29. Jorolv Moren, Abraham Hallenstvedt and Tom Christensen, *Norske organisasjoner* (Oslo: Tanum, 1976).

30. Johan P. Olsen and Harald Sætren, *Aksjoner og demokrati* (Bergen: Universitetsforlaget, 1980).

31. Berit Bratbak and Johan P. Olsen, "Departement og opinion," in Johan P. Olsen, *Meninger og makt* (Bergen: Universitetsforlaget, 1980), pp. 86–167. Also, *Innstilling om den sentrale forvaltningens organisasjon* (Otta: Engers boktrykkeri, 1970).

32. Pål E. Lorentzen, *Undersøkelse om offentlighetsloven. Den offentlige forvaltning som informasjonskilde for pressen* (Bergen: Maktutredningen, discussion paper no. 74, 1978), p. 7.

33. Lorentzen, *Undersøkelse om offentlighetsloven*, pp. 124–126.

34. Bratbak and Olsen, *Departement og opinion*.

35. While parts of this criticism are officially accepted (Stortingsmelding no. 75, 1976–1977, p. 84), the public's attitudes are diffuse and contradictory. In general, Norwegians trust experts more than they trust politicians (Francesco Kjellberg et al., *Forvaltning, byråkrati og den enkelte* (Oslo: Institute of Political Science, University of Oslo, 1980)).

36. In this area, the level of openness is clearly lower in Norway than in the United States. Information that is "secret" in Norway may be found in congressional documents and then used in the political debate in Norway. A public committee considering this issue has recommended relaxing the rules (NOU 1980:51, *Nedgradering og offentliggjøring*).

37. Here we rely on Lægreid and Olsen, *Byråkrati*.

38. Johan P. Olsen, "Governing Norway: Segmentation, Anticipation and Consensus Formation," in Richard Rose and Ezra Suleiman (eds.), *Presidents and Prime Ministers* (Washington, D.C.: AEI, 1980), p. 246.

39. This analysis includes the occupation and education of the breadwinner of the family in which the respondent grew up; whether the breadwinner was publicly or privately employed; the region and the municipality where the respondent grew up; sex; age; level and type of education; language used; vocational experience; career expectations; party affiliation; union membership; membership in other interest groups; and participation in civic groups and ad hoc actions.

40. Innstilling fra *Komiteen till å utrede spørsmålet om mer betryggende former for den offentlige forvaltning* (Kragerø: Naper Boktrykkeri, 1958).

41. Resemblance to the role of a scientist is linked to educational background (economists, scientists, and social scientists), to functions performed (planning, making of laws and rules), ministry (Ministry of the Environment, Ministry of Foreign Affairs) and to contacts with the international level and with political institutions at the national level.

42. Renate Mayntz, *"German Federal Bureaucrats: A Functional Elite be-*

tween Politics and Administration" (in this book). Robert D. Putnam, "The Political Attitudes of Senior Civil Servants in Britain, Germany and Italy." *British
Journal of Political Science* 3 (1973): 257–290.

43. Graham Allison, *Essence of Decision* (Boston: Little, Brown, 1971). Re-
nate Mayntz and Fritz Scharpf, *Policy-making in the German Federal Republic*
(Amsterdam:Elsevier, 1975). R. L. Peabody and F. E. Rourke, "Public Bureauc-
racies," in James G. March, *Handbook of Organizations* (Chicago: Rand
McNally, 1965, pp. 802–837). Ezra Suleiman, *Politics, Power, and Bureaucracy in
France* (Princeton, New Jersey: Princeton University Press, 1974).

44. The respondents were given a list of activities. They were first asked how
much time they spent on each activity. Then they were asked which was their
major activity. The two questions give approximately the same results. The
boundaries between the various activities are, of course, somewhat obscured.
Lawmaking and planning may for example, involve some coordination. Nevertheless, significant variations are captured by such grouping.

45. Mayntz and Scharpf, *Policy-making.*
46. Mayntz, "German Federal Bureaucrats."
47. Bratbak and Olsen, "Departement," p. 109. Olsen, *Governing.*

48. Asked to characterize the level of conflict in their own work area on a
five-point scale, 14 percent say there is considerable/some conflict. A little more
than one-third use the middle category, and more than half the civil servants say
there is considerable/some agreement. The level of conflict reported by civil servants is strongly related to the respondents' integration in the ministry—the more
integrated, the less conflict perceived (Lægreid and Olsen, *Byråkrati,* pp. 151–
161).

49. Meritocracy conflicts here include conflicts between people, and between
bureaucrats and their clients.

50. Highley et al., "Top Civil Servants."

51. Young people just recruited; people who perceive conflicts with the political leadership in the ministry; who plan to leave the ministry; and who have
personally participated in civic groups/ad hoc actions, an activity that is contrary
to ministerial norms.

52. There are also some variations between ministries due to special situations.

53. Again the view of the civil servants coincides with the reports of other
participants and with case studies of specific policy-making processes.

54. Unpublished material from the study "Power in Norway."

55. Tom Christensen and Morten Egeberg, "Organized Group-Government
Relations in Norway: On the Structured Selection of Participants, Problems, Solutions and Choice Opportunities," in *Scandinavian Political Studies* 3 (2):239–
260. Robert B. Kvavik, *Interest Groups in Norwegian Politics* (Oslo:
Universitetsforlaget, 1976). Olsen, *Integrated.* Stein Rokkan, "Norway: Numerical Democracy and Corporate Pluralism," in Robert A. Dahl (ed.), *Political Oppositions in Western Democracies* (New Haven: Yale University Press, 1966).

56. St. meld.nr. 28 (1976–1977) NOU 1974:60, *Ansattes medbestemmelse i
offentlig virkscmhet.*

57. Those who already have representation are the most in favor of expansion. Representatives of smaller and less resourceful organizations are more negative, probably because they do not expect to be included. Among civil servants those least integrated in the ministries are most likely to favor more organizational participation.

58. Bull, *Norge.*

59. Richard Neustadt, "White House and Whitehall," in *The Public Interest,* 1966 (2), pp. 55–69.

60. Olsen, *Integrated.* Bergh and Pharo, *Vekst.*

61. Morten Egeberg, Johan P. Olsen, and Harald Sætren, "Organisasjonssamfunnet og den segmenterte stat," in Olsen, *Politisk organisering,* pp. 115–142.

62. Bergh and Pharo, *Vekst.*

63. Nils Petter Gleditsch, Øyvind Østerud and Jon Elster, *De utro tjenere* (Oslo: Pax, 1974).

64. Karl Mannheim, *Ideology and Utopia* (New York: Harcourt, Brace and World, 1949).

65. Olav Grimsbo, "Ekspertise og konflikter i utredningsutvalg" (Oslo: Institute of Political Science, University of Oslo, mimeo., 1973). Lægreid and Olsen, *Byråkrati.*

66. E. E. Schattschneider, *The Semi-Sovereign People* (New York: Holt, Rinehart and Winston, 1966).

67. James G. March and Johan P. Olsen, *Ambiguity and Choice in Organizations* (Bergen: Universitetsforlaget, 1976).

68. Olsen, *Governing.*

69. For a general discussion of such mechanisms in organizational decision-making, see Richard Cyert and James G. March, *A Behavioral Theory of the Firm* (Englewood Cliffs, N.J.: Prentice-Hall).

70. The most important organizational bases for coordination across segments have been the Ministry of Finance and the political twins—the Labor party and the Federation of Labor Unions.

71. Olsen and Sætren, *Aksjoner.* So far most civil servants do not consider ad hoc actions important in their work field.

72. This will be true as long as politicians are able to make choices. If they are not, the position of the civil servants may be strengthened. We may have a situation where politicians talk and civil servants run the system.

73. K. McNeil and James D. Thompson, "The Regeneration of Social Organizations," in *American Sociological Review,* 1971 (36), pp. 624–637.

PARTIES, POLITICS, AND THE STATE IN CHILE
The Higher Civil Service

Arturo Valenzuela

Even before the election of Salvador Allende to the presidency of Chile in 1970, and his abortive attempt to bring about a socialist society within the framework of democratic procedures, the Chilean state had evolved into an awesome set of structures and institutions active in all reaches of national life. No other Latin American country, with the exception of Cuba, had as prominent a public sector. Direct public investment represented well over 50 percent of all gross investment and state agencies controlled over 50 percent of all credit. Government expenditures accounted for 24.2 percent of the Gross National Product (46.9 percent if decentralized agencies and state enterprises are included), and the state bureaucracy employed over 13 percent of the economically active population. The government development corporation owned majority shares in 39 key productive enterprises and minority shares in another 80. Medical care was administered by a national health service, and over 150 public and semipublic agencies managed a vast network of pension plans and social security programs. The state played an important role in labor disputes by regulating closely the collective bargaining system and monitored and controlled all wages, prices, and exchange rates.[1]

The picture in the nineteenth century was vastly different. From independence until the beginning of the twentieth century the role of the state was a regulating one, confined to the administration of justice, foreign affairs, defense, and the levying of customs duties in what was primarily an export economy. As table 1 shows, in 1850 there were 1,273 employees of the central government in nondefense functions. Thirty years later the number of employees had increased to 2,408, an increase that exceeded the population increase by only 13 percent.[2] In 1875 about 1.6 percent of the active population worked in the public sector.[3]

By 1900, however, the growth of the central government began to exceed the population growth rate by a substantial margin. Whereas the population had increased an additional 28 percent, the bureaucracy jumped in size by over 226 percent, dwarfing the central decision makers and their staffs in the presidency and Congress. Indeed, it was under the Parliamentary Republic (1890–1925), when Congress became the unquestioned center of the policy-making process, that the state began its first real expansion, one that involved a new role of dispenser of public works. The increase in state activities and public employment responded to vigorous log-rolling among legislators to divvy up the vast wealth from nitrate exports for the benefit of their constituencies through massive projects built by private contractors. As a result, the customs service expanded sharply to the point that in 1900 that office alone had as many employees as the entire government had in 1850. Functionaries in the burgeoning state-owned telegraph and post office business increased from 325 in 1880 to 1,650 in 1900. And in the field of education, employment increased dramatically as secular forces succeeded in wresting from the church its monopoly over public instruction.[4]

But it would not be long before the state would take on even more functions, marking a second and more fundamental shift in its orientations. The devastating economic crisis of World War I and the invention of synthetic nitrates, which destroyed the country's premier export industry, coupled with the growing importance of middle-class political parties and the challenge of an increasingly militant labor movement, led to the creation of several semiautonomous institutions aimed at providing social benefits and credit to low- and middle-income sectors. Credit institutions were also set up to help private enterprise in mining and industry. The *Caja de Crédito Salitrero* (Nitrate Credit Bureau) (1907), the *Caja Nacional de Ahorros* (National Savings Bureau) (1910) and the *Caja de Crédito Popular* (Popular Credit Bureau) (1920) were followed in the 1920s by close to fifty new agencies in health, social security, labor, and in public works and transport.[5] From 1920 to 1930 the number of state em-

TABLE 1.   Number of Employees in the Chilean Centralized Public Sector, by Ministry from 1850 to 1967

	1850	1880	1900	1919	1931	1941	1951	1961	1967
Presidencia	6	6	5	8	9	68	131	92	121
Congreso	90	191	170	259			272	336	377
Interior	208	568	1,935	3,828	4,359	7,100	9,231	12,495	14,355
Hacienda	519	729	1,564	2,481	2,149	2,237	6,205	7,913	8,322
Justicia					1,630	3,754	4,613	5,245	6,883
Relaciones Exteriores	15	47	784	813	180	166	262	328	427
Obras Publicas y Transportes					131	229	507	3,317	7,133
Salud Publica					704	835	2,488	14	36
Education Publica					11,127	16,583	24,385	39,266	50,634
Tierras y Colonización					116	191	277	384	349
Trabajo Prev. Social					—	137	663	495	650
Economia Fomento y Reconst.					—	—	1,100	1,099	1,851
Mineria									
Vivienda y Urbanismo									

Source: Data for 1850–1919 from Carlos Humud, "El sector público chileno entre 1830 y 1930" (Memoria de Prueba, Facultad de Ciencias Económicas, Universidad de Chile, 1969), p. 180. Data for 1931–1967 gathered from information scattered through Germán Urzua V. and Anamaría García B., *Diagnóstico de la burocracia chilena* (1818–1969) (Santiago: Editorial Jurídica de Chile, 1971). Information on congressional staff for 1951, 1961, 1967 from Anexo del Personal, Ley de Presupuesto for the respective years.

Note: Members of armed forces and police not included.

ployees doubled, while the population increased 15 percent. And, by 1930, 7.6 percent of the active population worked for centralized or decentralized state agencies.[6]

As Osvaldo Sunkel has noted, two earthquakes, a natural one that devastated much of southern Chile, and a political one that saw the election of the Popular Front (1938–1941), led to a fourth redefinition of the role of the state. To its regulatory, public works, and social welfare functions were added economic planning and industrial development through direct involvement of the state in the creation and operation of agricultural and industrial enterprises.[7] Succeeding governments continued to build and expand all four functions culminating in 1972 with the *Unidad Popular*'s (UP) incorporation into the public sector of over 250 of the country's largest industrial firms representing 22 percent of all industrial production and almost 20 percent of industrial employment.[8] In the process, the centralized administration (shown in table 1) gradually lost ground to the decentralized and semiautonomous agencies and enterprises. By 1970 45 percent of all public employment and 54 percent of public spending were in institutions not directly dependent on executive authority and outside of the central government budget.[9]

The military commanders who overthrew Allende in September of 1973 came into office with the avowed purpose of putting an end to the violence and confrontation which marked the UP's attempt to shift the Chilean state to an even more central role in the life of the nation. But the military has surprised both its opponents and early supporters by embarking on a far more radical policy. It has steadfastly attempted to dismantle not only the programs of the Popular Unity government, but the very nature of the interventionist Chilean state that had evolved over several generations. It is too early to tell whether the junta will succeed in its efforts and difficult to assess when and whether Chileans will be able to reimpose a political system of stable democratic politics that set them apart from all but a few countries in the world.[10] Despite the military's efforts there is considerable evidence that they have not succeeded in dismantling the key feature of Chilean politics—a strong party system with significant roots at all levels of civil society.[11]

The goal of this essay is to describe the higher civil service in Chile at the height of the power of the interventionist state. Because of the ad hoc quality of the current regime, which makes it difficult to judge the extent of irreversibility of junta policies, the essay will deliberately avoid discussion of the higher civil service under the military government.

Research into the Chilean bureaucracy and civil service is a difficult task because of the paucity of secondary materials and the difficulty of obtaining some of the most elementary primary sources, such as organizational manuals and the names and biographies of the administrative elite in different time periods. Students of Chilean politics have concentrated most of their attention on party politics and social change, to the neglect of state institutions.[12]

The essay will begin by describing the recruitment of ministers and under secretaries, noting their distinctly political character. It will then turn to a discussion of the educational backgrounds, recruitment, and promotion of higher civil servants—agency heads and bureau chiefs—stressing the mixture of professional training, agency experience, and partisan politics that characterized the Chilean bureaucracy. This assessment will be followed by a brief description of the relationships between higher civil servants and ministers, and a more detailed consideration of the crucial interactions between higher civil servants and legislators. The essay will conclude with a survey of the principal characteristics of the Chilean higher civil service, and some general observations on those factors that contributed to shaping the character of a service markedly different from most of its European counterparts.

PRESIDENTIAL CABINETS: MINISTERS AND UNDER SECRETARIES

On coming into office, a Chilean president had a very delicate balancing act to perform in making the key appointments of his government. Cabinet posts were filled by turning to prominent leaders with some familiarity with the subject matter of each ministry, but also with the necessary political credentials to make the appointment palatable to the governing coalition. Coalition politics was the fundamental characteristic of contemporary Chile. None of the six major political parties had majority support in the electorate. Since the Chilean system was a presidential one, coalitions were formed either before the election, to assure the broadest possible appeal for a particular candidate, or after the election to muster the necessary congressional support to ratify the election of the front runner and to ensure a working coalition in the Congress for the new administration.[13] Table 2 summarizes the coalition support of the last five constitutional governments in Chile. In the first three governments, as well as in most of their predecessors, coalitions fell apart mid-way through a presidential term, requiring new coalition arrangements. At the same time, most presidential coalitions were minority coalitions, requiring bargaining with parties outside of the presidential alliance to get legislative programs approved. Only in 1961–1963 did a presidential coalition have a majority in both houses of Congress. Finally, the table also shows that the Christian Democrats departed sharply from traditional practices by attempting to govern as a single party, particularly in the period 1965–1969 when they temporarily gained outright control of the Chamber of Deputies.

With the 1925 constitution, ministers were no longer held responsible to passing majorities in either house of Congress. However, Congress still retained the right to impeach ministers, and most contemporary presidents repeatedly faced successful and unsuccessful impeachment proceedings designed to keep the presidential coalition honest and the congressional opposition happy. This guaranteed that ministerial appointments would be drawn from a pool of individuals with impeccable party ties. Indeed, the parties further assured their influence by requiring that candidates nominated for cabinet posts be given official party permission (*pase*) to serve in office. Presidents could not simply appoint militants from various party organizations, they had to bargain with party central committees to gain their consent. The result of this appointment process is that cabinets were highly unstable. Table 3 provides information on the number of full and partial cabinet changes and the average duration in office of ministerial cabinets from 1932 to 1973. With the exception of the Jorge Alessandri government, which managed to structure a coalition with majority support in the legislature, and the Frei administration, which attempted to govern without coalition support, cabinets lasted in office for an average of less than one year. Individual cabinet members lasted in office on average for only a few more months.

While the Frei government exhibited a much higher level of ministerial stability, an examination of the backgrounds of all the ministers in office in 1968 reveals that they were also first and foremost party appointees.[14] None could be classified as a civil servant, though the minister of the interior had served as a minister in an earlier government under a Radical party president. Another had held an important post in the nationalized steel industry. All the rest came from the private sector or from universities. Four of the ministers had been prominent Christian Democratic party leaders, and five had begun their careers as important party leaders within the university. The ministers of health, public works, and agriculture were the only nonlawyers in the group. Five held university appointments, signaling the preference among Christian Democrats to turn to the universities for high-level political appointments. This contrasts with the Alessandri and Ibañez administrations, which sought their ministers in the private sector. Under Allende, the universities were also prime recruiting grounds for cabinet officials, though the coalition requirements of the Popular Unity government brought into ministerial positions men of very diverse backgrounds, including individuals who had made careers in the labor movement and a few who were blue-collar workers.

Though only two of Frei's ministers had served in Congress, this was due in large measure to the fact that the Christian Democratic party, a relatively new party, had had few congressmen in previous periods and

TABLE 2. Recent Presidents and Approximate Status of Coalition and Congressional Support

PRESIDENT	YEARS	PRESIDENTIAL COALITION PARTIES	MAJORITY/MINORITY STATUS	CORE SUPPORT
G. Gonzalez Videla 1946–1952	1946–1949	Radical Communist Falange Nacional	Minority	Radical
	1949–1952	Traditional conservatives Liberal Radical	Minority	Radical
Carlos Ibañez 1952–1958	1952–1955	Agrarian-Labor Popular Socialist Other Left & Right Fragments	Minority	Agrarian-Labor
	1955–1958	Agrarian-Labor Other Shifting Support	Minority	Agrarian-Labor

President	Period		Status	
Jorge Alessandri 1958–1964	1958–1960	Liberal (Informally) Conservative (Informally) Independent	Minority	
	1961–1963	Radical Liberal Conservative	Majority in Chamber Majority in Senate	Liberal Conservative
	1963–1964	Conservative Liberal	Minority in Chamber Minority in Senate	Liberal Conservative
Eduardo Frei 1964–1970	1964–1965	Christian Democrat	Minority	Christian Democrat
	1965–1969	Christian Democrat	Minority in Senate Majority in Chamber	Christian Democrat
	1969–1970	Christian Democrat	Minority	Christian Democrat
Salvador Allende 1970–1973	1969–1973	Socialist Communist Radical	Minority	Socialist Communist

Source: The most useful source in compiling this table was Lía Cortés and Jordi Fuentes, *Diccionario Político de Chile* (Santiago: Editorial Orbe, 1967). Many other secondary works were also consulted. It should be noted that the table is only approximate. It does not include more complex yearly variations, or variations on specific issues.

TABLE 3.   Cabinet Changes and Ministerial Turnovers in Chilean Presidencies

PRESIDENTS	NUMBER OF INTERIOR MINISTERS	NUMBER OF PARTIAL CABINET CHANGES	NUMBER OF MAJOR CABINET CHANGES	TOTAL NUMBER OF MINISTERS	AVERAGE LENGTH OF CABINETS	AVERAGE LENGTH OF MINISTERIAL SERVICE
Arturo Alessandri 1932–1938	6	2	3	59	10 months	12 months
Pedro Aguirre Cerda 1938–1942	7	2	2	44	9 months	11 months
Juan Antonio Rios 1942–1946	8	3	5	84	6½ months	6 months
Gabriel González V. 1946–1952	4	2	2	73	7 months	11 months
Carlos Ibáñez 1952–1958	8	3	5	75	7 months	12 months
Jorge Alessandri 1958–1964	2	1	1	20	29 months	43 months
Eduardo Frei 1964–1970	3	2	1	22	31 months	40 months
Salvador Allende 1970–1973	9	1	5	65	5⅚ months	7 months

Source: For the first four administrations data drawn from information available in Luis Valencia A., *Anales de la república*, 2 volumes (Santiago: Imprenta Universitaria, 1951). For the rest the *Hispanic American Reports*, *Facts on File*, and the *Mercurio Edicion Internacional* were consulted.

was reluctant to draw on their newly gained strength in the Congress for ministerial posts because it would reduce their congressional numbers. However, historically, ministers were often drawn from the ranks of congressmen and former congressmen. During the period of Radical party dominance (1932–1951), a third of the ministers had had congressional experience while in the nineteenth and early twentieth century over two-thirds of all ministers had served in Congress.[15]

Occasionally in periods of significant crisis, or in an attempt to gain the respect of opposition groups for presidential initiatives, Chilean presidents would constitute cabinets of "administration" with a few "technicians"—individuals with prestige who have remained at the margins of active party politics. These ministers were often brought into the more "technical" ministries having to do with mining or more often the economy. Though most came from the private sector, a few had made careers in the public sector, most notably as top administrators of state-run enterprises under the aegis of the Corporación de Fomento (State Development Corporation—CORFO). Alessandri appointed several ministers with CORFO backgrounds and good ties with Chilean industrial interests. Frei also appointed a few higher civil servants during his term in office. The most prominent was Raúl Saez, who had spent most of his career with CORFO and came to the ministerial position after serving as one of the "wise men" of the Alliance for Progress. Another prominent civil servant was Sergio Molina, who was one of the first professional economists to serve in the Ministry of Finance and was responsible for setting up Chile's modern Bureau of the Budget. After serving as minister of finance, he stepped down to become the head of CORFO. Unlike Saez, however, Molina was closely identified with the party. Allende also appointed some prominent civil servants in his unsuccessful attempt to diffuse opposition to his government. The most prominent individual was Carlos Briones, brought into the cabinet just before the military coup. Briones had served for years as superintendent of the social security system under various presidents and was highly regarded by all political groups. Like Molina, Briones was, however, a member of the Socialist party. Indeed, the only really "neutral" civil servants that Chilean presidents have occasionally turned to to fill ministerial posts were the high-ranking members of the armed forces. Allende followed the practice of Radical presidents and of President Ibañez by appointing military men to the post of minister of the interior. But, he went farther than his predecessor when he brought into his cabinet all of the commanders of the various services. This gave his embattled government some breathing space, but eventually contributed to the politicization of the armed forces.

A new president not only appointed the cabinet, but was required to designate the under secretaries who served as the directors of ministerial

TABLE 4.   Background Characteristics of Chilean Under Secretaries in 1968

Place of Birth		Age at Appointment	
Santiago: 5		20–30:	0
Provinces: 7		30–40:	10
		40–50:	1
		50– :	1
University Training		*Profession*	
U. of Chile: 8		Law:	10
Catholic U.: 3		Engineering:	1
No Univ.: 1		Economics:	1
Years in Public Administration		*Years in Agency*	
None: 5		8	
1–5: 2		2	
6–10: 3		2	
11–15: 0		0	
16–20: 0		0	
21– : 1		0	

Source: Lists of under secretaries obtained from José Manteola, *Guía de la administración pública de Chile y de los principales organismos del sector privado* (Santiago: Ediciones Guía, 1968). Biographical information is from the *Diccionario Biográfico de Chile,* 13th edition (Santiago: Ediciones Ercilla, 1967).

cabinets. The under secretary dealt with the day-to-day coordination of the ministry and was influential in personnel, financial, and juridical matters.[16] Though in the nineteenth century the predecessors for the under secretary, the "Official Mayor" established in 1853, were often career civil servants, in the twentieth century the post became increasingly "politicized" as appointees were brought in to balance the political appointments of the governing coalition.[17] More recently, under secretary positions were filled by younger men—generalists—who worked with the study and technical committees of the various political parties and were associated with university departments or research institutes. This was clearly the pattern in the Frei and Allende administrations. (Under the military government, the military has reserved the position of under secretary for itself, but there is evidence that military under secretaries have little influence.) Thus as table 4 shows, in 1968 Frei's under secretaries were overwhelmingly lawyers, with law degrees from the prestigious school of law of the University of Chile. Most of the under secretaries were in their early thirties and had had little experience in government service. Indeed, only two had served in the government for over ten years (though only one had served in the same agency for ten years), and four had had no previous government experience. Four of the twelve under secretaries were serving as university faculty before being appointed. All had close party ties.

THE HIGHER CIVIL SERVICE: CIVIL SERVICE CAREERS AND EDUCATIONAL QUALIFICATIONS

Examination of the careers of bureau chiefs and agency heads, including the decentralized agencies, suggests a very different picture. Rafael Lopez has noted that there are far more insiders among those leadership groups than among ministers and under secretaries. As table 5 shows only one quarter of the "Directors Generals" and heads of public enterprises were outsiders—whereas almost 64 percent of the ministers and almost half of the under secretaries were classified as such. A more detailed examination of the backgrounds of all directors of centralized agencies in the Ministry of Finance and Public Works and decentralized agencies in the Ministry of Finance confirms these observations. With the exception of the key post of director of the Central Bank, a position filled by a university professor, table 6 shows that all of the other decentralized agencies of the Ministry of Finance were led by individuals with over twenty (most with over thirty) years in public service. Half of these individuals had served only in the agency they now directed. Most of the directors of these agencies were over fifty. Frei had appointed five directors to their posts; the other four were reappointed to posts they had held from previous administrations. A similar picture is suggested by the directors of the key public works agencies of the Ministry of Public Works who command a third of the national budget. The five directors of agencies in the centralized sector of the Ministry of Finance, which include such

TABLE 5.   Rates of Insiders and Outsiders for Top Echelons in the Bureaucracy, 1968 (Percent)

	MINISTER	UNDER SECRETARY	GENERAL DIRECTOR	TOP EXECUTIVE PUBLIC CORPORATION
Insiders	36%	56%	79%	76%
Outsiders	64	44	21	24
Total	100	100	100	100
N	14	16	24	21

Source: Rafael López Pintor, "Development Administration in Chile" (Ph.D. Dissertation, University of North Carolina at Chapel Hill, 1972), p. 68.

TABLE 6.   Background Characteristics of Agency and Bureau Heads in the Centralized Sector of the Ministry of Finance and the Decentralized Sectors of Finance and Public Works

	AGENCY			
BACKGROUND	Finance Centralized	Finance Decentralized	Public Works Decentralized	Total
Place of Birth:				
Santiago	2	4	3	9
Provinces	3	6	5	14
Age at Appointment:				
20–30				
31–40	1	1	1	3
41–50	2	2	2	6
51–	2	6	5	13
University training:				
Univ. of Chile	1	4	6	11
Catholic Univ.	3		2	5
None	1	5		6
Profession:				
Law	1	1		2
Engineering	2		6	8
Architecture			2	2
Economics		3		3
None	2	5		7
Years in Public Admin.:				
1–5			1	1
6–10				
11–15	3			3
16–20	1		2	3
21–	1	8	5	14
Frei Appointment:				
Yes	5	6	4	15
No	0	3	4	7

Source: Information obtained from *Diccionario Biográfico de Chile*, 13th edition (Santiago: Ediciones Ercilla, 1967). Names of agency heads obtained from José Manteola, *Guía de la administración pública de Chile y de los principales organismos del sector privado* (Santiago: Ediciones Ercilla, 1967).

important agencies as Internal Revenue, the Bureau of the Budget, and the Customs Bureau, while career individuals, tended to be younger and had served fewer years within their own agencies. All, however, had more than ten years in the public sector. The significant difference with the other two groups is that all of the directors were appointed by Frei. This is not surprising for, as with the head of the Central Bank, these agencies deal with broader policy questions of interest to a new administration.

The biographical material on the directors of agencies in Public Works and Finance provides, not only information on the appointment process to higher posts, but information on civil service careers in Chile. Though individuals born in Santiago, with about one-third of the country's population, have close to 40 percent of the posts, the provinces are not as underrepresented as might be expected. Indeed, examination of other agencies, such as the decentralized agencies in the Ministry of Economics and Mining, suggests that in the more technical agencies there may be an overrepresentation of provincials—individuals who follow civil service careers because they may have less entry into the private sector, which is more closely tied to the Santiago elite.

In one survey of Chilean civil servants with professional degrees, most said that they entered public employment because they were not able to find a good job in the private sector. Though 70 percent noted that they were satisfied with their jobs, a majority would leave public service if they could obtain a better salary in the private sector.

That the primary objection to the civil service is its low economic reward rather than low prestige is suggested by the ranking of occupational prestige in Chile by the same sample of bureaucrats. As table 7 shows, though bank and industrial executive was ranked higher than

TABLE 7.   Occupational Prestige as Perceived by Officials of the Chilean Ministry of Housing

OCCUPATION	RANK ORDER	MEAN SCORE
Medical Doctor	1	2.5
University Professor	2	3.1
Bank or Industrial Executive	3	3.8
High Executive in the Bureaucracy	4	3.9
Lawyer	5	5.2
Technical Employee in the Bureaucracy	6	6.2
Landowner	7	6.8
Merchant	8	6.9
Priest	9	7.6
Military Officer	10	7.8

Source: Rafael López Pintor, "Development Administration in Chile" (Ph.D. Dissertation, University of North Carolina at Chapel Hill, 1972), p. 163.

higher civil servant, the rankings were extremely close. Higher civil servants, in fact, were ranked closer to the second-ranking university professors than to the fifth-ranking lawyers, a position of traditional prestige in Chile. Professionals ranked their middle-level positions in the administration as carrying more prestige than those of landowner, merchant, priest, and military officer. Since they could aspire to promotion to the higher civil service, they perceived their status to be comparable to colleagues in the private sector who could aspire to be industrial executives.[18]

In Chile there is no civil service commission and no uniform system of recruitment and promotion of personnel. Each agency administers its own personnel system. The *Estatuto Administrativo* on civil service regulation provides some basic requirements for entry (such as completion of the tenth grade) and spells out a series of "rights" that guarantee all public employees with employment stability and provide a system of advancement in which both merit and seniority are key factors.[19]

Though the Estatuto allowed many high school graduates to find employment in the state bureaucracy, in practice promotions went to those individuals with high-level technical or university training. Indeed, over the years the laws setting the organizational lines of each agency (including the level and number of positions to be filled and their respective salary levels) have increasingly called for professional degrees as minimum requirements to fill middle- and upper-level jobs. Thus the Decree Law on the internal organization of the *Servicio de Explotaciones de Puertos* (an agency administering Chile's ports) specified that the agency had to hire four economists in category 4 of the pay scale and five civil engineers in grade 1. Article 5 of the same law specified that the position of director required university degrees in either civil, industrial, or commercial engineering.[20] Likewise, by law, only graduates with degrees in law, civil or commercial engineering were allowed at one time to take the highly competitive examinations administered by the Ministry of Foreign Relations.[21]

Both through legislation and internal agency policy, professional groups with university training succeeded in flexing enough political muscle to establish virtual fiefdoms in public agencies.[22] As table 8 shows, public works was dominated by civil engineers and architects, the public health service was populated by doctors, the Ministry of Economics had a large number of economists and engineers. Lawyers had a strong presence in Finance, Justice, and Labor, as well as a monopoly of positions in the Comptroller General's Office not dependent on the executive. With the creation of the Ministry of Housing in 1967, architects came to dominate that ministry, leaving Public Works as a bastion for engineers. Surveys of professionals within public agencies confirm the proposition that loyalty to the profession took precedence over loyalty to the institution.[23]

And the importance of the public sector as an employer of individuals

TABLE 8. Distribution of Selected Professions by Ministry

	INTERIOR	FOREIGN RELATIONS	ECONOMICS	FINANCE	EDUCATION	JUSTICE	PUBLIC WORKS	AGRICULTURE	LANDS AND COLONIZATION	LABOR AND SOCIAL WELFARE	PUBLIC HEALTH	MINES	TOTAL
Architects	2	—	8	20	11	1	278	1	—	5	31	—	357
Agronomists	—	—	70	27	11	—	5	404	16	—	1	—	534
Civil Engineers	7	—	72	4	13	—	272	1	2	2	15	28	416
Commercial Engineers (Economists)	1	—	68	25	7	—	2	5	—	—	1	3	112
Doctors	207	—	4	1	26	61	3	—	—	6	5,633	—	
Dentists	92	—	1	—	20	1	6	—	—	—	1,040	—	
Teachers	5	—	—	—	8,178	1	56	16	1	—	182	—	8,439
Lawyers	58	3	90	182	19	115	99	11	17	155	48	18	815
Public Administrators	110	169	35	65	19	18	6	4	2	8	1	2	439

Source: INSORA, *Recursos humanos de la administración pública chilena: Informe complementario—clasificación ocupacional* (Chile: Santiago, 1965), pp. 67, 70.

257

with university degrees or highly specialized technical degrees is attested to by the fact that public agencies employed 19,762 such individuals, 15 percent of the total employment in the public sector. Table 9 shows that two-thirds of all doctors worked for the government, 36 percent of all agronomists, 27 percent of all architects, 19 percent of all dentists, and 13 percent of all economists. The table does not include civil engineers and lawyers, two large occupational groups among university professionals.

In the late 1960s only in some of the more traditional agencies of the central government were civil servants without university training able to ascend to bureau or agency head. Such was the case, for example, with some of the decentralized agencies of the Ministry of Finance where, as table 6 showed, over half of the directors were career people with training provided by their own agencies, either as inspectors or customs officials. It is not surprising that individuals without university credentials were more likely to make their careers in a single agency.

Concern over the increased importance of highly trained but narrow, professional specialists in the middle and upper leadership positions of public agencies led to the creation of a separate School of Political Science and Administration at the University of Chile in 1954. The founders of the school, primarily lawyers associated with the prestigious *Contraloría General* (Comptroller General), hoped that it would become an avenue for training competent generalists who could eventually staff the higher civil service with careers not restricted to individual agencies.[24] The school, however, was not able to compete with the professional schools in attracting the best students, and its graduates tended to move into middle-level ranks of the public service with few prospects for promotion. Indeed, the school had difficulty convincing public agencies to hire their graduates, a majority of whom had to find jobs in the private sector. Nor could the school compete with some of the well-entrenched training programs within the more prestigious agencies. Thus the Ministry of Foreign Affairs continued to insist that Foreign Service officers, in addition to their university training, complete courses in the Academia Andrés Bello associated with the ministry. The Ministry of Finance preferred to train its own inspectors in its *Escuela Nacional de Administración* (National School of Administration) which, despite the title, was a school restricted to its own middle-level functionaries. The well-entrenched professional associations, and the practice of individual agencies setting their own recruitment standards, clearly mitigated against the success of the new school.[25]

CIVIL SERVICE CAREERS: THE UBIQUITY OF POLITICS

The fact that most higher civil servants in Chile had university degrees and were professional civil servants does not mean, however, that promo-

TABLE 9.   Distribution of Professionals in the Public and Private Sectors

PROFESSION	TOTAL NUMBER PROFESSIONALS	PROFESSIONALS PUBLIC SERVICE	PROFESSIONALS PRIVATE SECTOR	% PROFESSIONALS PUBLIC SERVICE	% PROFESSIONALS PRIVATE SECTOR
Architects	1,327	357	970	27.0	75.0
Dentists	2,819	528	2,291	18.7	81.3
Agronomists	1,495	534	961	35.7	64.3
Economists	845	112	733	13.3	86.7
Foresters	55	2	53	3.6	96.4
Doctors	4,809	3,327	1,482	69.2	30.8
Total	11,350	4,860	6,490	42.8	57.2

Source: INSORA, *Recursos humanos de la administración pública chilena: Informe complementario—clasificación ocupacional* (Chile: Santiago, 1965), p. 26.

tions to top-level posts were determined solely by merit. Experience in public service and advanced training, while necessary credentials, were not sufficient for a successful career. There were no *grands corps* as in France that automatically selected those few individuals who could aspire to the higher civil service posts. To rise to the top, civil servants had to build political credentials through active involvement in a political party and the establishment of contacts with party leaders in and outside of the Congress.

Indeed, the merit system did not even work at the lower levels of the bureaucracy. Given the necessary credentials, political influence, such as the recommendation of a regional party leader, a congressman or a senator was very useful and often determinative in obtaining the job in the first place. Eighty-six percent of the respondents in one survey of civil servants said that political considerations were important in recruitment to public office.[26] With regard to promotions, the qualifications committees set up in each agency in order to judge the performance of personnel routinely gave 80 or 90 percent of the employees the highest possible scores. It is clear that, once the basic criteria for a position were defined by the professional credentials needed to fill it, promotion was based either on seniority or on political clout—and the latter was clearly indispensable to reach the top. Ambitious individuals, highly qualified in their fields of expertise, were the least likely to neglect the important political dimensions, so that the "best and the brightest" combined professional and political achievement.

Political parties in Chile were ubiquitous. They penetrated all levels of every organization in the society from unions to student groups, professional colleges, neighborhood associations, soccer clubs, and Protestant churches. The bureaucracy was obviously not immune. In every ministry and agency, public functionaries identified closely with one or another political party. The law gave civil servants full political rights and permitted party membership and party leadership provided that it did not lead the functionary to make use of state facilities or functions for narrow partisan purposes.[27]

In the period before 1938, though middle-class elements identified in the Radical party had already made significant inroads into the public sector, the conservative and liberal parties had a strong presence in the civil service, a presence that continued in later years in the Ministry of Foreign Affairs and in the judiciary. With the Popular Front in 1938 the Radical party became the principal force in several coalition governments and the master of bureaucratic patronage. Radical party members dominated most agencies, and continued to be strongly entrenched in the Comptroller General's Office and in the Ministry of Education after their fortunes began to decline in the 1950s. The working-class Democrats and later the Socialist party were able to gain something of a foothold in the Ministry of Labor and had strong representation in the social security sector. The Christian Democrats, drawing great strength from a new generation of university-trained technicians in nontraditional fields such as economics, sociology, and agronomy began to make inroads in the public sector even before the advent of Eduardo Frei to the presidency.[28] The only party to neglect to find a niche in the public administration was the Communist party, and the leading theoretician and long-time senator of the party recently told the author that this was a strategic mistake of major proportions going back to the 1930s.[29] These remarks should not be taken to mean, however, that parties carved out specific enclaves. While some were more dominant than others in particular agencies, all agencies had active members from all major parties among their employees. In fact, party allegiance outweighed professional identity in structuring individual loyalties. So as not to antagonize the faithful within each of the professions, parties tended to support the quest by professional associations for special privileges. However, party cleavages were clearly dominant and cut across professional and agency lines.

In a survey of *tecnicos* conducted in the early 1970s (48 percent were employed in the public sector and another 22 percent had served previously in the government) 83 percent identified themselves as party sympathizers or members. Of these, 28 percent were party leaders and advisers and another 24 percent were active party members. By contrast, in a similar sample in Argentina 52 percent of the respondents claimed no party affiliation. In Argentina the strong party identifiers were more likely to be outside the government, whereas in Chile they were equally divided between those serving inside and outside the public sector. In Argentina 63 percent of the sample argued that active membership in political parties reduced individual influence, whereas in Chile only 18 percent advanced that view. By contrast, 50 percent of the Chilean tecnicos (as opposed to 12 percent in Argentina) held that party affiliation was important in increasing an individual's influence. The rest argued that partisan affiliation made no real difference.[30]

A sample of individuals drawn from the professional and semiprofessional staff of the Ministry of Housing ($n = 230$) yielded similar evidence of partisan affiliation. In response to an open-ended question asking party preference, only 15 percent indicated that they were "apolitical." Among the party identifiers the largest percentage, almost 50 percent, identified with the Christian Democrats, which was to be expected in a new agency set up by the Frei administration. They were followed by the Socialists, Radicals, Nationals, and Communists in that order.[31]

The importance of partisan attachment is evidenced by the fact that union elections and elections to agency boards was generally structured along party lines. In 1972, the election of the steering committee of the elite Oficina de Planificación Nacional (National Planning Office— ODEPLAN), dependent directly on the presidency, yielded 40 percent of the 210 votes cast for the Christian Democrats, 30 percent for the Socialists, 25 percent for the Communists and the rest to minor party candidates.[32] Indeed, partisan divisions within agencies increased further with attempts in the late 1960s to introduce an element of democratization in public institutions. Partisan divisions were also exacerbated by the growing political polarization of the Allende years.

In promoting individuals to bureau and agency chiefs, presidents looked within each agency for competent individuals who also met the requisite political qualifications. This did not mean, however, a wholesale dismissal of agency heads from previous administrations. The same restrictions on the president's latitude with appointments of cabinet members and under secretaries affected the appointments at other levels of the bureaucracy. Presidents were wary of dismissing agency heads or of making new appointments without clearing matters with all of the parties in the coalition. Presidents also had to ensure that they would not unduly antagonize other elements that could conceivably become members of the presidential coalition should there be a falling out with the current partners. Since Chile was not a parliamentary system, and a president remained in office for a fixed term, presidents realized the fragility of their position. The next congressional election might undermine a partner in the coalition, or policy disputes might lead to coalition shifts. An excessively vindictive treatment of partisans of other political organizations was simply impossible. Coalition politics thus guaranteed an element of continuity, as parties bargained to ensure that a few of their members be promoted to important public posts. And the coalition nature of the process was an incentive to parties to put up some of their best people for promotion so as to make a stronger case to their coalition partners.

Promotion of new individuals from within the agencies was facilitated, in turn, by the strong inducements that existed for agency and bureau heads to retire. Civil servants could retire in Chile with fifteen years service and a relatively good pension. Agency heads, however, could retire with what was known as *la perseguidora*—a pension that kept pace with the salary of the current occupant of the post retired from. This was an extraordinary fringe benefit and a particularly attractive one in a society with extremely high inflation. It meant that one could continue to enjoy a high salary automatically readjusted for inflation. Agency heads were thus appointed as a culmination of their careers and could be persuaded to retire to allow a new president to make new appointments—and give colleagues within the agency a chance to earn, not only status and influence, but permanent financial security.

That parties did not fear that a president would use his appointment power to unjust political advantage is evidenced by the congressional practice of empowering incoming presidents with sweeping powers to reorganize the bureaucracy. In what was probably an unconstitutional practice, Congress would delegate a broad authority to the chief executive allowing him to redefine the functions, location, internal structure, personnel requirements of all agencies, with the exception of agencies specifically exempted by the law. Employees to be dismissed would be given special and very attractive severance pay.[33] This did not mean, however, that large numbers of employees would be dismissed. More often than not it meant that new agencies, or reorganized agencies, that could carry forth new program initiatives of the new administration were brought into existence without having to abolish older ones. Even the conservative and austerity-minded Jorge Alessandri added 35,000 new employees to the public sector during his tenure in office.[34]

It is revealing to note that the Frei administration was rebuffed when it sought the same authority. The Christian Democrats, though achieving the presidency with coalition backing, made it plain that they intended to rule the country as a *partido unico*. Opposition parties, concerned that Frei would ignore the usual procedures and appoint his own people to administrative posts, were reluctant to provide him with the sweeping authority over administrative reorganization.[35]

In fact, on coming into office the Frei administration confirmed its detractors' fears. Though in the first year it did not control the Congress, and after 1965 it controlled only the lower chamber, it proceeded to make appointments with little regard for coalition politics. Indeed, the Christian Democrats explicitly criticized traditional politics in general, and the Radical party in particular, for the particularism and inefficiency of a public sector not inspired by technical expertise. The Christian Democratic government, confident that it was the wave of the future and would be in office for years to come with a solid majority, thus marked an important turning point in modern Chilean politics. The bitter antagonisms that it engendered, particularly among followers of the other centrist party, the Radicals, contributed in no small measure to the growing polarization and confrontation that eventually would lead to regime breakdown. When the Christian Democrats failed to achieve their goal of becoming a majority party (which would have broken the historical stalemate of Chilean party politics) it was too late to recreate the center coalitions that the Radicals had forged for much of the twentieth century.[36]

The pressures for a tough stand on traditional politics came not only from leaders but from followers. Frei found that in many cases he could not reappoint competent higher civil servants because of strong opposition from Christian Democratic functionaries in the agency in question who felt it was their turn to be promoted.

Despite their claims, the Christian Democrats engaged in traditional political practices except that new appointments were almost exclusively to members of their own party with no effort to balance appointments among potential allies.

Only a few notable exceptions to this pattern can be cited. Frei resisted pressure to move four or five steps down the seniority system and appoint a Christian Democrat to the post of comptroller general, preferring to give the position to the second-ranking official of the agency, a Radical, and one of the country's most prominent experts in administrative law. Likewise, Carlos Briones, a Socialist, and superintendent of the Social Security Administration, was kept on because of his outstanding reputation. Sergio Chaparro, the head of the National Institute of Statistics, an agency that like the Electoral Tribunal was considered to be above politics, was also reconfirmed to his post. Frei also maintained several bureau heads in the more technical but less prominent agencies, particularly in the decentralized sector as table 6 indicates.

In those cases where bureau and department heads were unwilling to resign from the public office, the Christian Democrats made use of an old bureaucratic practice of respecting an individual's job security, but of depriving him of any real leadership functions. The *huesera* (or common grave), a series of offices for individuals with no official responsibilities beyond paper responsibilities, became a feature of many agencies. The author, while conducting interviews with civil servants in Chile in 1969, came across several bureaucrats, mainly Radicals, who had many years of experience but nothing to do.

Since Frei was not granted statutory authority to conduct a broad reorganization of the executive branch, he turned to another old practice—the creation of new agencies designed to carry out priority programs. New life was put into agrarian reform organizations that had been on the books since the early 1960s, and statutory authority was obtained to create a new Ministry of Housing and Urban Development, though Frei failed to move out of public works all of the agencies he sought for the new ministry.[37]

Thus in sharp contrast with the directors of the Ministry of Finance and Public Works described earlier, 40 percent of the directors in the Ministry of Housing were between thirty-six and forty years of age and only 3.6 percent were over fifty. Over half had been in public service for less than five years. Indeed of 312 individuals sampled from the professional and administrative staff, 67 percent had been in public service for less than five years. Most were brought in directly from universities, or from other agencies in the housing field. Only 7 percent came from the private sector.[38] The law setting up the ministry did not require that hiring and promotion practices accord with the Estatuto Administrativo, giving the president more latitude. In other agencies, notably the Instituto de Desarrollo Agropecuario (Institute of Agrarian Development—INDAP), and to a more limited degree in the Corporación de Reform Agraria (Agrarian Reform Corporation—CORA), the key agencies in the Christian Democratic party's major agrarian reform effort, outsiders predominated among staff. Indeed, the school of sociology of the Catholic University, which had been attracting some of the brightest students in the university, became an important recruiting ground for the agrarian reform agencies and other priority agencies dependent directly on the presidency.

When the Allende government came to office it was also denied statutory authority to make transformations in the executive branch. The Christian Democrats, supported by the rightist National party, feared that the Popular Unity government would follow its lead and only make appointments of its own people. In fact, the Allende government resembled much more closely traditional political practices because of its coalition nature—an unwieldy alliance of Socialists, Communists, Radicals and assorted splinter parties. However, the UP deviated from traditional practices because it also sought to exclude opposition elements, particularly Christian Democrats. Furthermore, the Allende government outdid its predecessors in the extent to which it followed an explicit quota system to justify appointments at all levels of the government from ministers to department heads. Conflicts often ensued within government agencies as militants of particular parties within the coalition objected to directorial appointments of militants of other parties. Changes in electoral fortunes of the parties in the municipal elections of 1971, in various by-elections, and in the congressional elections of 1973 further complicated the situation because the quota system tended to follow the relative electoral strengths of the coalition partners. The requisition of a large number of industries brought into the public sector only added to the confusion as parties jockeyed with one another to have their people appointed as "intervenors." Much of the administrative chaos during the Allende years can be directly attributed to political polarization and the ensuing search for partisan advantage.

It is clear that, with the rise of the Christian Democrats as an ideological center in Chilean politics differing from the more pragmatic center represented by the Radicals, coalition politics were severely undermined. And, with the demise of coalition politics, the traditional checks on the potential excesses of a politicized promotion system in the public sector also disappeared. During the Allende period the twin qualifications of professional expertise and party credentials gave way to a preponderance of the latter.

MINISTERS AND CIVIL SERVANTS

The most important variable affecting the relationship between ministers and higher civil servants was the marked instability of ministerial positions. As noted in table 3, ministers served in their posts for only a few months, hardly enough time to become familiar with the intricacies of large bureaucratic organizations.

However, while ministers and cabinets came and went, higher civil servants had security of office for at least the six-year presidential term. This gave the upper reaches of the administration significant continuity and influence as ministers were forced to rely on the expertise of their bureau and agency heads.[39] "Departmentalism" set in early in a minister's tenure. Many ministers were forced to deal with under secretaries appointed by a predecessor, individuals who had already established a rapport with the career people within the agencies. As noted earlier, in most Chilean governments coalition requirements meant that under secretaries were often from other political parties.

Ministers in important ministries that set policy directions for the government as a whole, such as the Ministers of Finance and Economics, had considerable influence by virtue of their role as spokesmen for the president and the coalition majority. Critical decisions, such as price control and wage readjustments, were hammered out at the highest level of the government and involved active participation of influential ministers. Likewise, priority areas of a new administration, such as industrial development under Aguirre Cerda, agrarian reform under Frei, or public enterprises under Allende, catapulted the relevant ministers into positions of importance. Generally speaking, however, even in important ministries, higher civil servants had considerable latitude in their day-to-day activities. Thus, 56 percent of the directors and department heads in the Ministry of Housing, during the Frei years, indicated that they had considerable autonomy in carrying out their functions (4 percent thought that it was illimited) while another 21 percent thought that their autonomy was adequate. The same group of directors ranked the minister as fourth in overall influence within the agency, after the bureau and agency directors, the under secretary and the department heads in that order. The minister ranked first only in general policy matters and in budgetary affairs, while the bureau chiefs ranked first in technical matters, purchasing, accounting, and matters of efficiency. It is interesting to note that in personnel questions, as well as in purchasing and juridical questions, the under secretary had the most influence, followed closely by the directors. Indeed, most communications within the agency went from the directors to the department heads. Fifty-four percent of those interviewed said that they became aware of the existence of problems from their immediate supervisor, and 17 percent said that this information came from subordinates. Only 8 percent mentioned the minister and 2 percent the under secretary.[40] Even though Housing was supposed to be a new and innovative agency, it was very hierarchical and professional in its day to day operations.

Peter Cleaves documents well the entrenched character of public agencies and the difficulties that a government faces in attempting drastic reorganization in his account of the attempt by the Frei administration to dismantle the Ministry of Public Works and to incorporate some of its major services into the new Ministry of Housing and Urban Development. As Cleaves notes, the minister and the government were simply not able to overcome the resistance of agency heads, including the head of the Bureau of Public Works, a prominent Christian Democrat who had made a long career within Public Works. The minister's clout was simply not enough to move against both the interests of the agency and its successful attempt to enlist allies in the Congress anxious to protect their ties to programs with important ramifications for their constituencies.[41] For while agencies were relatively self-contained, they also had close ties to other organizations and groups that provided them with additional avenues of support and autonomy. The most important was the Congress and, through the Congress, the political parties.

CONGRESSMEN AND HIGHER CIVIL SERVANTS

If the parties were important in Chilean politics, and had a strong impact on recruitment and promotion in the public bureaucracy, it was in the final analysis due to the fact that they derived formal authority from their base in the legislature. And Congress as a body, and congressmen and senators as individuals, had considerable influence over the bureaucracy. Congress could create or abolish agencies. It also could set the internal personnel system and structure of each agency, specifying the salaries and formal qualifications for advancement. Congress also determined the functions and the operating procedures of each agency. Agencies consequently were continuously submitting proposals for legislative action that would benefit agency personnel or give the agency broader jurisdiction and institutional autonomy. The proliferation of autonomous agencies is due in no small measure to the efforts of individual agencies with powerful allies in the Congress who succeeded in gaining a measure of independence from the executive through the creation of separate accounts, earmarked tax revenue, special fees, or investment sinking funds. As an example, the professional staff of the Ministry of Transport successfully managed to obtain congressional support to designate inspection fees on trucks for the exclusive purpose of providing salary increases for the ministry professionals, assuring them of a stable source of income not tied to Ministry of Finance action.[42] Congress was also critical in the budgetary process. In a society with endemic inflation, it was not enough to ensure that an agency receive adequate funding in the appropriations law but that the agency receive a significant portion of the funding during the first quarter when the money was worth substantially more than in the last quarter. Though the executive clearly had the upper hand in designing the budget, congressmen and senators could help out, not only in approving budgetary legislation, but in pressing for advantages in the implementation stage. Even more important than the national budget was the yearly salary readjustment legislation—over which organized groups jockeyed to obtain salary increases that would offset the ravages of inflation. The 1968 readjustment law, which began with 300 articles, eventually was expanded to 800 as members of Congress added 2,114 amendments favoring particular groups and agencies.[43]

In addition, deputies and senators played an important role in supervising the operations of executive agencies. For many years they had direct influence because Congress would appoint four deputies, and beginning in 1946 two senators, to supervisory bodies of each of the autonomous agencies. These were among the most sought-after positions in Congress because they gave individual legislators considerable clout over appointments and other internal agency matters. Even though the *consejerías parlamentarias* (parliamentary advisory bodies) were abolished in 1961 because of growing criticism over political meddling and patronage abuse, Congress continued its supervisory role through the institution of investigatory committees.[44] Though committees did not have subpoena powers, civil servants and ministers always responded to an invitation to testify because the political cost of ignoring a congressional request was deemed too great.[45] It was widely believed in Chile that higher civil servants could not lie to a congressional committee. Congressmen and senators had such close contacts of their own with staff at all levels of the bureaucracy, that they could easily check up on information presented in formal hearings by agency superiors. There simply was no "official secrets" act in Chile as parties and congressmen had bridges to their party counterparts in the ministries.[46]

Finally, legislators were influential in promoting the careers of individual civil servants who had close party ties, or who had been particularly diligent in responding to requests for constituency service. Obviously, civil servants who became important party leaders or advisers with direct contacts in the upper levels of the party organizations were in the best positions. But, individuals could also seek help from congressmen they knew well to represent their case to more important leaders with more direct access to the centers of the policy-making process.

It would be a mistake, however, to argue that civil servants only opened their doors to congressmen because of the political clout the latter might have over their agencies and careers. Occasionally, members of Parliament were very successful in providing agencies with important

TABLE 10. Scores of Most Influential Actors on Several Policy Areas in Ministry of Housing as Perceived by Agency Officials

POLICY ACTOR	GENERAL POLICY	TECHNICAL MATTERS	PERSONNEL MATTERS	BUDGET MATTERS	PURCHAS-ING	ACCOUNT-ING	JURIDI-CAL	EFFI-CIENCY	TOTAL
Minister	364	258	264	364	199	152	231	277	2,109
Under Secretary	268	187	358	249	335	181	372	252	2,202
Personnel Secretary	129	160	112	118	116	108	112	114	969
Bureau Head	331	364	327	283	314	281	289	318	2,507
Department Head	264	333	285	262	227	227	220	297	2,115
Supervisory Commission	281	283	134	181	120	100	168	187	1,454
External Agencies	272	216	185	331	241	245	249	179	1,918
Government Employees	152	212	166	116	145	118	133	172	1,214

Source: INSORA, "El proceso de toma de decisiones en el Ministerio de la Vivienda y Urbanismo" (Santiago: INSORA, 1969), p. 6.

269

information, financial aid, and community support for agency projects to be carried out in their constituencies. To the chagrin of elements trying to introduce "rational planning" mechanisms within the bureaucracy, bureau chiefs in charge of line agencies were often more willing to follow informed political pressure than the unrealistic planning targets they knew to be based on faulty and unrealistic data and premises.[47]

The influential position of senators and deputies over agencies is underscored by table 10, in which professional staff in the semiautonomous housing agencies ranked the relative influence of various individuals and organizations. Over general policy, and personnel matters, senators and deputies ranked second in importance to the politically appointed governing board of the agency and above department heads, technical personnel, and other agency professionals. Senators and deputies also ranked a close third to the funding agencies in influence over financial allocations and a close third to mayors and prefects (intendentes) in the allocation decisions for specific projects. Indeed, the success of mayors, who were much more important than prefects, was in turn due to their ability to receive support from political allies in Congress.[48]

In his survey of tecnicos in Chile, Ascher found that 72 percent of the respondents listed Congress as among the three most important decision-making centers in the country, followed by 65 percent for parties and 22 percent for the president. When asked to specify the single most important decisionmakers, the largest number (42 percent) specified political parties, followed by top regime leaders (33 percent) and the president (8 percent). Congress was second or third on two-thirds of the lists.[49]

While legislative ties were crucial to higher civil servants and higher civil servants were active in partisan politics, congressional careers, like ministerial careers, were very distinct from careers in government service. An examination of the biographies of all forty-five senators serving in the Congress in the late 1960s reveals that no senator had moved into electoral politics after a career in the civil service. The party organization, and not the government, was the base for their political careers. This does not mean that senators did not serve in some capacity in high-level administrative posts. In fact nine had served as minister in previous governments before being elected to the Senate. Six other senators held important government posts at one time or another for short terms. These ranged from a private secretary to President Juan Antonio Ríos, to directors of the Post Office and the Statistics Bureau, to an under secretary of the Ministry of Finance. Twenty-five other senators had no previous ministerial or public service experience.[50] An examination of biographical material for all candidates who ran for Congress in 1973 suggested no trend against this pattern.[51]

CONCLUSION

From a comparative perspective, the most salient characteristic of Chilean public administration was its permeability to party politics and its subordination to the legislature, factors that sharply distinguished it from its major Western European counterparts and Japan. Strictly speaking, there was no higher civil service in Chile—no body of government officials with a highly developed esprit de corps, recruited through special schools or screened by rigid examinations, insulated from party politics and Parliament and the changing fates of governments. The Chilean civil service was recruited and promoted through a Chilean version of the spoils system: party recommendations, and legislative support, in addition to formal credentials, were important in gaining entry and crucial in rising to higher office. The civil service was fragmented, not only by differing professional loyalties, but more importantly by strong partisan loyalties that prevented the development of institutional loyalties. Though career civil servants provided continuity to the public business, leadership was defined by, and responsive to, the distribution of political forces, parties, and coalitions, whose strength was ultimately determined by the electorate. Ministers and under secretaries were first and foremost political elites—and successful bureau and agency heads were those individuals who combined formal training and experience with active party work.

This is not to say that there was no such thing as a civil service career in Chile. The administration was not merely populated by political hacks. The formal requirements for entry and promotion and the incentives for political parties to select the best people ensured that agencies were often led by extremely competent individuals, many of whom became authorities in their lines of service as attested by their frequent affiliation with universities as part- or full-time lectures. Civil service careers did provide job security, and when job security was lost through promotion to the top, retirement was at full pay, providing a powerful incentive for ambitious individuals to end their careers as agency heads. Indeed, the mixture of professional and political factors ensured that the Chilean higher civil service, while perhaps less competent, was more responsive to democratic political forces than the more elitist managers of public bureaucracies in other countries.

But why did Chile, which developed a labor movement, a party system, and an interventionist state so similar to that of several European countries, develop a higher civil service more akin to the one found in the United States? Hans Daalder has argued that the degree of party permeation of state bureaucracies is a function of the relative timing of the emergence of these institutions in different national settings. The permeation is greater in those situations in which the parties preceded the development of administrative bodies.[52]

However, the key to a politicized administration is not so much the development of a party system as such, as the formation of a strong legislative body before the development of large-scale state bureaucracies. The elected officials in time became the leaders of fledgling party organizations that, in order to survive in an era of growing democratization, had to extend their roots out of the halls of Congress and into an expanding body politic. Where the Congress and mass parties emerged before the administration they were in a better position to create institutions that would be more responsive to congressional control and more permeable to party influence. Furthermore, elected officials became the key political elites with a monopoly over policy formulation and implementation before their functions began to be delegated to administrative authorities. Private groups intent on influencing policy gravitated to the legislature and to party organizations, and through them built ties to administrators whose fortunes remained at the mercy of politicians.

The capacity of congressional and political elites to mold the public sector in Chile did not simply result from the provisions laid down in early nineteenth-century documents, particularly the 1833 constitution. It also resulted from the fact that the War of Independence, a violent struggle lasting over several years, left the country with few administrators and military leaders from colonial times. The revolutionary elites did not have to contend with the presence of an established cadre of governmental, judicial, and military officials performing their traditional functions as they sought to forge new republican institutions. And Chile, unlike most of its neighbors and many European countries experimenting with republican and democratic institutions at the same time, managed to consolidate from a very early date a constitutional form of government. After 1830, all presidents, with the exception of several chief executives in the tumultuous years of 1924 to 1930, were elected to office and served out their constitutional mandates. And, what is more important for the purpose of the argument at hand, the Congress gradually consolidated its position as the center of gravity of Chilean politics. From 1860 to 1925 the government of Chile was for all intents and purposes a parliamentary government.[53]

Table 11, which examines all ministers who have served in Chile from the founding of the Republic until 1953, shows the close interrelationship between Congress and the top managerial leadership. In the early period no ministers served who would not serve either before or after in the legislature, and in the other two periods of the nineteenth century ministers who served first in Congress were clearly the most numerous, and a stint in a ministry often meant a return to the legislature afterward. After

TABLE 11. Ministerial Recruitment in Chile: Congressional Ties of Ministers in Selected Periods

	1831–1861	1861–1891	1891–1925	1925–1932	1932–1953
Congressmen before or simultaneously while serving as minister	21	70	164	19	37
Congressmen after serving as a minister	9	9	17	8	11
No congressional experience	20	14	57	66	76
Congressmen before and after serving as a minister	20	49	111	9	9
Total	50	142	349	102	133

Source: This table was compiled by making a list of all ministers and juxtaposing it to lists of congressmen and senators to determine prior and subsequent service by ministers in the legislature. Lists were drawn from Luis Valencia A., *Anales de la República*, 2 Volumes (Santiago: Imprenta Universitaria, 1951).

1925, when simultaneous service was outlawed, presidents continued to name individuals with congressional experience to ministerial posts—though ministers with no congressional experience became the dominant number as congressmen and senators were reluctant to give up seats in the legislature to serve for a brief period in a presidential cabinet.

In the early nineteenth century, higher civil servants not occupying ministerial positions were often indistinguishable from the political elites. An examination of the biographies of the top administrators in 1850 reveals that of sixteen individuals, eleven were also either deputies or senators at some point in their careers, and six held the congressional post before assuming the administrative post. Of those who did not serve in Congress three were not prominent enough to be mentioned in biographical dictionaries, one was a foreigner, and one served in the government for only a short period of time.

By the turn of the century the twentieth-century pattern had begun to impose itself. Only eight of the thirty-four top administrators in 1903 (24 percent) ever became ministers, and 10 (29 percent) served in Congress. Administrators were becoming a more distinct group—one subordinate to the political elite—a pattern that would hold until the overthrow of the regime in 1973.

With the advent of the military government, the public bureaucracy was purged of many of the most prominent supporters of the Popular Unity government, and eventually of the opposition Christian Democratic party. Parties were severely restricted or outlawed, and the Congress was shut down. For the first time in Chilean history, the administration would function without the supervision and interference of political elites. However, despite the claim that "technical" and "neutral" criteria for appointments would be used, military leaders have clearly used similar standards in designating the top ranks of the government and civil service. Active and retired military officers have moved into many ministerial posts and have monopolized the positions of under secretary. Agency and bureau heads have also come from military ranks. Support for the regime is the basic qualification for service, though government has sought to promote competent individuals from agency staffs. Personal acquaintance with an important general or with the leaders of the economic–policymaking elite who are guiding the country, is as helpful to an ambitious civil servant as party contacts were before the coup.

At the same time, it is clear that most individuals in civil service have not dropped their party identification and, indeed, in most agencies a majority of the civil servants oppose the government. Even in the elite Bureau of the Budget, where ninety percent of the budget analysts retained their jobs, opposition elements predominate with the largest contingent identifying with the Christian Democratic and Socialist parties. So far it would seem that a major reformulation of the relationship between administration and politics has not been attained.

NOTES

I wish to acknowledge the aid of J. Samuel Valenzuela in the preparation of this paper. Historical materials are drawn from a larger collaborative project, *The Origins of Democracy: Theoretical Reflections on the Chilean Case,* to be published by Cambridge University Press. I am also grateful for the advice of Luis Quiroz, Jorge Tapia Videla, Iván Auger, and Claudio Orrego, whose intimate knowledge of Chilean politics and bureaucracy helped to provide some important insights. Finally, this work owes a great deal to the excellent study of Rafael López Pintor, "Development Administration in Chile" (Ph.D. Dissertation, University of North Carolina at Chapel Hill, 1972).

1. Sergio Bitar, *Transición, socialismo y democracia: La experiencia chilena* (Mexico: Siglo XXI Editores, 1979), p. 36. An invaluable source for these statistics is ODEPLAN, *Plan de la economía nacional: Antecedentes sobre el desarrollo chileno,* 1960–1970 (Santiago: ODEPLAN, 1971).

2. Population figures are drawn from Chile, *Censo de la República de Chile* (Santiago: Sociedad Imprenta y Litografía Universo, 1908), p. XVII.

3. Rafael López Pintor, "Development Administration in Chile" (Ph.D. Dissertation, University of North Carolina at Chapel Hill, 1972), p. 100.

4. The best study of the evolution of Chilean budgets and employment in the nineteenth century is Carlos Humud, "El sector público chileno entre 1830 y 1930" (Memoria de Prueba, Facultad de Ciencias Económicas, Universidad de Chile, 1969). The classic study of the Parliamentary Period is Manuel Rivas Vicuña, *Historia política y parlamentaria de chile,* 3 vols. (Santiago: Ediciones Biblioteca Nacional, 1964). The best full treatment that breaks new ground in interpreting the period is Julio Heise G., *Historia de chile: El periodo parlamentario 1861–1925,* Vol. 1 (Santiago: Editorial Andres Bello, 1974).

5. For a detailed description of the development of the public sector, see Germán Urzúa V. and Anamaría García B., *Diagnóstico de la burocracia chilena* (1818–1969) (Santiago: Editorial Jurídica de Chile, 1971), and Germán Urzúa V., *Evolución de la administración pública chilena* (1818–1968) (Santiago: Editorial Jurídica de Chile, 1970).

6. López, "Development Administration in Chile," p. 100.

7. "Cambios estructurales, estrategias de desarrollo y planificación en Chile (1938–1969)," *Cuadernos de la Realidad Nacional,* No. 4 (June 1970), pp. 31–49. A more detailed discussion, which draws on Sunkel's work, is Osvaldo Contreras

Strauch, *Antecedentes y perspectiva de la planificación en Chile* (Santiago: Editorial Jurídica de Chile, 1971).

8. Bitar, *Transición, socialismo y democracia*, p. 177. Another excellent account of the economy under Allende is Stefan de Vylder, *Allende's Chile: The Political Economy of the Rise and Fall of the Unidad Popular* (Cambridge: Cambridge University Press, 1976).

9. The most comprehensive, though flawed, study of employment in the public sector is INSORA, *Recursos humanos de la administración pública chilena* (Chile: Insora, 1962). See p. 37. It was complemented by INSORA, *Recursos humanos de la administración pública chilena: Informe complementario—clasificación ocupacional* (Chile: Santiago, 1965). On expenditures see ODEPLAN, "Plan de la Economía," p. 388.

10. Studies are only now beginning to appear evaluating the junta years. For a discussion of the changes in the state since 1973, see Pilar Vergara, "Las transformaciones del estado bajo el régimen militar," paper presented at the conference Chile Under Military Rule, Woodrow Wilson International Center for Scholars, Washington, D.C., May 15–17, 1980.

11. See Arturo Valenzuela and J. Samuel Valenzuela, "Party Oppositions Under the Chilean Authoritarian Regime," paper presented at the conference Chile Under Military Rule, Woodrow Wilson International Center for Scholars, Washington, D.C., May 15–17, 1980. This study and the Vergara study mentioned in note 10 will be published in Arturo Valenzuela and J. Samuel Valenzuela, *Military Rule in Chile* (Baltimore: The Johns Hopkins University Press, forthcoming 1984).

12. The few general studies in English in addition to the dissertation by López mentioned earlier include the discussion of the bureaucracy in Federico Gil, *The Political System of Chile* (Boston: Houghton Mifflin Co., 1966); Charles Parrish, "Bureaucracy, Democracy, and Development: Some Considerations Based on the Chilean Case," in Clarence E. Thurber and Lawrence S. Graham (eds.), *Development Administration in Latin America* (Durham, N.C.: Duke University Press, 1973); and Richard A. Fehnel, "Chile" in John C. Honey, *Toward Strategies for Public Administration Development in Latin America* (Syracuse: Syracuse University Press, 1968). An excellent study which, though focusing on the social security system, provides rich information on the political context of the administration is Jorge Ivan Tapia and Luis Quiroz, "El subsistema político de la seguridad social en Chile," Instituto de Ciencias Políticas, Universidad Católica de Chile, *Serie de Documentos de Trabajo* Año IV, No. 5 (September 1974). Unfortunately this book-length manuscript was never published. The only case study, in addition to those by López and Tapia and Quiroz, is the excellent work by Peter Cleaves, *Bureaucratic Politics and Administration in Chile* (Berkeley: University of California Press, 1974). Treatments of the juridical basis of public administration are much more plentiful. The best is Enrique Silva C., *Derecho administrativo chileno y comparado*, 2 Volumes (Santiago: Editorial Jurídica de Chile, 1969). An excellent earlier treatment is Manuel Jara C., *Derecho administrativo* (Santiago: Artes y Letras, 1953).

13. For a fuller treatment of coalition dynamics in Chile, see Arturo Valen-

zuela, *The Breakdown of Democratic Regimes: Chile* (Baltimore: Johns Hopkins University Press, 1978).

14. The only comprehensive source of names of higher civil servants is the list provided in Jose Manteola, *Guía de la administración pública de Chile y de los principales organismos del sector privado* (Santiago: Ediciones Guía, 1968). Biographical material was obtained from the *Diccionario Biográfico de Chile, 1968* (Santiago: Empresa Periodística de Chile, 1968) and Jordi Fuentes and Lía Cortes, *Diccionario político de Chile* (1810–1966) (Santiago: Editorial Orbe, 1967).

15. Data for the most recent period are being analyzed. For a table that shows for earlier periods the extent to which ministers are drawn from Congress and the extent to which they return to Congress after serving in the ministry, see table 11 and the concluding section of this essay.

16. For evidence on the role of under secretaries, see INSORA, *El proceso de toma de decisiones en el ministerio de la Vivienda y Urbanismo* (Santiago: INSORA, 1969).

17. López, "Development Administration in Chile," pp. 170, 196.

18. Such perceptions were no doubt reinforced by the fact that the respondents considered themselves upwardly mobile. Fifty-seven percent thought they had higher status professions than their fathers. Only 17 percent thought their status was lower. See López, p. 146.

19. See the Estatuto Administrativo (DFL 338) in Contraloría General de la República, *Recopilación de los Decretos con Fuerza de Ley,* Volume 48, No. 2 (Santiago: Contraloría General de la República, 1960), pp. 1303–1392. This law brought into one document several disparate pieces of legislation and thus replaced legislation from 1942, 1953, and 1958.

20. See DFL 216, in Contraloría General de la República, *Recopilación,* pp. 919–923.

21. See DFL 338, in Contraloría General de la República, *Recopilación,* p. 1378.

22. It must be noted that agencies had considerable leeway in practice. Only in 30 percent of all agencies had the "organic regulations" to implement the law been approved, and most were out of date. See Urzúa V., and García B., *Diagnóstico de la burocracia,* pp. 199–200.

23. López, "Development Administration in Chile," p. 170.

24. In part the creation of the school was a response to the inroads that the School of Economics at the University of Chile had been making in training high-level personnel for the decentralized sector and for centralized agencies dealing with economic issues. The lawyers attached to the Contraloría and the Law School rejected the premise that a training designed to serve large enterprises in the private sector could be extended to the public sector.

25. It was difficult to establish a new program because of the advent of widespread reform efforts in the university that pressed, not for further elite training, but for greater democratization. The climate did not favor the expansion of the school in the direction of the French ENA. I am indebted to Jorge Tapia Videla for these observations.

26. López, "Development Administration in Chile," p. 118. James Petras in his *Politics and Social Forces in Chilean Development* (Berkeley: University of California Press, 1969) notes that 70 percent of the respondents to a broad survey of administrators said that promotions involved personal, family, and political considerations. Unfortunately, the political variable is not isolated from the others. See p. 308. The Petras survey was not very helpful to this study because it did not focus specifically on higher civil servants and because the sampling techniques are very questionable.

27. See DFL 338, Article 99, in Contraloría General de la República, *Recopilación,* p. 1325.

28. Arturo Aylwin was a case in point. A member of a prominent Christian Democratic family and a professor of the Catholic University Law School, he eventually became general counsel of Contraloría.

29. Volodia Teitelboim in a conversation with the author on October 18, 1980.

30. William Louis Ascher, "Planners, Politics and Technocracy in Argentina and Chile" (Ph.D. Dissertation, Yale University, 1975), pp. 233–235.

31. López, "Development Administration in Chile," p. 120.

32. Ascher, "Planners, Politics and Technocracy," p. 252.

33. A case in point is Law 13.305, which authorized the executive to "reorganize all the branches of the Public Administration, with the exception of those indicated in article 208 . . . to indicate their functions and faculties and their dependency or relationship with each ministry, and by implication to structure, create, decentralize, fuse, divide, fix internal plant, expand, reduce and eliminate services, posts and jobs." See Contraloría General de La República, *Recopilación,* Volume 48, No. 1, p. 7.

34. Jorge Tapia and Luis Quiroz, "El subsistema político," p. 92.

35. Frei was also prevented from implementing his centralized planning objectives when Congress refused to go along with his objectives for ODEPLAN, the National Planning Office. See Sunkel, "Cambios estructurales, estrategias de desarrollo."

36. For an elaboration of this point and its implications for the collapse of the constitutional order in Chile, see Valenzuela, *The Breakdown of Democratic Regimes.*

37. An excellent discussion of this can be found in Cleaves, *Bureaucratic Politics,* pp. 160ff.

38. Arturo Hein and Jaime Contreras, *El funcionario público: Caso-Ministerio de la Vivienda y Urbanismo* (Chile: INSORA, 1971), pp. 26–31.

39. For a description of relations between ministers and civil servants, see Tapia and Quiroz, "El subsistema político," pp. 26–32.

40. INSORA, "El proceso de toma de decisiones," pp. 6, 10.

41. Cleaves, *Bureaucratic Politics,* pp. 159–160.

42. For discussions of the budgetary process, see Cleaves; Hugo Araneda D., *La administración financiera del estado* (Santiago: Editorial Jurídica de Chile,

1966) and Arturo Valenzuela, *Political Brokers in Chile: Local Government in a Centralized Polity* (Durham, N.C.: Duke University Press, 1977).

43. Tapia and Quiroz, "El subsistema político," p. 59.

44. A good account of these appointments can be found in Gil, *The Political System of Chile,* pp. 109–110.

45. Tapia and Quiroz, "El subsistema político," p. 33.

46. These observations are derived from interviews conducted by the author with congressmen from a five-province region in 1969. Similar observations were made by Iván Auger, who served for over twenty years as a Senate staff member directing the staffs of several key commissions.

47. Valenzuela, *Political Brokers,* p. 143.

48. Valenzuela, chapter 6.

49. Ascher, "Planners, Politics and Technocracy," p. 161.

50. Lists of senators were obtained from Chile, Senado, Oficina de Informaciones, *Boletín de Información General,* December 31, 1968. Biographies were traced in the sources listed in note 5.

51. Biographical information compiled for an unpublished project by staff members of the Instituto de Ciencias Políticas, Universidad Católica, 1974.

52. Hans Daalder, "Parties, Elites and Political Development," in Joseph Lapalombara and Myron Weiner (eds.), *Political Parties and Political Development* (Princeton, N.J.: Princeton University Press, 1966), p. 60. I am grateful to Samuel Valenzuela for information presented in this section.

53. For an explanation of this phenomenon, see Valenzuela, *Political Brokers,* chapter 8.

ABOUT THE AUTHORS

EZRA N. SULEIMAN is Professor of Politics at Princeton University, where he is also Chairman of the Council on International and Regional Studies and Chairman of the Committee for European Studies. He has held awards from the American Council of Learned Societies, the Ford Foundation, the Guggenheim Foundation, and the German Marshall Fund. He is the author of *Politics, Power, and Bureaucracy in France,* and *Elites in French Society: The Politics of Survival,* and coeditor, with Richard Rose, of *Presidents and Prime Ministers.*

SABINO CASSESE is Professor in the Political Science Department of the University of Rome. He also serves on both the Superior Council of Public Administration and the Steering Committee of the European Group of Public Administration. He is president of the governmental commission for the transfer of public corporations to the regions. He has written on public enterprises, on the history of administrative culture and Italian public administration, and on the formation of the administrative state in Italy. He is author of *Il sistema amministrativo Italiano* (Bologna: Il Mulino, 1983).

HUGH HECLO is Professor of Government at Harvard University. He received his Ph.D. from Yale University. He was formerly a Senior Fellow at the Brookings Institution, Washington, D.C., and is the author of *A Government of Strangers: Executive Politics in Washington* and *The Private Government of Public Money.*

PER LAEGREID is Assistant Professor at the Institute of Public Administration and Organization Theory, University of Bergen, Norway. He has published several articles on central bureaucracies and personnel mobility and policies. He is the coauthor, with Johan P. Olsen, of *Byråkrati og beslutninger* (1978).

RENATE MAYNTZ, Professor of Sociology at the University of Cologne, received a B.A. from Wellesley College, a doctorate in sociology at the Free University in Berlin, and honorary doctorates from the universities of Uppsala and Paris. She has held chairs at the Free University in Berlin and the Hochschule für Verwaltungswissenschaften in Speyer. She has taught at Columbia University, the New School for Social Research in New York, Stanford University, the University of Edinburgh, and at FLACSO (Facultad Latino-americana de Ciencias Sociales) in Santiago de Chile.

JOHAN P. OLSEN is Professor of Public Administration and Organization Theory at the University of Bergen. He has been a Visiting Professor and Fellow at Stanford University and at the University of California, Irvine. He is coauthor of *Ambiguity and Choice in Organizations* and has written several books in Norwegian on political macroorganization, public bureaucracies, corporatism, and direct actions and movements.

T. J. PEMPEL is a Professor of Government and Director of the China-Japan program at Cornell University. He has written extensively on the Japanese bureaucracy. His latest book is entitled *Policy and Politics in Japan: Creative Conservatism.* He has received two Fulbright fellowships and other grants that have provided support for several years of research in Japan.

RICHARD ROSE is Director of the Centre for the Study of Public Policy at the University of Strathclyde, Glasgow. He is also Secretary of the Committee on Political Sociology of the International Political Science and International Sociological Associations. He has been a visiting scholar at the American Enterprise Institute, the Brookings Institution, and the Woodrow Wilson International Center in Washington, D.C., and a visiting professor at the European University Institute, Florence, Italy. He is the author or editor of, among others, *Politics in England; Governing without Consensus: An Irish Perspective; Electoral Behavior: A Comparative Handbook; Managing Presidential Objective; Can Government Go Bankrupt?, Do Parties Make a Difference?,* and *Understanding Big Government.*

ARTURO VALENZUELA is Professor of Political Science and Chairman of the Council of Latin American Studies at Duke University. He is the author of *Political Brokers in Chile: Local Government in a Central-ized Polity* and *The Breakdown of Democratic Regimes: Chile,* and coauthor and coeditor of *Chile: Politics and Society* and *Military Rule in Chile* (forthcoming). He is currently working with J. Samuel Valenzuela on a book on the origins of democratic regimes.

INDEX

283

advancement, 92–93, 94, 96
career patterns, 87, 94–95, 97
comparison with other countries,
74–75, 90, 92, 95
entrance exam, 89, 91
entrance requirements, 89–92, 93
history, 78
interministerial competition, 94–95,
97–98
job security, 93
Civil service, Norway, 206–241
careers, 213–18
confidentiality, 219–20
discipline, 214–17, 230
hierarchical control, 230, 232
history, 210–13, 219, 220
norms, 216, 220–22
organization of authority and interests, 225–234
organization of knowledge and beliefs, 218–225
promotion, 213–15
recruitment, 213–16
law degree and recruitment, 225
relationship with the media, 219–20
rules and procedure, 230
rules of competence and authority,
212
socialization into, 217–18
working conditions, 226
World War II, 212–216
Civil service, United States, 8–34
absence of central leadership, 9
administrative management, 9–10,
13–14
and the presidency, 24–30
career positions, 14, 16–21, 22–23
educational background, 16
comparison with other countries, 10,
11, 12, 15–17
dual role as informal personnel system, 9–10, 21
history, 10–12, 17–18, 27
political parties, 14, 16–21
political role of civil servants, 21–24
public careerists, 18–21, 22
temporary staff positions, 18, 20
years of experience, 19
Civil service, West Germany
careers, 185–88, 190–91

comparison with other countries,
178–79, 183, 193
distinction between administrative
and political careers, 188–191
elite, 174–205
Federal Personnel Committee, 182
higher civil service, 175–76
history, 175–77, 180–81, 184–85,
189–90, 193
laws and legislation, 185
promotion, 182–87
ranks, 180
recruitment, 180–81, 187, 188–89
Civil Service Appointment Ordinance
(Japan), 80
Civil Service College (Britain), 147
Civil Service Commission (United
States). See Office of Personnel
Management (United States)
Civil Service Commission (West Ger-
many), 187
Civil service reform. See under indi-
vidual countries
Civil Service Reform Act of 1978
(United States), 31
Cleaves, Peter, 267
Cohn, Samy, 121
Committee on the Present Danger
(United States), 22
Communist party (Chile), 261, 262, 265
(France), 124, 129, 130, 132
(Germany; KDP), 185
Comparisons between civil service in
different countries. See under in-
dividual countries, i.e., Civil ser-
vice, Britain, etc.
Comptroller General (Chile), 258, 260
Concept of a united elite, 233
Conférence des Grandes Ecoles
(France), 109–10
Congress (Chile), 247, 251, 262, 263,
267–70, 272–73
Congress (United States), 11, 12–13,
21
Congressmen in civil service (Chile),
267–70
Connally, John, 23
Conseil d'Etat (France), 120
Conservative party (Britain), 139, 140–
41, 160, 162, 165, 167

conflicts between generalists and
specialists, 211
occupational backgrounds, 211
responsibility, 234–35
Ministries (Italy), Heads of, 61
Ministries (Norway), 214
Ministry for Coordination and Plan-
ning (Norway), 235
Ministry of Agriculture (Italy), 56, 66
Ministry of Agriculture and Forestry
(Japan), 87, 100
Ministry of Commerce (Norway), 223
Ministry of Construction (Japan), 100
Ministry of Cultural Goods (Italy), 57
Ministry of Defense (Britain), 162
Ministry of Defence (Italy), 49, 50, 56,
60
Ministry of Economics (Chile), 255,
256, 266
Ministry of Education (Britain), 159
(Chile), 260
(Italy), 60, 66
(Japan), 73
Ministry of the Environment (Britain),
164
(Norway), 225
Ministry of Finance (Chile), 251, 253–
55, 256, 258, 264, 266, 270
(Japan), 73, 95, 97
(Norway), 214
(Italy), 45, 56, 57
Ministry of Foreign Affairs (Chile),
258, 260
(Italy), 60
(Norway), 223
Ministry of Foreign Commerce (Italy),
56
Ministry of Foreign Relations (Chile),
256
Ministry of Health (Britain), 159
(Italy), 66
Ministry of Health and Welfare (Ja-
pan), 85, 87
Ministry of Home Affairs (Italy), 49
Ministry of Housing (Chile), 255, 256,
261, 269
Ministry of Housing and Urban De-
velopment (Chile), 264, 267
Ministry of Industry (Britain), 164
(Italy), 56, 66
Ministry of International Trade and In-

dustry (Japan), 73, 87, 97
Ministry of Justice (Chile), 256
(Italy), 60
(Norway), 225
Ministry of Labor (Chile), 261
(Italy), 66
Ministry of Mining (Chile), 255
Ministry of Public Works (Chile), 253–
55, 256, 264, 267
(Italy), 56, 57, 66
Ministry of Student Affairs (Italy), 49
Ministry of Tourism (Italy), 66
Ministry of Transport (Chile), 267
(Italy), 54, 66
Ministry of Transportation (Japan), 73,
87
Ministry of the Treasury (Italy), 44, 45,
49, 50, 57, 65, 67
Mitterrand, François, 108, 112–13
Molina, Sergio, 251
Mussolini, Benito, 47

Nara Period (Japan), 78
National Assembly (France), 118, 122,
123, 127
National Institute of Statistics (Chile),
264
National Park Service (United States),
17
National Personnel Authority (Japan),
82, 88, 91
National Planning Office (Chile), 262
National Public Service Law (Japan),
82–83
National Rescript to Soldiers and
Sailors (Japan), 79
National Savings Bureau (Chile), 243
National School of Administration
(Chile), 258
(France), 109, 111, 113–18, 126, 128–
29, 130–31
National Security Council (United
States), 25, 26
National Socialist State (West Ger-
many), 177, 188
Nationalist Party (Chile), 261
Nazi Party, 177, 185, 193
Nettl, Peter, 164
New Deal (United States), 9
Nitrite Credit Bureau (Chile), 243
Nixon, Richard M., 9, 29, 30, 87